About the Author

In 1964, John Philip Rothacker was dramatically and radically converted to the Lord Jesus Christ. Born in Fremont, Ohio, in 1935, he graduated from the College of Dentistry at Ohio State University in 1963, and completed an internship in pedodontics at Children's Hospital a year later, following which he met the Lord.

He then practiced dentistry for two years, dividing his time between private practice and working with children at the Columbus State School for the mentally retarded. Following a desire to serve the Lord full time, and stimulated to fasting and more prayer, John left to do missionary dentistry for three months in the summer program of Project Compassion in the West Indies in 1966. After this ministry, while travelling and working with other missionaries, God led John into the gifts of the Holy Spirit, and he experienced the power of God in many exciting, miraculous, and life changing ways.

After returning home, he was ordained in 1967 by the Lord Jesus **"through prophetic utterance with the laying on of hands by the presbytery"** (I Tim. 4:14). John was set apart as an apostle, "to plant the church," which is what this book on *The church*, and his whole life and ministry, are all about. His first of three other major publications, *The Public Ministry of Women*, teaches about the biblical role that women are to have in the body of Christ, specifically in the assembly, along with many other foundational truths. The second, *A Woman's Headcovering*, is a booklet expounding "a biblical custom practiced faithfully by all godly women from the beginnings of recorded history until our present generations." The third, *A Woman's Dress*, is another booklet, teaching what God has to say from the creation of man in "Genesis" to "The Revelation of Jesus Christ" about modesty and dress for both men and women, but primarily the biblical and secular emphasis that is upon women.

i

In 1976, the Lord Jesus led John out of nine years of part-time dental practice (for Paul, it was making tents, Acts 18:3) and into a radio ministry where he has been "on call" teaching and discussing the scriptures and health related subjects over the air live. An original "talk radio" format according to Acts 19:9, the "Truth for Today" program is an outreach through the media of radio, tapes, and literature to "plant the church" in Christ, in His love, faith, holiness, righteousness, health, and healing, always endeavoring to speak the truth in love.

After having been called to be celibate for many years, the Lord gave him a helpmate to minister with him. God is healing both naturally and supernaturally as John teaches; and his wife, Dulce, is given manifestations of the Holy Spirit such as "**a word of knowledge**," "**gifts of healings**," and "**spiritual songs**" (Ex. 15:26; I Cor. 12:7-11; Eph. 5:19). As they minister together, the operation of "**faith**" and "**the working of miracles**" bring wonderful surprises.

Among various ministries available is a Basic Disciples Course on audio cassettes together with his books called "Apostolic Foundation Series." This series of teachings from the Lord's direction is very helpful for anyone who desires to build his life and God's church in love and scriptural truth. These and other programs from Truth For Today are available upon request.

Another specific ministry given by special revelation is "Holy Nutrition." Through the "Health for Today" program, literature, instructions, and products about health and healing are obtainable. "Manna From Heaven" Whole Leaf Aloe Vera is the first in their own line of products that the Lord has directed them to provide for the "health and healing" of His people.

John is also active in various ministries working to preserve our American Christian heritage and regain religious freedom at home, and promoting unity, revival, and restoration in the body of Christ worldwide.

About the Cover

The cover developed gradually over many months, the same as the church has over centuries. First, there was a pastoral scene with the flock of God shepherded by the five-fold ministry, with the Lord Jesus present in Spirit as reflected in the cool still waters so wonderfully portrayed in Psalm 23. The lush green grass for our health with caring oversight brings contentment where we can be fed and ruminate on the Word of God (Psa. 1:2), and properly digest "our daily bread" (Mt. 6:11).

The vine and the grapes are of course an oft symbol of the Lord and His people, for He is the vine and we are the branches, and as we abide in Him, we bear much fruit (Jn. 15). Unfortunately, often the vineyard is not kept by the vine-growers as it should be (Lu. 20; Isa. 5; Jer. 12:10).

So then, the back of the book, which once was the same as the front, gradually developed into a Babylonish scene. The grass is not as green, briars and thorns cropped up, and we have a Babylonian ziggurat with a lamb being taken for slaughter and the sacrifice of false worship. Storm clouds are coming, completely unawares by the fat, overindulgent leader depicted as Ezekiel saw it, as a fat sheep which has not only trodden down the pasture with his own feet but is now drinking of the clean water and fouling the rest with his feet (Eze. 34).

Perhaps if you look closely you can see some thrusting the others with their sides, shoulders, and a few with horns. And perhaps you can spot the wolf lurking to pounce on its prey (Eze. 22:27; Hab.1:8; Mt. 7:15; Acts 20:28-30).

This is just a portion of the picture given in the scriptures and this book, which we have portrayed on the cover. The church has degenerated into a Babylonish disgrace, but wake up church, the Lord is at work!

"He will purify the sons of Levi and refine them like gold

and silver, so that they may present to the Lord offerings in righteousness" (Mal. 3:3 NAS). Yes, "Christ also loved the church and gave Himself up for her; that He might sanctify her, having cleansed her by the washing of water with the word, that He might present to Himself the church in all her glory, having no spot or wrinkle or any such thing; but that she should be holy and blameless" (Eph. 5:25-27 NAS)!

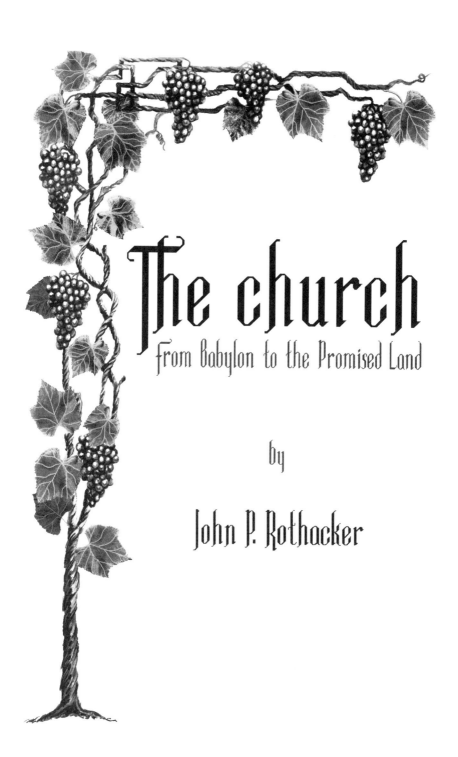

The church
From Babylon to the Promised Land

by

John P. Rothacker

Available from:

John Rothacker Ministries
Box 3219
Columbus, Ohio 43210

www.JohnRothacker.org

(NAS) indicates New American Standard Bible © 1960, 1962, 1963, 1968, 1971, 1972, 1973, 1975, 1977 by the Lockman Foundation and used by permission.

International Standard Book Number 0-9674869-4-7

Printed in the United States of America

Contents

Thank You!

First, I want to thank the Lord for everything! His instruction, enlightenment, the wonderful way He leads us into truth is amazing, and fills life with so much wonder and excitement. When writing on subjects such as are found in this book, to reflect on the direction, the inspiration, revelation, all of God's marvelous ways of bringing truth to us, it's just simply wonderful. Thank you Father, thank you Lord Jesus, and thank you Holy Spirit!

Also, I want to thank my wife, Dulce, for her years of patience while writing this book, and for her reading and help.

Thank you Brian, for your thorough, consistent, time consuming, and greatly appreciated meticulous editorial assistance. Without it this work would not be as precise, or as clear as I trust it is. What a tremendous help you have been!

To my friends, Wilma, Linda, Gladys, and Jim, for their input, help, prayers, and support, I shall always be grateful!

And to Tom, because your artistic ability and skills in making the cover and graphics have been so amazing, working with you and the Lord and seeing the work develop has been also wondrously surprising! Thanks to you, and thanks again to all!

Preface

What is "**the church**"? What does it do? What is it for? What is its structure? How do we get in? How is it named? How does it operate? Who is its head? How does it get direction? How is it led? How is it financed? These are just some of the questions that we must know the answer to if we are to live successfully in this life and for eternity!

The format of the different chapters is one of teaching with scriptural references; the first chapter also has a section of questions and answers.

Let us begin this most important study in prayer.

"Lord God, maker of heaven and earth, we praise thee and thank thee that thou art the ruler of the universe, and we desire to be ruled by thee, by thy great and mighty power and love and holiness and righteousness. We confess our own inadequacies in the light and knowledge of your supreme wisdom and truth. Make us to be thy servants in building your church, for thy glory and for thy honor, both now and forever. Amen! Illuminate us, teach us, guide us, strengthen, enable, and inspire us by thy Holy Spirit to do thy will and not our own, for Jesus' sake and in His precious name we pray. Amen, and Amen!"

Introduction

In introducing this work on "the church," I would like to outline briefly its contents. The first chapter teaches us what the church really is, and then how one is to enter it scripturally. It contains questions and answers at the end for bible teaching purposes.

The second chapter tells us what Babylon is, the false church, so that we can then be able to understand properly the true church and how we are to function in it.

The third chapter explains what the true church is and how it differs from the false in many significant ways. After chapters two and three we should be able to better understand the true and the counterfeit which all of us are involved with in one respect or another.

Chapter four is a doctrine the scripture refers to as "**one mind, and one accord**," which any group of Christians, even in Babylon, can follow to find the Lord's mind and will, but is absolutely essential for building the kingdom of God unto perfection.

Chapter five is then a teaching on discipline which is also essential for bringing about the perfecting of the church and the maturing of God's people in order to accomplish His will at the end of this age!

There are many teachings for the church which are outside the scope of this one on "**the church**" itself, but are vital in perfecting the saints. Other books which I have written are available and address some of these issues.

Now, as we get into "**the church**" together,

"May God bless our hearts and minds, and give us the courage and strength to walk in His ways, being faithful unto the end, is my prayer! Amen!"

CHAPTER 1

The church:
Definitions & Baptisms

The church, what is it?

The first thing we must do, I believe, is to define what we are talking about. Jesus said, "I **will build My church; and the gates of hell shall not prevail against it**" (Mt. 16:18 KJV). So we are talking about the Lord's church and not our own. It does not belong to us; it belongs to Him; it is His church. It does not belong to any man other than the Lord Jesus Christ Himself!

Now, the word "**church**" in Greek, εκκλησια, *ekklesia,* means literally, "the called out ones." The prefix *ek* meaning "out," and *klesia* from the root meaning "to call" or "the called." So then, the church is "a people who are called out."

In the scriptures of the original Greek New Testament, as well as in the Greek Septuagint version of the original Hebrew "Old Testament" (which was the translation that the New Testament church used primarily and that the apostles often quoted from in writing the New Testament scriptures in Greek), the word *ekklesia* is used in a number of ways. We must understand them all and be able to interpret properly which way it is being used if we are to interpret properly the scriptures; and build with "**gold, silver, precious stones**" instead of "**wood, hay, stubble**" (I Cor. 3:10-15 KJV). It is essential if we are to receive reward and blessings both now and forever rather than to suffer loss and judgment both now and forever.

1

The word *ekklesia* was originally used in the Septuagint version of the Old Testament scriptures to refer most often to a group of people called to assemble together. Consequently, it is used in the New Testament to refer sometimes to a secular, non-Christian gathering in a public place, often translated "assembly" (Acts 19:32, 39, 41), as well as for the physical gathering of God's people, translated "**church**" (Acts 7:38 KJV; I Cor. 11:18) or "**congregation**" (Acts 7:38 NAS).

However, in the New Testament, *ekklesia* is usually used to refer to the spiritual group of God's people, whether assembled or not assembled, the children of God, the ones called out of darkness into His marvelous light, out of sin and into righteousness, out of unbelief and into faith, out of Satan's kingdom and into the kingdom of God! In this latter sense, the word "church" is used concerning four different size groups, each progressively larger size group usually consisting of a number of the smaller size groups. First, the word "church" is used several times to refer to a small group of Christians that gather regularly in a house (I Cor. 16:19b); or secondly, a larger group that gathers in a larger place (I Cor. 11:18-22); but it is most often used to refer to either all the non-assembled Christians that live in a city (I Cor. 1:2; 16:1, 19a); or to all the people of God that live in heaven and in earth combined (I Cor. 10:32; 12:27-28; 15:9; Heb. 12:12-29).

In Ephesians, Paul writes that God has put all things under the feet of the Lord Jesus and "**gave Him to be the head over all things to the church, which is His body, the fulness of Him that filleth all in all**" (Eph. 1:22-23 KJV). We read similarly in Colossians of Christ that, "**He is before all things, and in Him all things hold together. He is also head of the body, the church; and He is the beginning, the first-born from the dead; so that He Himself might come to have first place in everything**" (Col. 1:17-18 NAS). Then Paul wrote, "**Now I rejoice in my sufferings for your sake, and in my flesh I do my share on behalf of His body (which is the church) in filling up that which is lacking in Christ's afflictions**" (Col. 1:24 NAS).

It is very significant that the word *ekklesia* is never used for a building; and very interesting that William Tyndale, who in 1525 was the first to translate the New Testament from the original Greek into English and print it, translated *ekklesia* uniformly "**congregation**," and translated the Greek word for heathen temples in Acts 19:37 as "**churches**," which still remains today in the King James Version. A root of the Greek word used for "**churches**" here, *hieron*, meant "a sacred place" and "a temple for the worship of god." The word "church" in English is believed to have come from the Greek words for "house of the Lord," *oikos*, meaning "house," and *kuriakon*, "of the Lord [kurios]." The word *kuriakon* does not appear in the Greek Old Testament at all, and when it appears two times in the Greek New Testament, it does not refer to a house or a building, but is a possessive term referring to either the "**Lord's supper**" (I Cor. 11:20) or the "**Lord's day**" (Rev. 1:10). The word "house" has always referred to both people, such as the "**house of Israel**" (Lev. 10:6) or the "**house of David**" (II Sam. 3:1), as well as a place of worship (Gen. 28:17; Ex. 23:19), such as eventually the temple building (I Chr. 6:32). Although the phrase *"oikos kurios,"* "**house of the Lord**," appears many times throughout the Greek Old Testament in referring to a building, primarily the one true place of worship which was a type of the temple in heaven that we are to come to now during this New Testament period (Ex. 23:19; Deut. 23:18; I Sam. 1:7, 24; I Ki. 3:1; I Chr. 22:14; II Chr. 3:1; 36:7, 10, 14, 18; Ezra 1:5; Hag. 1:2), it never appears in the New Testament. The phrase *"oikon tou Theou,"* "**house of** [the] **God**," also appears quite often throughout the Greek Old Testament, similarly referring to the tabernacle or the temple; but when it appears in the New Testament, it never is referring to a building of the New Testament, but only to either the tabernacle of the Old Testament (Mt.12:4; Mk. 2:26; Lk. 6:4) or to the people of God during this New Testament period (Heb. 10:21). Thus we can see that although the Greek word translated "church" in many modern English Bibles, *ekklesia*, was never used for a building in scripture (in either the Greek Old or New Testaments), but most often referred to the people of God, by 1525 the word "church" began to be used for a building in English, but even then only as a heathen temple. Unfortunately, the word "church" not only came to have the dual meaning of "the people" as well as "a building," but by 1828 in Webster's first edition of the <u>American Dictionary of the English Language</u>, "church" came to have nine different meanings; thus our language has been corrupted, and the true meaning of scriptures consequently confused!

It is also significant that the Greek word συναγωγη, *sunagoge*, synagogue, means either "a gathering, a bringing together, an assembly of people" (Num. 16:3; 20:4; 27:17; Josh. 22:16; Acts 13:43) or "a place of gathering, a place of assembly" (Gen. 1:9; Mt. 4:23; 6:2, 5). Although it is used primarily for the Jews in both the Old and New Testament scriptures, it is used even once in the New

Testament for an assembly of Christians by James (Jam. 2:2), "the apostle who maintained unbroken to the latest possible moment the outward bonds connecting the synagogue and the church" (Trench's Synonyms of the New Testament). Therefore it is not difficult to understand how it has become a contributing factor in the dual meaning of the word "church" (although unscriptural), referring both to "the people" and to "the place of worship." When we also realize that the word "synagogue" became used primarily for the religious buildings of the system that arose during the Jewish Babylonian exile (which took place in several phases), we can also come to understand how the word "church" has become used primarily for the buildings of the various Babylonish systems that have arisen during the Babylonian exile of Christians (which has many different phases and exilings).

So then, we have found that the true church of the Lord Jesus Christ is the people of God, often referred to in the scriptures as the body of Christ, with Christ as its head. It is a living organism that we will find is organized, but it is not an organization of man, but of God. It is the spiritual group of people who exist all over the world and in heaven who are indwelt by the Spirit of Jesus Christ (Eph. 3:14-21). The church is not a physical building, but a spiritual building, a "**spiritual house**" not made up of physical stones but "**living stones**," which Peter says have "**been born again**" and are "**now the people of God**," a "**holy nation**," a "**holy**" and "**royal priesthood**" (I Pet. 1:22 - 2:10 NAS).

The church throughout the scriptures is also referred to in many other ways, and is descriptively called, "**the household of God**," "**the building**," a "**holy temple**," and a "**habitation** [dwelling, NAS] **of God**" (Eph. 2:19-22 KJV); the "**church**," the "**church of God**," the "**churches of Christ**" (I Cor. 1:2; Rom. 16:16); the "**body of Christ**" (Eph. 4:12), the "**bride**" of Christ, His "**wife**," "**the Jerusalem from above**," "**the holy city**," the "**new Jerusalem**" (Gal. 4:26; Rev. 19:7; 21:2, 9).

The Lord's church, How do we enter?

Now, how do we enter the body of Christ, His church? Again Paul wrote: "**For by** [Gk. $εν$, *en*, **in**] **one Spirit we were all baptized** [Gk. $εβαπτισθημεν$, *ebaptisthemen*, indicative passive form of $βαπτιζω$, *baptizo*, meaning "**immersed**"] **into** [$εισ$, *eis*, into] **one**

4

body, whether Jews or Greeks, whether slaves or free, and we were all made to drink of [$\varepsilon\iota\sigma$, into, KJV] one Spirit" (I Cor. 12:13□NAS). So we see that we enter the Lord's church, the true church, the people of God, the body of Christ, by being immersed "into" it by being immersed "in" the Holy Spirit. The scripture says, "there is one body, and one Spirit" (Eph. 4:4), so knowing this, we could say, "We were all immersed in the Holy Spirit [and thus] into the body of Christ"; or by rearranging the structure of the sentence without changing the meaning, we could say, "We were all immersed into the body of Christ by being immersed in the Holy Spirit."

Our next question might be then, "Who baptized us, that is, who immersed us in the Holy Spirit [and thus] into the body of Christ?" In other words, who put us in the true church of the living God? The answer can be found in the gospel according to Matthew the apostle when we read that John the Immerser said, "I immerse [baptizo] you in [en] water into [eis] repentance, but He who is coming after me is mightier than I . . . He [Himself] will immerse you in [en] the Holy Spirit and fire" (Mt. 3:11 lit.). Here again the Greek participle en means "in," but is sometimes translated "by" or "with," which makes properly understanding these and similar scriptures about the Holy Spirit somewhat difficult until we know this! (Jn. 1:33; Acts 1:5; 11:16; I Cor. 12:13). Sadly, the simplicity of the truth of scripture is often confused. Again, the Greek word eis, translated "for," could be translated, "immerse into repentance." The element in which John baptized was water; the element in which Jesus baptizes is the Holy Spirit; and consequently, Jesus immerses us into His church and we become members of His body.

Next, we might ask, what part does water baptism play in entering the Lord's church? Did not John the Baptist connect water baptism and spirit baptism? Yes, and so did Peter when he said, "Repent, and let each of you be baptized in [$\varepsilon\nu$, en] the name of Jesus Christ for [$\varepsilon\iota\sigma$, eis, into] the forgiveness [remission] of your sins; and you shall receive the gift of the Holy Spirit" (Acts 2:38 NAS). We must understand that this is exactly what Jesus meant when He said, "Truly, truly, I say to you, unless one is born again [$\alpha\nu\omega\theta\varepsilon\nu$, anothen, lit. "from above," but sometimes used in repetition, therefore "again" is acceptable (Gal. 4:9)] he cannot see the kingdom of God." Then when He further explained this He said, "Truly, truly, I say to you, unless one is born of water and the Spirit, he cannot enter into the kingdom of God" (Jn. 3:3, 5 NAS).

Now, lest one think this is not referring to water baptism, please check the context. After Jesus ended His discourse on being born of water and the Spirit in verse 21, immediately we are told that He baptized with His disciples in Judea, verse 22. In the next verse we have John the Baptist again baptizing in Aenon, because there was much water there. Then we have a discussion between John's disciples and the Jews about purification which we are told was about water baptism. Immediately after this discourse in verse 36, we read that, **"Jesus was making and baptizing more disciples than John (although Jesus Himself was not baptizing, but His disciples were)"** (Jn 4:1-2 NAS).

You see, dear reader, when Jesus spoke about being **"born of the water,"** He was not speaking about being born of the amnionic fluid of your mother's womb. The context disproves this, and so does common logic. The Lord would not state a fact of our natural birth as a requirement of our spiritual birth; neither would He combine something that occurs in our natural birth together with something that happens in our spiritual birth as requirements of entering His spiritual kingdom. That would confuse us. The teaching of confusion is of Babylon. Neither did Jesus mean figuratively that He was referring to the Word because we read where Paul said that Jesus will sanctify the church **"and cleanse it with the washing of water by the word"** (Eph. 5:26 KJV). One does not use something literal like **"the Spirit"** and something figurative in the same sentence. We could never understand anything if the Lord did this in His Holy Word! Please note that Paul explained his figure of speech, **"the washing of water,"** immediately and in the same sentence when he added, **"by the word."** To take the phrase, **"of water"** in John 3 out of context is like saying that because Jesus said, **"I am the door"** in John 10:7, 9, and in Revelation 3:20, **"Behold, I stand at the door and knock,"** that He was knocking on Himself. Nonsense! Water is literal, the Spirit is literal, and the Blood is literal, and that is what the same author of the scripture, an apostle, John, meant when he said, **"This is the one who came by water** [His baptism] **and blood** [His death], **Jesus Christ; not with the water only, but with the water and with the blood. And it is the Spirit who bears witness, because the Spirit is the truth. For there are three that bear witness, the Spirit** [who descended at His baptism like a dove] **and the water** [of His baptism] **and the blood; and the three are in agreement"** (I Jn. 5:6-8 NAS). These three are the beginning, anointing for the duration of, and ending of the 3 1/2 years of His earthly ministry.

Jesus is our primary example, and He included us when He insisted that He Himself be baptized in water by saying, "**In this way it is fitting for us to fulfill all righteousness**," and then as He was coming up out of the water of baptism He was anointed with the Holy Spirit for ministry (Mt. 3:15-17 NAS). He then was declared by the Father's voice from Heaven that He was His Son! What a beautiful demonstration of being "**born of water and of the Spirit**," being "**born from above**" so as to be declared by our Heavenly Father as His children!

You see, we are born into the spirit realm in a similar way as into the natural. In the natural we have the natural seed, then a natural birth through water followed immediately by receiving the breath of life. In the spiritual birth, the Word of God is the incorruptible seed that works in our hearts until we are brought to repentance (I Pet. 1:23); then we are born of the water (water baptism — the covenant sign (Gen. 9:9-17; 17:9-14; Acts 7:8; Rom. 4:11; Eph. 1:13; Col. 2:11-12), which is a portrayal of what's next; and then we are born of the Spirit (Spirit baptism, the birth of spiritual life and reality; Jn. 3:3-8; Gal. 4:29; Rom. 6:3-4).

This was God's method in type in the Old Covenant when we read that they "**all were baptized into** [ειϛ, *eis*] **Moses** [a type of Christ] **in** [εν, *en*] **the cloud** [a type of the Holy Spirit] **and in** [εν, *en*] **the sea** [a type of water baptism] . . . **and all drank the same spiritual drink . . . Christ**" (the Spirit of Christ, the Holy Spirit, I Cor. 10:1-4; compare with 12:12-13).

This harmonizes perfectly with what Peter the apostle taught and practiced when he opened the door of salvation, first to the Jews. He said to those who asked what they were to do: "**Repent, and be immersed every one of you in the name of Jesus Christ for the remission of sins, and you shall receive the gift of the Holy Spirit. For to you is the promise, and to your children, and to all who are afar off, as many as the Lord our God shall call. And with many other words he earnestly testified and kept on exhorting them, saying, 'Be saved from this crooked generation!' So then, those who gladly received his word were immersed; and there were added that day about three thousand souls**" (Acts 2:38-41 lit.). Again, when he opened the door (singular, because there is only one door, Jesus, Jn. 10:9) of the church with the keys of the kingdom to the Gentiles, the Holy Spirit fell on them as he spoke of salvation in Jesus' name, and he then "**ordered them to be immersed in the name of Jesus Christ**" (Mt. 16:18-19; Acts 15:7; 10:43-48 lit.).

Peter further explained about baptism when he wrote, "**The patience of God kept waiting in the days of Noah, during the construction of the ark, in which a few, that is, eight persons, were brought safely through the water.** And corresponding to that, <u>baptism now saves you</u> — not the removal of dirt from the flesh, but an appeal to God for a good conscience — through the resurrection of Jesus Christ**" (I Pet. 3:20-21 NAS).

Baptism is absolutely essential according to Jesus and the New Testament apostles. Jesus said, also, **"Go ye into all the world, and preach the gospel to every creature. He that believeth and is baptized shall be saved; but he that believeth not shall be damned"** (Mk. 16:15-16 KJV). And He also said, **"All authority has been given to Me in heaven and on earth. Go therefore and make disciples of all the nations, baptizing them in the name of the Father and [of] the Son and [of] the Holy Spirit, teaching them to observe all that I commanded you; and lo, I am with you always [all the days], even to the end of the age"** (Mt. 28:18-20 NAS).

Paul, the apostle, wrote, **"Know ye not, that so many of us as were baptized into Jesus Christ were baptized into His death? Therefore we are [were] <u>buried</u> with Him by baptism into death: that like as Christ was raised up from the dead by the glory of the Father, even so we also should walk in <u>newness of life</u>. For <u>if</u> we have been <u>planted</u> together <u>in the likeness</u> of His death, we shall be also in the likeness of his [the] resurrection"** (Rom. 6:3-5 KJV). Please note that as one arises out of the water in water baptism, it is described as arising into a new life; this is exactly why Jesus used the expression of being "**<u>born</u> of the water.**" This new life is made real by receiving the Holy Spirit, and this is why Jesus said you must "**be born of water and the Spirit.**" Together, this being born of the water and of the Spirit make up being born-again, "**from above**"; the commandment and the faith being given from the Father above, in heaven, and the Spirit sent from above, and both received here below, now (Jn. 3:3-5).

Again Paul writes, "**In Him you were also circumcised with a circumcision made without hands, in the removal of the body of the flesh by the circumcision of Christ; having been <u>buried with Him in baptism</u>, in which you were also raised up with Him <u>through faith in the working</u> [operation] <u>of God</u>, who raised Him from the dead**" (Col. 2:11-12 NAS).

Continually throughout the book of Acts we find examples given to us of the necessity and practice of immediate baptism by

8

immersion as commanded by our Lord Jesus Christ when people are being brought to God. On the day of Pentecost (Acts 2:38-41), by Philip the evangelist's ministry to the city of Samaria and then to the Ethiopian eunuch (Acts 8), in Paul's own conversion (Acts 9:1-18 & 22:6-16), with Cornelius and his kinsmen and near friends (Acts 10; 11), by Lydia and her household (Acts 16:14-15), by the Philippian jailer and his household (Acts 16:25-34), and the disciples at Ephesus (Acts 19:1-7); in all these scriptural conversions we have God's record of people being born of water and the Spirit in order for them to enter the kingdom of God, the Lord's church.

Now, let us consider several other important aspects concerning water baptism. It is important to note that baptism was given as a command, not an option! Peter commanded it of the Jews on the day of Pentecost, and it is even stated as such to the Gentiles years later, for it is written, "**He ordered [commanded] them to be baptized in the name of Jesus Christ**" (Acts 2:38 & 10:48 NAS). Paul also was ordered to be baptized by Ananias, a devout disciple, who brought him into the kingdom of God (Acts 22:16).

Another aspect of water baptism is that although converts usually received water baptism before the Spirit baptism as instructed by Peter in the first record of God's command to us, this is not always the case. In the conversions of Cornelius and his company, the Holy Spirit was given first, before water baptism (Acts 10). The circumstances made this necessary as Peter and the rest of the Hebrew Christians were very reluctant about ministering to the Gentiles, so in God's time He gave Peter a vision and then spoke to him to go and minister to Cornelius, an Italian Gentile. Peter understood the meaning of the vision, that God was not cleansing everything that could be put in one's mouth, but "**God has shown me that I should not call any man unholy or unclean**" (Acts 10:28-29 NAS). Then God gave him and the other Hebrew Christians another sign by giving the Gentiles the Holy Spirit just as He had the Jews on the day of Pentecost, that is, with a wonderful outpouring accompanied with the receiving of the gift of tongues. Since the Gentiles had received the reality of the baptism in the Holy Spirit, Peter asked who could forbid water in order that they also receive the picture of this spiritual baptism and the sign of the New Covenant, water baptism (Acts 10:47). He had to defend his actions before those of the circumcision when he returned to Jerusalem; so he related the whole affair, how God had given to the Gentiles the gift of the Holy Spirit just as he had them; and therefore he defended his action to the Jewish believers with the question, **"Who was I that I could stand in God's way?"** (Acts 11:17 NAS). Those of the circumcision then acknowledged that by the Gentiles receiving the Holy Spirit, proven by the sign of also receiving the gift of tongues, that God had granted unto them **"repentance unto life"** (Acts 11:18 KJV; I Cor. 14:22), not "a second work of grace," nor "power for service," but had obtained <u>salvation</u> and were to be accepted in the New Covenant! Although we find this example in scripture of Spirit baptism preceding water baptism (and for the just cause we have discussed), whenever instruction is given in scripture as to how people coming to Christ are to enter into Him, water baptism is commanded first, and then Spirit baptism. However, in this day of lukewarmness, lack of real commitments, and true discipleship, the scriptural method is not only not used, but repentance, water baptism, and Spirit baptism may one or all be ignored. We are never told in scripture to have people ask Jesus into their hearts, although this is a most vital accomplishment of conversion, because this method so often either fails or is incomplete as to all of the purposes of God. Rather, we are told to instruct them about repentance toward God and from sin, water baptism (which is their confession of faith before man that Jesus died for their sins, was buried, and was raised again from the dead), and the receiving of the Holy Spirit, usually ministered by the laying on of hands (which not only accomplishes the receiving of Jesus into one's heart, but these and many other things as well). A new convert is then well on the way of learning the six basic doctrines of Christ given to us in Hebrews 6:1-3, which are:

[1] **"repentance from dead works,**
[2] **and of faith toward God,**
[3] **of the doctrine of baptisms,**
[4] **and of laying on of hands,**
[5] **and of resurrection of the dead,**
[6] **and of eternal judgment."**   (KJV)

Without these foundational principles, these A,B,C's of the Christian life, God says we <u>cannot</u> **"go on unto perfection!"** Because they are so ignored, neglected, and rejected today, is it any wonder why we have so much immaturity, carnality, and backsliding; so much spiritual infant mortality?

Water baptism, as we have stated, is our testifying before

10

man of our faith in what God has done in Christ to save us from our sins and prepare us for all eternity. Jesus commanded His disciples to baptize new converts and said, "**He that believeth and is baptized shall be saved; but he that believeth not shall be damned**" (Mt. 28:19-20; Mk. 16:16 KJV). It is therefore a fulfillment of what God requires when Jesus said, "**Whosoever therefore shall confess me before men, him will I confess also before my Father which is in heaven. But whosoever shall deny me before men, him will I also deny before my Father which is in heaven**" (Mt. 10:32-33 KJV). And again, "**Whosoever shall be ashamed of me and of my words, of him shall the Son of man be ashamed, when he shall come in his own glory, and in his Father's, and of the holy angels**" (Lu. 9:26 KJV).

The importance of water baptism can especially be seen overseas. In India for example, where the Hindus have millions of gods, they think nothing of it if someone says they have asked Jesus into their heart, just one "god" among their millions. But, when one takes the public stand of water baptism, all know the seriousness of their decision, and they are then considered by the unbelievers as real Christians and subject to all kinds of persecution. This vital decision and the results are also true among the monotheistic Moslems.

In Nepal, predominantly Buddhist and Hindu, it was for years only after someone was water baptized that they were considered Christians by the believers or the government. What makes this remarkable is that for many years it was against Nepalese law for anyone to change their religion; they were subject to one year's imprisonment. Therefore, many were imprisoned for becoming a Christian. Also, it was three years imprisonment for anyone evangelizing, plus three more years for a total of six if you baptized anyone. What makes it thrilling is to realize how vital, how pure, and how much more apostolic the church in Nepal was — was until recently when some of the law was changed and its enforcement relaxed, and now every sect of Christianity has invaded with their divisive doctrines! Moreover, what makes it amazing is that although the founding apostle to this nation spent over 10 years in prison under horrible conditions on three separate occasions because of these original laws, he travelled abroad and saw the church in our country and others many times and consequently did not particularly want the law changed, because it resulted in a purer, more commited church! What a powerful witness to the truth of God's Word!

What can we learn from Philip's ministry about baptism, the only record of a New Testament evangelist (Gk. ευαγγελιστασ, *euaggelistas,* bearer of the *euaggelion,* "good news") in all of the Word of God? (Acts 8; 21:8; 6:1-6). One, we learn that after Philip preached to the city of Samaria, the Lord working with him and confirming the word with signs following, that they "**gave heed**" to Philip as they had to Simon, the sorcerer, and then believed the good news "**concerning** [Gk. περι, *peri,* "what relates to, can be said about"] **the kingdom of God, and the name of Jesus Christ**" (Mk. 16:20; Acts 8:6, 10, 12 KJV). They did not believe into Christ, but believed things concerning Christ. And here we must bring out a very simple but profound truth, and that is the difference between believing "about" Christ and believing "into" Christ. We know a lot about many historical figures, but we do not have a personal relationship with them, and yet we may believe "in" them if we agree with their life and teaching, or we may not believe "in" them if we do not accept their philosophy or life style. However, when the scriptures state that people believed or are to believe "in" Christ, it often uses the Greek participle *eis,* meaning "into" (Jn. 3:16, 18, 36). There is a very significant difference. For example, let us suppose someone is drowning and they see a lifeboat. They may "believe in" lifeboats, but they will still drown and be lost unless they "believe into" the life boat — get into the lifeboat! One is strictly intellectual, an understanding of the purposes of lifeboats, the other is the real experience of being saved by one. So, too, is it with Christ! We must get "into" Christ, not just believe "in" Him, His teaching and purposes to save us but without commitment "to" Him; but we must get "in+to" Him, and get "into" Him by His way, not ours; nor according to our mistaken church traditions, understanding, or instruction about scripture, or culture; but according to His understanding of His Word, as revealed by His Holy Spirit! His Word says we must:

[1] "**Repent**";
[2] "**be baptized in the name of Jesus Christ for** [*eis,* into] **the forgiveness of** [our] **sins**"; and then,
[3] "**receive the . . . Holy Spirit!**"

(Acts 2:38 NAS).

Today's vernacular expression of stating that one "is into something," meaning that one is very involved in some thing, or consumed by some thing, is very accurate and appropriate, and

12

we might well ask ourselves, "Am I really into Jesus (my very personal involvement with the very living person of the Lord Jesus Christ), or am I just into religion (Christianity, as a religious, moral, or philosophical teaching of Christ), or into some other worldly activity?"

Another important aspect that we can learn from Philip's ministry to the Samaritans is that after they came to an intellectual acceptance of "**the good news about the kingdom of God and the name of Jesus Christ**," and were baptized in water, they still had not received the Holy Spirit, and thus were not yet fully into Christ (Acts 8:12 NAS). They had "**received the Word of God**," but "**they had simply been baptized in the name of the Lord Jesus**" in water only, not the Spirit (Acts 8:14-16 NAS). They had done everything they had been told to do, thus far, but had not as yet had the Holy Spirit ministered to them (Gal. 3:5). (This is the present state of so many in the institutional church and those sitting under the traditions of men; and this is also the state of multitudes of those who have left the powerless rituals and lifeless agendas of church experience, and no longer attend the show.) But, praise God, when the apostles at Jerusalem heard about it, they sent men of God to pray and lay hands on them to receive the blessed Holy Spirit. It had to be some days before they arrived and "**then they began laying their hands on them, and they were receiving the Holy Spirit**" (Acts 8:17 NAS).

Please notice, here it is not called the "baptism of the Holy Spirit," but a "**receiving [of] the Holy Spirit**", because these terms are describing the same experience, but from different aspects (Acts 1:5; 8:15, 17, 19; 10:47; 11:16). However, because the receiving of the Holy Spirit is the same as being baptized in the Holy Spirit (the initial experience of being immersed in the Spirit of God), it does not mean that there is not more to receive. If one reads the scriptures carefully, one realizes that there is what is called a "pouring forth of the Spirit," and a receiving of the gifts of the Spirit, usually tongues and prophecy. When the Spirit is spoken of as being "**poured out**," "**coming upon**," or "**falling upon**" someone, you will also notice that manifestations of the Spirit accompany the experience (Acts 2:17, 18, 33, 4; 10:44-46; 11:15; 19:6). This is actually a receiving of a particular "**anointing**," meaning "a pouring upon," of the Holy Spirit that is given for serving (I Jn. 2:20, 27; I Cor. 12:7-11).

So we see, dearly beloved, the problem of confusion concerning experiences in the body of Christ today is usually the result of the confusion, mixed-up meaning, and inaccurate meaning, of scriptural terms. And this may surprise you, but this is what God has judged necessary, because it is a product of our Babylonish systems. God is going to continue His judgment of confusion upon our language, our spiritual vocabulary, until we come out of these systems in order to build His church in unity, righteousness, and holiness according to His Word; until we are willing to see that "the local church" is not "our local church," but "His local church," (that is, all the born-again Christians in our locality, our local city); and we decide to work in harmony and love, pursuing righteousness and holiness in all that we do with everyone we can. Until then we will not be out of Babylon, our confusion, or be working in ways pleasing to God! Consequently, we will be building with a lot of "**wood, hay,** [and] **stubble**" instead of "**gold, silver,** [and] **precious stones,**" and we will regret our selfishness on the Day of Judgment, hang our heads in shame, and will suffer loss for it forever! (I Cor. 3:12-15).

Another term often used concerning the Holy Spirit is for one to be "**filled**" with the Spirit, or interestingly in one place, "**filled in** [εν, *en*] **spirit**" — our spirits are to be filled up with God's Holy Spirit (Eph. 5:18). This experience may or may not happen when one first receives the Spirit, and it is an experience that needs to be continually sought (Acts 2:4; 4:31; 9:17). Sometimes a person receives the Holy Spirit and a gift of the Spirit as well, and yet is not filled. This is the case when someone receives the Holy Spirit and the gift of tongues, and yet does not experience any particular change in spirit. They might even feel rather dry and unfulfilled. This is because they need to be filled in spirit, with the Spirit of God. However, praying with one's spirit by praying in tongues edifies the believer, and thus facilitates being filled with the Spirit, and then the edified Christian can better edify the church (I Cor. 14:4, 15). Paul gives us some much needed instruction when by the Spirit of God he writes to us in the Greek present tense (that means, now), imperative (a command), passive (that means, it is to be done to us by someone else): this means we are now to submit ourselves to God and have the Holy Spirit fill us (Eph. 5:18). Paul here gives us some ways to help the Spirit do this for us. Namely:

[1] "**speaking to one another in psalms and hymns and spiritual songs,**
[2] **singing and making melody with your heart to the Lord;**

14

[3] **always giving thanks for all things in the name of
our Lord Jesus Christ to God, even the Father;
and**
[4] **be subject to one another in the fear of Christ."**

(Eph. 5:18-21 NAS)

So we learn from Philip's ministry to the Samaritans that receiving the Holy Spirit is not automatic upon confession of the Lord Jesus nor after asking Him into one's heart as is so commonly taught today. Neither is it automatic after valid water baptism (although He may come in); but the Holy Spirit may well be waiting for us to see that He is ministered to the one coming to Christ, the same as He waits for us to proclaim Christ to someone who is lost and without the gospel. We need to note, also, that by the Lord sending the apostles to minister the Holy Spirit, the new converts were established upon the foundation of apostles and prophets, and their proper relationship with the rest of the body was assured (Eph. 2:20). This is important for any evangelist to know so that his work is scripturally fruitful and lasts.

As we look at Philip's ministry to the Ethiopian eunuch, we wish to point out several things concerning our discussion of being born of water and the Spirit. When the eunuch asked for guidance in the scripture because he did not have the Holy Spirit to teach him, Philip started there at Isaiah 53:7 where the eunuch had been reading, and "**told him the good news, Jesus**" (Acts 8:35 lit.). This gospel obviously included water baptism for we find that as they came upon some water the eunuch said, "**Look! Water! What prevents me from being baptized?**" (v. 36 NAS). God in His love and providence had amazingly provided some water along a desert road. And God always will provide for us to obey His Word, no matter in what circumstances we find ourselves. Then the Holy Spirit is "**given to them that obey Him!**" (Acts 5:32 KJV). Notice also, that Philip and the eunuch both went down into the water for the baptism, and after the immersion they came up out of the water (vv. 38-39). My friend, can anyone ignore the relevancy, the immediacy, the importance, the method, the necessity of water baptism in being born again, after careful study, unless he is willfully blinded by his traditions and unscriptural allegiances? Oh, the credentials of man (licenses and ordinations of man-made organizations) that rob men of the credentials of God (true, powerful anointings of God)!

Several additional aspects of water baptism can be gained

15

from Paul's conversion (Acts 9:1-22; 22:3-16). In Paul's case, he was persecuting the church when he was apprehended by the Lord Jesus while walking on the road to Damascus. When an apprehensive Ananias was sent to a blinded, praying, fasting, spiritually hungering and thirsting Saul of Tarsus, God was teaching Paul and us. Although Paul was three days without Christ within (the living bread and drink), and without food or drink (physical nourishment), he was healed by Jesus when Ananias put his hands on him; and it was possibly at this time that Paul was filled with the Holy Spirit as Ananias had spoken. But, it was <u>after this</u> that he was told to "**arise, and be baptized, and wash away your sins, calling on His name**" (Acts 22:16 NAS). If Paul did not receive the Holy Spirit when Ananias first laid his hands on him, then it would have been immediately after his baptism in water that the Lord Jesus baptized Paul in the Holy Spirit. He may have received the gift of tongues then or else later, but we do know that this mature apostle had and used this precious gift more than all of the immature Corinthians (I Cor. 14:18). After being spiritually fed, Paul received something physically to eat. These facts should tell us a few things. Specifically, one is not "**born again**" when one finds out who Jesus is, but one must be born of water and the Spirit. Paul did not fall off a horse, but they led him by the hand as they walked to Damascus (Acts 9:8; 22:11). Those that hunger and thirst after righteousness, spiritually and physically, shall be filled (Mt. 5:6)! Water baptism is vitally important, and when done in faith, involves the washing away of our sins by calling on the name of the Lord Jesus. It is our part in the physical of what God does in the spiritual. It is not recorded that he received the gift of tongues at the time he was filled with the Holy Spirit, as it is not the evidence of this experience. The witness of the Spirit, the fruits of the Spirit, and the revelation of the Spirit within our hearts that Jesus Christ is indeed the Son of the living God are evidences of being born into the family of God, and of having been baptized, immersed, in the Holy Spirit (Rom. 8:16; I Jn. 4:7; 5:1-13; Gal. 5:19-24; I Cor. 12:13).

In the conversion of the men at Ephesus (Acts 19), we can learn also that the baptism of John the Baptist was similar to Christian baptism — both baptisms being for the remission of sins after repentance (Mt. 3:1-17; Acts 2:38; 19:1-7). However, whereas John's baptism could only point to Jesus who was yet to die and be raised from the dead, and to the Holy Spirit which was not yet given (Jn. 7:39), Christian baptism in the name of Jesus Christ the Baptizer makes the experience of being baptized in the Holy Spirit (into the death, burial, and resurrection of the person of Christ) a wonderfully possible present reality! Notice also, since they had not even heard about the Holy Spirit, Paul knew that there was something incomplete about their water baptism, because if they had been baptized according to the commandment of the Lord Jesus recorded in Matthew's gospel, "**in** [*eis,* **into**] **the name of the Father, and of the Son, and of the Holy Ghost** [**Spirit**]," they would have certainly known about the Holy Spirit (Mt. 28:19 KJV). Then "**they were baptized in** [*eis,* **into**] **the name of the Lord Jesus. And when Paul had laid his hands upon them, the Holy Spirit came <u>on</u> them, and they began speaking with tongues and prophesying**" (Acts 19:5-6 NAS). Thus we can also learn that receiving gifts of the Holy Spirit is no indication of spiritual maturity as these Ephesians received them at the very time of their being born again, but it certainly is an indication of wonderful New Testament spiritual life!

At this point it would be good to bring out the fact that the words Jesus instructed the apostles to use in baptism, as recorded in Matthew 28:18-20 where they were commanded to baptize "into" the name of each of the three persons of the Godhead, is not in disharmony with what is recorded throughout the book of Acts where we only find it recorded that they baptized in the name of the Lord Jesus (Acts 2:38; 8:16; 10:48; 19:5; 22:16). Confusion concerning this issue arises because of: (one) a misunderstanding of the Godhead; and (two) a failure to remember that all scripture is given by inspiration of God, and that we need all of the Word of God because a true doctrine will not be found by only considering one or a few passages of scripture. The examples we find in the book of Acts are each a part of the truth, but not all of it. When we put all the instructions and examples together, understand the nature and doctrine of the Godhead, we will understand how to baptize and not be confused by those who see only a small part of the truth and want to emphasize that part to the exclusion of the part that they do not see nor understand. When Jesus told them to baptize in the name of the Son, He didn't need to mention His own name. But when the Jews needed to be baptized on the day of Pentecost, they needed to acknowledge Jesus as the Son of God, their personal Lord and Saviour. The Jews already believed in God the Father and God the Holy Spirit, but they had not been willing to acknowledge Jesus as God the Son; in fact they were responsible for crucifying Him, Peter said (Acts 2:36). So it was necessary for them and all the others recorded in the book of Acts who had the same scriptural background to identify the Son as Jesus, Jesus Christ of Nazareth, and we would do well to do so today! But in doing this, we should not deny the distinct reality of God the Father and God the Holy Spirit, as some do who do not understand the Godhead.

In closing this section on water baptism, it would be good to consider one of the most frequent attacks against it. That is, some say that to require water baptism as a part of salvation makes salvation of works and not of faith. Nothing could be further from the truth. We have a wonderful example given to us in the scriptures that refutes such false reasoning and unscriptural teaching. In II Kings, chapter 5, we read about Naaman the leper, the captain of the army of the king of Syria, who came down to Israel because of the testimony of a little Israeli maiden to be healed of his leprosy. The prophet Elisha gave him a word to go and wash seven times in the Jordan river where many years later God would have another prophet, John the Baptist, baptizing people for their cleansing from the leprosy of sin. The Greek Septuagint translation reads that after he "**baptized**" himself "**according to the word of the man of God**," he was cleansed of his leprosy. Naaman did not earn the salvation of his body, and by his testimony the salvation of his soul, by baptizing himself; how much less do we earn our salvation by having someone else baptize us! He was saved by putting his faith in the words of a man of God, and his faith was fulfilled when he obeyed them. And I say unto you according to the scripture that "**faith without works is dead**"; and unless you obey the Word of God you will not be saved! (Jam. 2:20, 26 NAS; Jn. 3:36). Obedience is not dead works, but true, living faith in action! When Abraham obeyed the Lord by offering his son Isaac upon the altar, it was then "**the scripture was fulfilled which saith, Abraham believed God, and it was imputed unto him for righteousness: and he was called the Friend of God. Ye see then how that by works a man is justified, and not by faith only**" (Jam. 2:23-24 KJV). We are not saved by works, but unto good works, and by them we are justified as they prove that our faith is living, saving faith — not dead (Eph. 2:8-10). Again, Naaman was not healed by works, but because by faith he obeyed the Lord in water baptism. And since we now have the opportunity, we also will not be saved unless by faith we obey the Lord in water baptism — never! The only exceptions would be when a proper prayer of repentance and salvation is offered just before death, and there is no time nor water available at that time (Lk. 23:39-43); or there is total ignorance about water baptism; and such cases are extremely rare! 18

Questions

Q: What is the church? (Please give the scriptural references for your answer to this and the following questions.)

Q: How do we enter the church?

Q: When should we baptize someone?

Q: Who should do the baptizing, and why?

Q: How should we baptize?

Q: What is meant by "obedience of faith?" (Rom. 1:5; 16:26)

Q: How does one receive the Holy Spirit, and is it "automatic"?

Q: What are at least 15 special terms describing experiences of the Holy Spirit which are distinct and specific, and describe them?

Q: Why does Paul say that there is one baptism when in fact there are a number of different baptisms mentioned in the scripture?

Q: What are some of the other baptisms mentioned in the scripture?

Questions and Answers

Q: How should we baptize?

A: We should baptize according to the Lord's instruction as found in Matthew's gospel and the examples found in the book of Acts together with the understanding given in the other gospels and epistles; understanding the Godhead as composing three distinct beings: the Father, the Son, and the Holy Spirit — and identifying the Son as the Lord Jesus Christ. Therefore, to say, "I baptize you in the name of the Father, and of the Son, the Lord Jesus Christ, and of the Holy Spirit, for the remission of your sins. Amen!" is an excellent way to baptize. And it satisfies all but the most narrow of false theology (Mt. 28:19; Acts 2:38; 8:16; 10:48; 19:5; 22:16; Jn. 1:1; 8:16-18; 16:13-14; Col. 1:1-2; 2:2, 9). Also, we immerse one time with the person lying back because we are portraying the burial and resurrection of one person, Jesus the Son of God. To deny scriptural variations and to institute some sectarian form or method of baptizing is to deny the reality of what is to be accomplished, and to confuse and take captive for selfish reasons the babe in Christ.

Q: What are at least <u>15</u> special terms describing experiences of the Holy Spirit which are distinct and specific, and describe them?

A: 1. **"Born** of the Spirit." Being born of the Holy Spirit is when one first receives the Holy Spirit, when the Holy Spirit joins with one's human spirit and one receives a new life from above, from God, and becomes a new person spiritually. The Greek term γεννηθη ανωθεν, *gennethe anothen,* "born *anothen,"* can be literally translated "born from above," from heaven, as well as "born again," or "born anew," and is when one becomes a true child of God and is the possessor of eternal life in Christ Jesus the Lord (Jn. 3:3-5; I Pet. 1:23 - 2:2).

2. **"Receiving** the Holy Spirit." Receiving the Holy Spirit is the initial act of receiving the Holy Spirit into one's own spirit and becoming born again (Acts 8:17; 10:47; 19:2).

3. **"Baptized in** or **with** or **by** the Holy Spirit." Baptized in the Holy Spirit, from the Greek word εν, *en,* meaning preferably "in," is also the initial experience of receiving the Holy Spirit, and describes to us that it is an immersion into the Spirit of God, thereby placing us henceforth in the person of the Holy Spirit, as well as He in us. Jesus is the baptizer, and His baptizing someone in the Holy Spirit is a completely spiritual baptism, symbolized in water baptism which is recorded in scripture as baptizing someone into Jesus (Mt. 3:11; Acts 1:5; 11:16; I Cor. 12:13; Rom. 6:3-5).

4. **"Filled** with the Holy Spirit." Disciples are said to be filled with the Holy Spirit when God so fills the heart with His Spirit of love, grace, peace, joy and all of the fruit of the Spirit in such a fullness that divine life just flows out in word and deed. As we look at the examples in God's Word we find an expression of boldness in worship and praise to God, preaching and singing to others in sharing the wonderful works and Word of God (Acts 2:4; 4:31; 9:17; 13:52; Eph. 5:18). We all need to seek this experience continually!

5. **"Anointing** of the Holy Spirit." This term is descriptive of Jesus anointing or pouring out His Holy Spirit upon us, and although we do receive an anointing at conversion, it is an experience that may and should occur many times after our initially receiving the Holy Spirit. It is a more accurate term that could be used when describing what one receives after conversion when someone dramatically receives the gift of tongues, or any other gift for that matter, which some theology inaccurately calls "the Baptism of the Holy Spirit" or simply

"The Baptism" (I Jn. 2:20, 27; Lu. 4:18; Acts 10:38).

6. **"Impartation** of the Holy Spirit." This term is descriptive of someone receiving something, such as a gift of the Holy Spirit within himself (Rom. 1:11; I Thes. 2:8).

7. **"Falling upon** of the Holy Spirit." This term is used to describe the Lord pouring out His Spirit upon people in a very dramatic way, in a usually sudden outpouring, and often with the accompanying impartation of some spiritual gift (Acts 8:16; 10:44; 11:15).

8. **"Pouring upon** of the Holy Spirit." God is spoken of as pouring the Holy Spirit upon people when, from heaven, there is a great abundance of the Spirit being ministered to the people (Acts 2:17, 18; 10:45).

9. **"Renewing** of the Holy Spirit." This term comes from the Greek word *ανακαινωσεωσ, anakainoseos,* which root *καινοσ, kainos* means "new, made superior, made of a new kind," and the prefix *ανα, ana* means "anew, over again." Thus, this word also describes the born again experience when our spirits are infused with the Holy Spirit and made completely new, in a way that they never have been before. **"If any person is in Christ, there is a new** [*kainos*] **creation; old things are passed away, behold, all things are become new** [*kainos*]" (II Cor. 5:17 lit.). Properly, it is not a renewing like a refinishing of an old table with a new finish, but is like the making of a brand new table, a new creation that never has existed before. Therefore, since the spirit of man is made "anew," the term actually could be better translated an "anewing of the Holy Spirit" rather than "renewing" (Tit. 3:5).

10. **"Washed** in the Spirit." This too is the experience that we all receive when we are born again. We are washed from all our sins and iniquities by the precious, cleansing blood of the Lord Jesus Christ, God's own Son and His sacrificial Lamb! Hallelujah! Thank you, Jesus! (I Cor. 6:11; Tit. 3:5).

11. **"Sanctified** in the Spirit." This term expresses a work of the Holy Spirit whereby one is moved by the Spirit to a closer and more consecrated relationship to God, becoming more holy, that is, like God in character. Sanctification includes many past experiences and a present process, and therefore will involve many future experiences (I Cor. 6:11; II Thes. 2:13; I Pet. 1:2; I Thes. 4:3-8; 5:23).

12. **"Justified** in the Spirit." To justify means "to show, declare, render, or make righteous; to judge and declare guiltless and

therefore acceptable to God." This also takes place when one is born-again (I Cor. 6:11 NAS; Rom. 5:17-21).

13. "**Sealed** with the Spirit." This term describes the fact that when we receive the Holy Spirit we receive God's mark of authentication — proof that we are His (Eph. 1:13; 4:30; II Cor. 1:22; Jn. 6:27).

14. "**Grieve** the Spirit." We are admonished not to grieve (Gk.: λυπεω, *lupeo,* meaning grieve, to make sorrowful, or sad) the divine person of the Holy Spirit by disobedience to Him or His Word, or by unbelief, or wrong actions or attitudes towards others, especially the brethren (Eph. 4:30; Isa. 63:10 NAS; Gen. 6:5-6; Psa. 78:40; Psa. 95:10 KJV; Heb. 3:10, 17 KJV).

15. "**Quench** the Spirit." Because the Spirit is often typified as fire which has a consuming power, we are instructed not to quench (Gk.: σβεννυμι, *sbennumi,* meaning quench, extinguish, suppress, stop, or deny) the power and moving of God's Holy Spirit; whether in assembly or when talking with one another, as He moves among us and in us to purify, enlighten, enliven, and empower us (I Thes. 5:19; Deut. 4:24; Heb. 12:29; Mt. 3:11-12; Acts 1:8; 2:3).

Q: Why does Paul say that there is one baptism when in fact there are a number of different baptisms mentioned in the scripture?

A: In order to understand the scriptures properly, one must always examine them in the context in which they were given. Paul makes the statement that there is only one baptism in the context of a seven-fold basis of unity for all true believers. Paul wrote: "**There is one body, and one Spirit, even as ye are called in one hope of your calling; one Lord, one faith, one baptism, one God and Father of all, who is above all, and through all, and in you all**" (Eph. 4:4-6 KJV). Therefore, he is talking obviously about our baptism into Jesus Christ, which consists of two <u>counterparts</u>, a baptism of water and a baptism of the Spirit; and means the same thing as when the Lord Jesus said Himself that one must be "**born again,**" and then explained it as being "**born of water and of the Spirit**" (Jn. 3:3, 5).

Q: What are some of the other baptisms mentioned in the scripture?

A: 1. The baptisms of the Old Testament — ceremonial and healthful physical washings for spiritual and physical purification and consecration (Ex. 29:4; Lev. 14:8, 9; 15; 16:26, 28; 17:15; 22:6; Num. 19; Heb. 9:10, βαπτισμοσ, baptismos, a washing, a purification by water, an act of dipping or immersion, a baptism).

2. The baptism of Naaman the Leper — for physical healing, and typifying sin (II Ki. 5:14, dipped; in Gk. Sept.: εβαπτισατο, ebaptisato, baptized, from βαπτιζω, baptizo, to baptize).

3. The baptisms of Jewish traditions, the "tradition of the elders" — religious, physical washings (Mk. 7:4 lit., βαπτισμοσ, baptismos).

4. The baptism in the cloud and in the sea into Moses, a type of our Christian baptism in the Holy Spirit and in water into Christ (I Cor. 10:1-4).

5. The baptism of John the Baptist — a baptism of repentance for the remission of sins (Mt. 3:7, βαπτισμα, baptisma, baptism; Mt. 3:1-17; Lk. 7:29-30; Jn. 3:25 - 4:2; Acts 19:3-4).

6. The baptism of suffering and persecution (Mk. 10:38-39; Lk. 12:49-53).

7. The baptism of fire — a purging, refining, consuming work (Mt. 3:10-12; Lk. 3:16-17; Acts 2:3).

23

CHAPTER 2

Babylon

The revelation and understanding of what "**Babylon**" is, for us today and in the future, is one of the most important truths that we can discover from God's Holy Word. This is because it involves every Christian every day; and a right understanding will enable one to build with "**gold, silver,** [and] **precious stones**" rather than with "**wood, hay,** [and] **stubble**" (I Cor. 3:12 KJV). This means that all the work we do for the Lord, all the labor of our lives, will someday be judged by the fire of God's Holy judgment according to His Word; consequently we will either receive rewards or suffer loss according to its quality (I Cor. 3:9-15 NAS). Unfortunately, the vast majority of the teaching today, both by precept and example, is neither instructing nor training Christians to build upon the foundation of our Lord Jesus Christ in God's way; and that is "**upon the foundation of the apostles and prophets, Jesus Christ Himself being the corner stone**" (Eph. 2:20 NAS). Consequently, it is with much sorrow that we can see the inevitable fulfillment of the words of our Lord and Master Himself when He said, "**Many that are first shall be last; and the last shall be first**"! (Mt. 19:27-30 KJV; Mk. 10:29-31; Lk. 13:24-30). If we are to receive rewards at the judgment seat of Christ, which is a fearful time according to our beloved brother Paul, we must be building upon the lives and teachings of God's holy apostles and prophets: those who have given us His Word in Holy writ, those who have lived since, and those who are alive and with us today.

They are the ones that give us a proper interpretation and example of scripture, and the anointed "rhema" (spoken) word of God's presence with us now (Heb. 6:11-12; 13:7, 17; I Thes. 1:5-10; II Thes. 3:6-9; I Cor. 4:14-17; 10:31 - 11:1; Phil. 3:17-20; 4:9; I Pet. 5:1-11; Rev. 2:2). Therefore, I repeat with Paul, **"We must all appear before the judgment seat of Christ, that each one may be recompensed for his deeds in the body, according to what he has done, whether good or bad. Therefore knowing the fear of the Lord, we persuade men"** (II Cor. 5:10-11 NAS). And I will attempt to persuade you, dear reader, of the extreme importance of this teaching and to obey from your heart and soul the truth of God's word to us all!

To begin this study then, let us begin with the proper definition of several scriptural words.

Babel: In the Hebrew language means "confusion," derived from "balal" meaning "to mix up."
In the Babylonian, Chaldean language it means "Gate of God" & "Gate of Gods."

Babel: Noah Webster's 1828 American Dictionary of the English Language.
n. [Heb.] Confusion; disorder.

Babel: The New Bible Dictionary.
Babel, as Babylon throughout its history, became a symbol of the pride of man and his inevitable fall. A city of tyranny.

Babylon: The O.T. Hebrew or Chaldee word is translated in the KJV and NAS Bibles as "Babel" 2 times & translated "Babylon" 302 times even though the transliteration of the word in all cases spells "Babel"; in the the N.T. Greek it is Βαβυλων, *Babulon;* but because in the Latin it is spelled Babylon, it is translated such in the N.T. the 12 times it occurs.

Babylon: The American Heritage Dictionary of the English Language.
1. Any city or place of great luxury and corruption.
2. Any place of captivity or exile.

Babylon: Thayer's Greek-English Lexicon of the New Testament.
Allegorically, of Rome as the most corrupt seat of idolatry
and the enemy of Christianity: Rev. xiv 8; xvi 19; xvii 5;
xviii 2, 10, 21, (in the opinion of some I Pet. v 13 also).

Babylon: Spiritual interpretation:
The recognized principle sin is spiritual fornication which
is idolatry.
A system of idolatry, a place where persons, places,
organizations, Churches, buildings, and things are served
over and against God and His Word! It is started by selfish
ambition, pride, rebellion, and unbelief and often sustained
by force and fear.

Babylonian: The American Heritage Dictionary of the English
Language.
1. Of or pertaining to ancient Babylonia or Babylon, their
people, culture, or language.
2. Characterized by a luxurious, pleasure-seeking, and
immoral way of life.

Babylonian or Babylonish: Noah Webster's 1828 American
Dictionary of the English Language.
1. Like the language of Babel; mixed; confused.
2. In ancient writers, an astrologer.

Babylonian Captivity: The American Heritage Dictionary of the
English Language.
1. The deportation of the Jews to Babylonia and their period
of exile there.
2. The period (1309-77) when the Clementine claimants to
the papacy resided at Avigdon. (A city on the Rhone in
southeastern France.)

Babylonian Captivity: New Testament spiritual interpretation:
A state of spiritual captivity and bondage where spiritual
fornication and idolatry predominate because of selfishness,
pride, rebellion, unbelief, and fear.

With these thoughts in mind, let us then proceed with the
teaching on "**Babylon**."

To best understand the meaning and importance of Babylon today, it is expedient to divide its chronology into six time periods, then we will consider how it influences us and consequently what we should do about it now.

First: Babylon in the beginning.
Second: Babylon after this and throughout the time of the
             Old Testament.
Third: Babylon in the time of the writing of the
             New Testament.
Fourth: Babylon from the New Testament until now.
Fifth: Babylon now.
Sixth: Babylon in the future, and its soon finish!
             Babylon: God's Word to Us Now!

Babylon: In the beginning!

We first find Babylon translated as "Babel," mentioned in the scriptures in Genesis chapters 10 and 11. Chapter 10 includes a listing of the genealogies of Noah and his sons; chapter 11 includes a listing of the precise age of each generation from Shem until Abraham, then called Abram. From a careful study we realize that the initial building of the city and tower of Babel, and God's judgment in chapter 11 takes place before Nimrod later established Babel into the first kingdom of man as recorded in the larger time frame of chapter 10. This account of God confusing the languages of the whole earth and the scattering of the human race at the beginning of chapter 11 is a detailed account of what is mentioned several times in chapter 10; for example, verse 5 says that "**the nations were separated into their lands, every one according to his language, according to their families, into their nations**" (Gen. 10:5 NAS, 18-20, 25, 31-32). The scriptures record that the judgment of Babylon and the division of the peoples of the earth was during the days of Peleg, who was born only 101 years after the flood at the time of this judgment; and thus, he was given his name which means "division" (Gen. 10:25; 11:10-16). Consequently, this was during the lifetime of Noah, who lived for 350 years after the flood, and the lifetimes of his sons (Gen. 9:28).

First let us read the detailed account of what really happened at the world famous "Tower of Babel."

Genesis 11 (NAS)

1. "Now the whole earth used the same language and the same words.
2. And it came about as they journeyed east, that they found a plain in the land of Shinar and settled there.
3. And they said to one another, 'Come, let us make bricks and burn them thoroughly.' And they used brick for stone, and they used tar for mortar.
4. And they said, 'Come, let us build for ourselves a city, and a tower whose top *will reach* into heaven, and let us make for ourselves a name; lest we be scattered abroad over the face of the whole earth.'
5. And the Lord came down to see the city and the tower which the sons of men had built.
6. And the Lord said, 'Behold, they are one people, and they all have the same language. And this is what they began to do, and now nothing which they purpose to do will be impossible for them.
7. 'Come, let Us go down and there confuse their language, that they may not understand one another's speech.'
8. So the Lord scattered them abroad from there over the face of the whole earth; and they stopped building the city.
9. Therefore its name was called Babel [Babylon], because there the Lord confused the language of the whole earth; and from there the Lord scattered them abroad over the face of the whole earth."

Now, let us take these verses and expound on them and glean spiritual truths that lie therein and make application for our lives today. We have quoted these verses first in the New American Standard, but now we will give them in the King James Version so that you can compare them for better understanding.

Genesis 11 (KJV)

1. "And the whole earth was of one language, and of one speech."

The literal translation of this given to us in the margin of the NAS is, "Now the whole earth was one lip and used one set of words." This means that all spoke, not only the same language, but that each word was defined exactly the same by every person. Today the corruption of language is done by the enemies of truth and righteousness by giving words different meanings than originally and usually defined. Therefore, people do not understand one another accurately because they mean different things when using the same words. And as we shall see, this confusion becomes quite obvious in religious Babylon.

2. "**And it came to pass, as they journeyed from the east, that they found a plain in the land of Shinar; and they dwelt there.**" (KJV)

As we travel through life, we come across Babylon. The NAS translates this verse "**journeyed east**" while the KJV is "**journeyed from the east**." Since "confusion" is evident here and in many other scriptures, both translations are by men who were involved in "Babylon." People so involved often "don't know whether they are coming or going."

As they journeyed they found a plain, meaning an area that was easy to cultivate, not rugged nor requiring "**violence**" to take as the kingdom of God does (Mt. 11:12). They "**dwelt there**," or NAS "**settled there**," meaning it is not a life of continuous journey, but of religious ease and complacency. Notice that they "**found**" their place to live. This is typical of Babylonish living as people are not committed to the absolute Lordship of Jesus Christ in all of their ways. Instead of "finding" a house to live in, God calls His servants, as children of Abraham, to go "**to the land which I will show you**"; and He leads them each step of the way (Gen. 12:1 NAS; Jn. 8:39; Rom. 4:11-18; Gal. 3:7; Psa. 37:23). We are to obey by faith as children of Abraham, who "**went out, not knowing where he was going,**" and we are to follow the cloud of the Holy Spirit (Heb. 11:8 NAS; Ex. 13:21-22; I Cor. 10:1). People who are committed to Babylon, practice doing what they want and not what God wants.

Shinar is a prior name for the land which later became known as Babylon. "Shinar" is believed to have come from two words: "shane," meaning "to repeat"; and "naar," meaning "childhood." Therefore, it reveals to us a spiritual meaning of "to repeat childhood"; and so, "Babylon" is a "land" where the "second birth" is either a counterfeit or a mixture of the true and false, where people live in spiritual immaturity. Babylon is always synonymous with BabyLand.

3. "**And they said one to another, Go to, let us make brick, and**

**burn them thoroughly. And they had brick for stone, and
slime had they for morter."** (KJV)

The KJV says "**Go**" and the NAS says "**Come**" meaning they
still do not know whether they are coming or going. Confusion in
direction! Now we see man beginning to build something more
permanent to dwell in than tents or temporary shelters. They had
travelled here to the land of Shinar, and now have decided to build
what first would have been houses to dwell in. Since they are still
aware of only the one true God, their worship of Him would have
been in their homes or in open air meetings. This is the pattern
that God gives in all the scriptures: that He is a Spirit, and that He
is to be worshipped everywhere in spirit and truth, and there is no
need for special buildings. God wants to dwell in our hearts and
homes, and house churches are God's perfect plan for maturing in
love His larger house and family. Centuries later when David
desired to build a house for the ark of God to dwell in, God said to
him, "**Thus saith the Lord, Shalt thou build me an house for me
to dwell in?**" The Lord went on to say that He never had dwelt in
a house and never asked any of His children to build Him a house
(II Sam. 7:5-7 KJV). Solomon, David's son, was allowed to build
one temple for worship for the entire nation of Israel in Jerusalem;
but it was at Jacob's well near Mt. Gerizim that the Lord Jesus said
to a Samaritan woman that she would not worship God in that
mountain (which the Samaritans considered holy) or even in
Jerusalem (where the temple of God was) because "**those who
worship Him must worship in spirit and truth**" (Jn. 4:20-24 NAS).
The prophet Isaiah had said, "**Thus says the Lord, Heaven is My
throne, and the earth is My footstool. Where then is a house you
could build for Me? And where is a place that I may rest? For
My hands made all these things, thus all these things came into
being, declares the Lord. But to this one I will look, to him who
is humble and contrite of spirit, and who trembles at My word**"
(Isa. 66:1-2 NAS).

To apply this spiritually, the true church is made up of
individuals which are likened in scripture to living stones (I Pet.
2:4-8). Brick is man-made and uniform, so they all look alike; this
represents the carnal attempt to shape people according to man's
thinking and will, conformity and uniformity. God makes an
infinite variety of people, according to His divine will, and they
are represented by stones which are never alike. Brick is man's
substitute for godly material. Clay is what man was made of in

31

the beginning before God breathed into him the breath of life. And in Babylon rich mud deposits are abundant around the Euphrates River, while stones are few. Bricks are made from surface mud, whereas stones are dug from a quarry. Obviously, carnality is superficial and shallow; whereas true spirituality is deep and requires effort to obtain.

Slime is a flammable liquid mixture of hydrocarbons which has come from the decomposition of dead plants and animals, and turns firm and hard when exposed to air (it is commonly called tar). In spiritual Babylon, slime is used to hold people together; which means carnal commitments such as unscriptural church names, memberships, and covenants. Slime is literally bitumen which is black and gooey, and is representative of Satan's slime which sticks to the fleshly nature of man; thus holding men together by carnal methods. Being inflammable, it never survives the temptings of Satan or the testings of God, but is burned up in the fires of God's Holy Spirit.

God's mortar when needed is lime; which is a white cement representing the love of God, the only thing that can hold living stones together (II Cor. 5:14). Lime is made from the grinding of limestones together and intense heat. When used, water is needed, which is symbolic of the Holy Spirit. So God's people are to be made of, as well as held together by, love, perfected in the crucible of life by the Holy Spirit. If the stones are large and shaped perfectly enough, no mortar is needed, thus revealing that when we have grown in love and into more maturity, only the invisible spirit of love that is in our hearts is necessary to hold us together. It is a tactic of Satan to try to get God's people to add different carnal methods to God's love in order to hold themselves together. "S" for Satan, plus "lime" for love, equals SLIME!

Stone, not hewn by man, was the only kind allowed by God in building an altar for Him; for if man lifted up a tool to shape it, it was polluted (Ex. 20:25). True worship and sacrifice cannot be man-made and be acceptable to God. The temple, a picture of the true church, was made of huge stones, perfectly shaped, held together by their mass and large surface contact, representing daily intimate fellowship in God's love. The bricks used in Babylon were thoroughly burned with fire in order to make a stronger, more durable building. This fire was not ordered by God nor from God, so it is representative of "strange fire" (Lev. 10:1). This is in contrast to the true fire of the Holy Spirit (Mt. 3:11). Ritual is a strange fire, a counterfeit fire, that masks the shallowness of spirituality. When

32

the "strange fire" of Babylon is used on man-made bricks, the structure has a very hard surface and is difficult to penetrate or destroy. What we usually see today is the "strange fire" of Babylon mixed with the true fire of God, which is the traditions of men mixed with the true Word of God, and the cold mixed with the burning zeal of God resulting in a lot of lukewarmness in the church. It is very difficult indeed to change, and only by a revival of the intense heat of the Holy Spirit can it ever be changed! Also, in the NAS it says that they "**used**" the brick and tar, while the Hebrew lexicon states "and the bricks became (served as) stone for them" (Brown-Driver-Briggs-Gesenius, pg. 226b). This is also revealing to us that the carnal systems of man "use" the people of God. People are used and called to serve as they are supportive of the building of man's carnal kingdoms, but gifted ones and their gifts are suppressed if they do not contribute to the building of these kingdoms. It is wonderful to be used of God and serve Him, but how grievous it is to see people used and then discarded when they no longer suit the fancy or purposes of carnal leadership. The mixture of the true ways with Babylonish ways is very deceptive and usually undetected by the immature and the carnal mind. The hurt and damage to the saints of God who have been "used" by men and their systems is painful, and the cries of those who have been made to stumble are not always heard or often realized by the offenders on their way to "outer darkness"; or, if they are saved men, until on the day of judgment when they see their work go up in smoke as "**wood, hay,** [and] **stubble**" and "**the first will be last.**"

4. "**And they said, Go to, let us build us a city and a tower, whose top** *may reach* **unto heaven; and let us make us a name, lest we be scattered abroad upon the face of the whole earth.**" (KJV)

Here in this 4th verse is found the basic fundamental defects of sin in our fallen natures, the blinding and binding sins that are the cause of the building of Babylon, and the reason for the building of any of the idolatrous kingdom's of man on this earth! Quite simply, they are selfishness, pride, rebellion, fear, and unbelief!

These sins of the carnal nature are energized by Satan and his deceptive ways, often to the point of corresponding spirits entering into a person and driving him on in a relentless pursuit to try to completely satisfy and fulfill a corrupt human nature, which is an impossibility! Man is a spiritual being, and only the Spirit of

33

Root attitides and spirits of
Babylon

Fear

Pride

Rebellion

Selfish Ambition

Unbelief / Misbelief

God can truly and thoroughly satisfy the human spirit, soul, and body (Rom. 8:18-25). A person who has become a partaker of the divine nature can have victory over sin, but will still battle the spirits of the enemy, especially the spirits of Babylon, and may need deliverance from them (II Pet. 1:1-11; I Cor. 12:7-10; II Cor. 11:4; Eph. 6:10-18).

They said, "Go to, let us build us." This is selfish ambition, a root of all that is wicked and devilish. James made it so clear long ago when he said, "If you have bitter jealousy and selfish ambition in your heart" you do not have the wisdom of God, but the world, which is "earthly, natural [ψυχικη, psuchike, soulish], demonic"; and where this wisdom of the world exists there is "confusion and every evil work" (Jam. 3:14-16 NAS; KJV). Men have been trying ever since Babel, in varying degrees, to build God's kingdom by earthly ways, out of the reasonings of their own souls, and according to the deceptions and spirits of Satan. How tragic when men who are truly called of God still build out of their immaturity and carnality such "wood, hay, [and] stubble."

Not only do we find here the root of selfish ambition, but also a root of pride. This is another subtle sin that has infected us all; a sin that we must rid ourselves of by the Spirit of God, and put on true humility, which is humble obedience to the Word of God. They said, "Come, let us build for ourselves a city, and a tower whose top will reach into heaven, and let us make for ourselves a name" (NAS); and men are still striving to build for themselves (often in the name of God) thinking they are reaching God in heaven; competing with others to make for themselves a name everywhere, inside the church and out! The "edifice complex" has gripped the hearts of the multitudes as men seek to build larger and more beautiful buildings than others; and all the while the true buildings of God, the people of God, are neglected personally and used to fulfill a man's carnal imaginations. This is idolatry! Men complain of gamblers playing the "numbers game" and yet they play the numbers with each other and will lose the "gold" in the end — you can bet on it! Note also that the phrase "will reach" is in italic, meaning that it is not there in the original Hebrew; revealing their prideful confidence that the top of their tower will be in heaven, and that they are able to reach God their own way! Oh, how many people the whole world over believe they are actually reaching God in their own peculiar way, and yet it is a way of death, not life. God said, "There is a way which seems right to a man, but its end is the way of death" (Pro. 14:12

35

NAS). All Babylonish ways that are contrary to the ways of God as revealed in His Word are the deceptive, worldly ways of death! And it is pathetic how men who know what it is to be even filled with the Spirit of God still pray and ask God for a name to build under, a name of their own, rather than to build exclusively under His glorious name, the only name under heaven and in earth that can save and deliver a single living soul. We make up names by the thousands for a banner to go to war against the enemy, and he laughs at our feeble, misguided attempts. Oh, when will we unite under the Lord of Hosts, and in His glorious and victorious name, and put the enemies of our God to rout? It is scriptural to name buildings, but we, the people of God (the true building of God) are to wear none other than the name of the Master Himself, our wonderful Lord and Saviour, Jesus Christ of Nazareth. To say that you belong to any other church than His is pure carnality, and a result of ignorance and/or pride.

They said they wanted to build a city and stay put "**lest we be scattered abroad upon the face of the whole earth.**" Here we have <u>rebellion</u> and <u>fear</u>. This rebellion is the kind in which people fail to listen attentively to the Word of God in order to obey it. It is an unheedfulness, unwatchfulness concerning the will of God type rebellion, not necessarily the flagrant, defiant, fist in the face of authority type of rebellion that one often thinks of. God had originally said to Adam, and then again to Noah, and by implication to their posterity, "**Be fruitful and multiply, and <u>fill the earth</u>**" (Gen. 1:28; 9:1, 7 NAS). However, these Babylonian builders did not want to be scattered abroad upon the face of the earth; they did not want to do God's will; they were fearful of doing God's will; so of course God would accomplish it by confusing their languages so that they could no longer live and build together.

We might ask ourselves, would man so rebel against God if he knew and believed that God would judge him for it? Not usually, and so we have here the evidence of another of man's sins, <u>unbelief</u>. And not only did they not believe in God's judgment and justice, but they believed in error that they could actually "*reach into* **heaven**" by their own doing; and so it was not only unbelief but <u>misbelief</u>, as we could call it here and in many of its applications. Mankind had just been through the most destructive judgment the world had ever known, the flood, which had been only about 100 years before, and Noah and his sons were still living and giving testimony to it, and yet man still rebelled against the Word of God! This is unbelief! This is a basic character fault of man, for if Eve would have believed that God meant what He had said, she would not have been so quick to lust after the forbidden fruit and become deceived by Satan; and Adam would not have been so quick to disobey God in order to go along with his wife. We need to believe in both the goodness and severity of God! (Rom. 11:20-23). Man has a natural inclination to not believe in the judgment of an all wise and powerful God. He likes to believe in a God of love, but not in a God who will judge him for his sin, his rebellion, his refusal to obey His Word. Man is too short sighted. He only lusts after his immediate gratification, and not after the results of his choices in the long run. But God says that you can "**be sure your sin will find you out**"; "**for whatever a man sows, this he will also reap. For the one who sows to his own flesh shall from the flesh reap corruption, but the one who sows to the Spirit shall from the Spirit reap eternal life**" (Num. 32:23; Gal. 6:7-8 NAS). Unbelief and a lack of the fear of God (which is the beginning of all wisdom and knowledge) always leads to death and destruction (Pro. 1:7; 9:10; 10:27). Man still loves to believe in heaven, but stubbornly refuses to believe in hell, at least not for himself.

Notice from verses 3 and 4 that they started to make bricks before it was revealed what they were planning to build. So too with man, he starts working for God in his own way from his own human reasonings without really knowing what he is doing, or he is not willing to reveal to his followers what he is planning. When a supply of material is gained, he starts to fashion them into something that the Lord has not instructed him to do, or something contrary in fact to God's Word. And this is the heart of it, namely, man's rebellion. Couple man's rebellion with man's pride, unbelief, fears, and selfish desires, add Satan's deceptions, and you end up with all sorts of systems of error and confusion and suppression and manipulation and "**every evil thing**"! (Jam. 3:16). They range from the most subtle of errors within Christendom to the hideous extremes of Satanism. All along the way the Devil deceives, from eating the wrong food, as at the beginning in the Garden of Eden, to man's final flagrant rebellion, revealed prophetically in the book of The Revelation. Tragically, man's rebellion against the Word of the living God, stirred by Satan, is also being recorded in the lives of mankind today as it was in the beginning. Church, hear what the Spirit is saying!

Now, it is important to note that in their unbelief, selfishness, pride, rebellion, and fear, they chose to build "**a city and a tower, whose top *may reach* unto heaven.**" The first city was built by

Cain after he went out from the presence of the Lord. The root of the Hebrew word for city means "a fortified height, or place." The first times the words "city" or "cities" are mentioned in the scripture are: first the one built by Cain which he named after his son Enoch; then the one we are studying built with the tower and named Babel; then Babel as later established as Nimrod's headquarters and the other cities that he built in his kingdom; and then the cities of the plain, among which were Sodom and Gomorrah, which God destroyed (Gen. 4:17; 11:4; 10:10-12; 13:12; 19:25, 29; Deut. 29:23; Jer. 49:18). Man without God has war in his members and fortifies himself in fear from others, but brings destruction upon himself because of his own selfishness, pride, rebellion, and unbelief (Eze. 16:49-50).

Notice, also, that in building "**a tower, whose top *may reach* unto heaven**" how deceived they were in their vain imaginations, thinking they were reaching God. Oh, how men are deceived today by so many false religions which all have their roots here in Babylon. But what is most tragic is when people in the church think they are pleasing and serving God by building their beautiful buildings and not building the true temple, themselves and the people of God, unto Him who lives and rules in the true heaven.

Another very important revelation given to us here is the tremendous unifying power for either good or evil that there is in building a physical place, or a worship center, or building in a particular name! This is true in the world or in the church, whether it is a congregation, or a denomination, or an organization of any kind! What men do to unite God's people usually divides them! They unite their churches, actually their kingdoms, and at the same time cause a division in God's church, His kingdom. The people of God remain separated and divided by carnal methods and procedures. How true the words of our Lord Jesus are when He said, "**You are those who justify yourselves in the sight of men, but God knows your hearts; for that which is highly esteemed among men is detestable in the sight of God!**" (Lk. 16:15 NAS). Oh, how we need to get on our knees and seek the face of the living God in order that what we build will be only "**gold, silver, precious stones,**" which refers to building faith and godly spiritual attributes; and not "**wood, hay,** [and] **straw,**" which men use in building bricks and buildings (I Cor. 3:12 NAS; I Pet. 1:7; Rev. 3:18; II Tim. 2:20-21).

Another significant revelation is that they first spoke <u>individually</u>, "**one to another,**" or as we read literally in the Hebrew, "**<u>each one</u> unto <u>his</u> neighbor, 'Come, let us make',**" or as in the

Septuagint, "**a man said to his neighbor**," verse 3; and then secondly they spoke <u>corporately</u>, "**And <u>they</u> said, 'Come, <u>let us</u> build for <u>ourselves</u> a city, and a tower whose top *will reach* into heaven, and let <u>us</u> make for <u>ourselves</u> a name, lest <u>we</u> be scattered abroad over the face of the whole earth'**," verse 4. What this reveals is that it is within the soul of each individual person to build contrary to the will of God, and that these huge buildings or programs or organizations cannot be blamed upon just the leadership; leaders only lead where the people have first wanted or are willing to go. Children of God either want to pursue God only, and therefore allow the Spirit of God to knit them unto like minded individuals in building God's kingdom for His glory, or else because of their own unbelief, selfishness, pride, rebellion, and fears, they follow their own soulishness and choose to follow carnal leadership in building men's kingdoms for their own glory. This is a principle we must understand if we are to preach repentance and minister to people in order for them to change their building methods and programs in order to align themselves with God and His Word. We cannot blame all of this carnal building that we see around us only on carnal leadership; but must realize that each individual believer is responsible for how he builds and, therefore, with whom and how he builds together with others. Of course babes in Christ, who make up the vast majority of Christianity, will be easily taken in by carnal leadership because they either haven't had the time it takes to mature or else are not willing to grow, and thus be able to discern the true ways of God (Eph. 4:11-16).

Only as a believer gives himself totally to God in dedication and sanctification, in prayers, fastings, and giving to God with thankfulness and praise, will he become spiritual and see how and with whom he is to build for God. If a believer is yoked to those who are building properly for God, and he or she rebels against the truth of God, that person will be sent out of that spiritual fellowship into Babylon for a period of time for chastening and correction. Tragically, many people have never been out of spiritual bondage, and they die in Babylon, and will be raised on the last day to see for themselves the tragic waste of their lives that could have been spent in true worship and labor, of and for the Master Himself and not of and for themselves or someone else! Oh, the shame of idolatry!

It is also significant to realize that people fulfilling God's will in going to the ends of the earth are not like those who are building in Babylonish ways and going all over the world. The spiritual faith of those who go out under the leadership of the Holy Spirit, relying solely upon Him for their protection, provision, purposes, and path, is quite different from the faith of those sent forth under the names of Babylonish kingdoms which send forth men and women to build their "fortified cities," "worship towers," and "names." This difference in faith within the hearts of people is quite evident in doctrine and in methods, as well of course as in the spiritual life and accomplishments of those involved. What is remarkable also is the observable weaknesses of those who are building with a mixture of the true and the false, the spiritual and the carnal. Stop and meditate for a moment on this. There is quite a difference between those who are trusting in the security and support of one of man's organizations and the promises of people, versus those who are trusting in God alone and His promises only. There is in fact an eternal difference between: those who "**compass sea and land to make one proselyte**," and through insecurity, fear, and unbelief, build a city and a tower, and firmly attach names to their Babylonish creations, lest they "**be scattered abroad upon the face of the whole earth**"; and those who are set apart unto the Holy Spirit and sent to the ends of the earth, and whose attachments are only in and by the Spirit of the living God (Mt. 23:15; Acts 13:1-5). What a shame and what a shock it will be on that great day of the judgment of God Almighty when everything is revealed and the thoughts and intents of the hearts are made known.

5. **"And the Lord came down to see the city and the tower, which the children of men builded."** (KJV)

Here we have an expression that means that the Lord investigated the works of man. This reveals to us that God is just, in that he does not judge before thoroughly examining every circumstance of man. Also, it reveals to us the meaning and significance of what man accomplished apart from God. Notice that God had allowed man to build in his selfishness, pride, unbelief, rebellion, and fear for a period of time. Man is so nearsighted, but God sees the end from the beginning.

These builders were the children of men, not the children of God. And so it still is today, the children of men are busy about building their cities and religious towers apart from the living God. What is tragic, is when true children of God build after the carnal ways of men; thus showing themselves more interested in the physical buildings than building the true city of God, the church, as it has been prescribed to be built.

Another thing revealed here is that with all the efforts of man, they had not reached heaven, for "**the Lord came <u>down</u> to see**" their intentions.

6. "**And the Lord said, Behold, the people *is* one, and they have all one language; and this they begin to do: and now nothing will be restrained from them, which they have imagined to do.**" (KJV)

Here we are told that man can unify himself outside of the will of God, and when he does, he has great power and potential to accomplish anything he sets his mind to. Oh, how many are deceived because they see or experience unity, but it is no substitute of course for the confirmed unity which the Holy Spirit gives!

Notice, that without restraint, these unbelievers who are rebelling against God and His Word and thus following Satan, would eventually turn upon and destroy the true children of God who refuse to do so. Circumstances must be arranged that they will be set upon one another, and not God's people. And this is what has usually happened down through history as God's kingdom goes on. What a shame it is when children of God unite, however, in there demonic carnality, and fight against not only other carnal camps, but the true work and children of God.

7. "**Go to, let us go down, and there confound their language, that they may not understand one another's speech.**" (KJV)

Here we find that God will not forever continue to permit men to build contrary to His will, and he stops men by sending confusion among them. Here it was a confusion in language, but sometimes it is a spirit of confusion or another spirit that causes men to separate from one another in order for them to stop doing what God does not want done. Usually today in the church, God confuses the meaning of words in a language so that people do not understand the same thing by the same word. This judgment in "religious Babylon" causes Christians not to agree with one another so that they will not build together a larger Babylonish structure; but instead they stay divided until they agree to unite under the absolute headship and authority of the Lord Jesus Christ and His called, chosen, and confirmed servant authorities. These are godly men of faith who have been delivered from pride and rebellion, and who are committed to unselfishly serving the entire body of Christ with the vision and compassion of the Lord Himself; not desiring to be lords over God's heritage, as is common in a Babylonish structure.

8. **"So the Lord scattered them abroad from thence upon the face of all the earth: and they left off to build the city."**
(KJV)

God's original intention for man was for man to multiply and fill the earth. God is sovereign, and His will ultimately will prevail among the sons of men and not their own. When God judges man sufficiently, man stops doing that which is contrary to the divine will. The majority of the people quit building the city at this point, but we shall soon see that those bound by rebellion, pride, unbelief, selfish ambition, and fear do not heed God's lesser judgments and so will continue on and later suffer much more severe judgments from the hand of God!

9. **"Therefore is the name of it called Babel [Babylon]; because the Lord did there confound the language of all the earth: and from thence did the Lord scatter them abroad upon the face of all the earth."**
(KJV)

Let us summarize from this concluding statement. Whenever man builds a kingdom of his own, we will find there "Babylon," meaning "confusion," and ultimately the judgment of God. Christians have been judged for their own kingdom building; and their spiritual language and vocabulary has been confused, causing separation to prevent them from building a united kingdom that is not God's kingdom, and that does not have the Lord Jesus Christ as its King and lawgiver, its sustainer and life. Christians do not mean the same thing with the same words; the vast majority are in a state of spiritual confusion, a mixture of truth and error; and this will continue until we seek to build God's kingdom only with Jesus as the head and leading by His Holy Spirit in all endeavors. The Lord Jesus must be acknowledged and embraced as Lord in all areas of our personal lives and corporate lives if we are to build the true kingdom of God. The scattering abroad upon the face of the whole earth in a divided spiritual state is the continuing judgment of God and the direct result of man's idolatry, his pride, rebellion, unbelief, selfish ambition, and fears. Only a humble church, seeking God's will in all ways and God's glory only, will be found building with "**gold, silver, [and] precious stones**" that will endure the fires of God's judgment and be given rewards both now and on that great day when "**we must all appear before the judgment seat of Christ, that each one may be recompensed for his deeds in the body, according to what he has done, whether good or bad**" (II Cor. 5:10 NAS).

Also, please note that the city of "Babel" (a transliteration of the Hebrew word, which was derived from the root word "balal" meaning "confusion, mixed up," and later translated as Babylon), received its name from God because He did "balal" their one language. Therefore, most likely, Hebrew was the one language spoken when all the people were one. The land was known at the time of the judgment as Shinar, and then in the judgment of God the Babylonian language was created from which they then later made the name Babylon to mean "the gate of God" and even later as polytheism arose, "the gate of the gods." Eber, which means "beyond," was a great-grandson of Shem, and is the one from whom we get the name 'Ebrew or Hebrew, meaning "descendant of Eber" (Gen. 11:10-26). At the time of the judgment of Babel when God changed their languages and divided the people, Eber had a son born whom he then named Peleg, meaning "division" (Gen. 10:25). It is the language of Eber, later known as Hebrew, which Eber's descendant Abraham spoke who is honored as the head of the chosen people throughout all generations (Gen. 14:13).

It is important to note that when God confuses people, they become divided. Division therefore is upon occasion the judgment of God by the use of confusion! Again, whenever men build a kingdom of their own, there we have "Babylon," and ultimately find God's judgment of confusion and division, a scattering abroad.

Now that we have seen what happened at the beginning of the city and tower of Babel (Babylon) in what was then called the land of Shinar, and the righteous judgment of God upon the people, let us continue our inquiry to find out what happened next.

In the overview of chapter 10, we find that Noah begat Ham who begat Cush who begat Nimrod who then started his kingdom at Babel (Babylon). Please remember that the Hebrew "Babel" is transliterated as such only in these 10th and 11th chapters of Genesis, but elsewhere throughout the scripture it is translated in

English as "Babylon" (Hebrew: *Babel;* Greek: Βαβυλον, *Babulon;* Latin: *Babylon*). We read,

Genesis 10 (NAS)
8. "Now Cush became the father of Nimrod; he became a mighty one on the earth.
9. He was a mighty hunter before the Lord; therefore it is said, 'Like Nimrod a mighty hunter before the Lord.'
10. And the beginning of his kingdom was Babel [Babylon] and Erech and Accad and Calneh, in the land of Shinar.
11. From that land he went forth into Assyria, and built Nineveh and Rehoboth-Ir and Calah,
12. and Resen between Nineveh and Calah; that is the great city."

In these five verses we shall discover some wonderful truths concerning the kingdoms of man; so let us examine them more closely, using the KJV again so we can compare it with the NAS.

Genesis 10 (KJV)
8. "And Cush begat Nimrod: he began to be a mighty one in the earth.
9. He was a mighty hunter before the Lord: wherefore it is said, Even as Nimrod the mighty hunter before the Lord."

First, we find that "**Cush begot Nimrod**," is a literal translation. The name Cush means "confusion," and another recognized form of the name is Chaos (The Two Babylons). Later when paganism began to flourish and he and his son were deified, Chaos came to be known as "the god of Confusion." Cush has been reported to be the ringleader at the tower of Babel and responsible for God bringing about the confounding of languages; consequently Cush is known also as "Bel," meaning "Confounder." The meaning of the name Nimrod is "rebel"! So we see that the one responsible for confusion, "Confusion," has rebellion in his loins and gives birth to "The Rebel."

And how true this is! When man becomes confused as to what God has said or as to what He means, or as to who God is, it often results in man rebelling against the Word of God! We see that throughout all of history rebellion is a root sin of all that is not of God; man simply refuses to obey God, to live and act like He wants and has told him to! Rebellion is a sin from which all of us

44

born of Adam's race must be delivered! It is usually unrecognized for what it is, and with Satan's deceptive ways and motivating influences, rebellion flourishes like a stinking weed in the nostrils of a Holy God! (compare with Psa. 92:7). But, we are to take heart! **"Foolishness is bound in the heart of a child; but the rod of correction shall drive it far from him"** (Pro. 22:15 KJV). And even though we were dead in our trespasses and sins, walking according to that rebellious prince of the power of the air, and living in the lusts of our mind and flesh; **"God, being rich in mercy, because of His great love with which He loved us, even when we were dead in our transgressions, made us alive together with Christ"** and saved us by His grace (Eph. 2:1-10 NAS). Hallelujah!

Now, Nimrod the rebel was the first to become a mighty one after the flood. We see that word **"mighty"** used once before this in Genesis 6:4 when the sons of God had children by the daughters of men who bore **"the mighty men who were of old, men of renown"** (NAS). These men were the first to make a name for themselves, and they did it by their might; and it was because of these mighty men who were not obeying the Lord, that God brought on the flood. The word for **"mighty"** in Hebrew is "gibbor," and literally means "to be strong, valiant, powerful, bold, forceful, able to subdue others by force." It is used in dozens of cases for those men who were **"mighty men of valour,"** men who were powerful warriors in battle, men who became chiefs over others (I Chr. 12:1, 4, 21, 25, 28, 30; II Sam. 23). It is used in reference to God such as in Deuteronomy 10:16-17 where we read: **"Circumcise therefore the foreskin of your heart, and be no more stiffnecked. For the Lord your God is God of gods, and the Lord of lords, a great God, a mighty, and a terrible [the awesome God (NAS)] . . ."** (KJV). God is telling us here to love Him with all of our hearts and to stop rebelling; because He will either bless us in love when we obey, or subdue us in judgment when we do not. It reminds me of Paul who asked the Corinthians centuries later from his position of authority under Christ whether they wanted him to come to them **"with a rod or in love"** (I Cor. 4:21). If the nations will not **"serve the Lord with fear,"** and **"kiss the Son,"** then He will **"shepherd them with a rod of iron"** (Psa. 2:11-12; Rev. 2:26-27; 12:5 KJV). "Gibbor" is used in other instances, and one instance is where we read about **"mighty men of wealth"** (II Ki. 15:20; Ruth 2:1). Godly men will use their money to help others and to build the kingdom of God; but oh, how some men have subdued others by the power and forcefulness that is available with money!

Concerning the first occurrence of the word "**mighty**," with the mighty men before the flood, we find the earth consequently filled with violence and God not pleased! And Jesus prophesied the same conditions would be in our day before His second coming (Mt. 24:37; Lk. 17:26). Men are trying so hard to rule each other by the wrong methods, and that is by the force of physical strength, soulish or carnal persuasions, or fears that are spiritually demonic; and not by the true spiritual strength of God's love, in the humble service of the fear of the Lord. They want to be served instead of to serve. How tragic when it's by might and not love! We must remember that the kingdom of God is built, "**Not by might, nor by power, but by My Spirit, says the Lord of hosts**" (Zec. 4:6 NAS). Not ours, but God's almighty and powerful Spirit; who is the Spirit of love and peace, grace and mercy. And the scepter of God's kingdom is righteousness. Jesus said, "**The kings of the Gentiles lord it over them; and those who have authority over them are called 'Benefactors.' But not so with you, but let him who is the greatest among you become as the youngest, and the leader as the servant**" (Lk. 22:25-26 NAS); "**just as the Son of Man did not come to be served, but to serve, and to give His life a ransom for many**" (Mt. 20:25-28 NAS).

The literal translation of the phrase in Genesis 10:8, "**he became a mighty one on the earth**" (NAS), is more accurately translated in the margin and by the KJV as "**he began to be**," revealing to us the natural growth of power that comes about in a man's life or ministry. Woe, what development from such a small beginning; but then woe, what development from such a small act of sin as Adam's in the beginning! Unless one is discerning, one does not see the character faults that will lead to the destruction of a man and his ministry. That is why an elder must "**not** [be] **a new convert, lest he become conceited and fall into the condemnation incurred by the devil**" (I Tim. 3:6 NAS).

Next, it is most important to note that Nimrod's might in subduing animals in the hunt, soon led to subduing men, and thus building a kingdom for himself. The exercise of Nimrod's prowess probably seemed rather innocent at first, but men were awed. They said, "**Like Nimrod a mighty hunter before the Lord**" (Gen. 10:9 NAS). The fact that they used the word "**like**" reveals to us that they were comparing themselves with Nimrod and desiring to be like him. This is very unwise! (II Cor. 10:12). This is another reason why there is so much kingdom building of man today. Because of the carnal examples and carnal state of the church set before the young (those who have not even had time to mature), and the fact that they are not only permitted but encouraged to be pastors and leaders, this condition helps in carnality being promoted, propagated, and maintained in the church. The young and those beginning ministry are energetic and ambitious, and they learn the ways of carnal leadership quickly, both by word and deed. (This may be true of older men as well.) Their character has been developed in the recognized sectarian fashion, and they set off with inadequate spiritual understanding, to make a name for themselves, and "to build a church for God." Their main purpose for entering "the ministry" was for "building God's kingdom"; when most, if not all, are really building their own kingdom or the kingdom's of other men! Or, what we will begin to understand is usually the case, a Babylonish kingdom — a mixture which is an inversely proportional ratio between God's true kingdom and the kingdom of man, often carefully controlled. When Babylonishness increases, we have more of man and less of God, until He is either left out or done away with completely.

I need to emphasize here that men building their carnal kingdoms do not usually start out the way they become. <u>As a spiritual structure helps develop true spirituality, so too a carnal structure helps develop carnality.</u> Many a man begins very small in his own eyes, building zealously for God. However, using the wrong methods, means, and structure, causes him to become a leader with undue power, and with improper checks and balances so as to keep him humble before the Lord and doing things only God's way. He could then become an autocratic tyrant, so that the saying comes to pass, "power corrupts, and absolute power corrupts absolutely." People feed his ego and pride, and soon a spirit of pride enters in; and then another type spirit as he spends more time running his carnal kingdom and less and less time seeking the face of God who brought him into ministry. Soon the lusts of the flesh predominate, and he loses the relationship with the Lord that is imperative if he is to succeed in the true ministry that the Lord has called him to. God may withdraw His Holy Spirit from him as He did King Saul; if so, oh, what a tragic and shameful end then awaits him!

Jesus says if we will not repent, He will come and take our candlestick out of its place (Rev. 2:5). Yes, and all this is done **"before the Lord," "before Jehovah"** our God! (Gen. 10:9). Yes, and God sees everything and judges accordingly!

Mankind is defiantly rebelling openly against God, and yet much rebellion in the religious realm is not done defiantly of God, but men think they are serving God when all the while they are rebelling against Him because they refuse to do things according to His ways, which are given to us in His Word. Jesus reveals this clearly when He says that the time would come when men would even put true disciples to death and yet think they were serving God (Jn. 16:2). What is worthy of note is that whatever type of rebellion it is, either defiant rebellion or that which is from the deception of sin, rebellion can cause one to be a "mighty one in the earth," and not be what God would have one to be! In this teaching about Babylon, we want to study the course of rebellion in the religious realm principally, specifically Christianity; but we could trace the history of Nimrod the rebel as a type of "The Antichrist" and the coming world ruler who is the complete embodiment of Satan and all that he is and stands for. One further note that is significant to realize is that Nimrod gained his reputation of being a leader of men from being a great hunter and not a great shepherd. And so today, many great men gain their positions even in the church by developing the skills of a hunter of men rather than a shepherd of men. They care how the sheep can feed themselves rather than how they can care for the sheep. This problem is not new among God's people, as Ezekiel and Jeremiah wrote about it centuries before Jesus Christ. They were told by the Lord to prophesy to the shepherds of Israel, that God was going to deliver His people from their hand and give them to other shepherds who would properly care for the sheep of God's pasture (Eze. 34; Jer. 23). This is being fulfilled in our day and will continue to be as never before as the end of the age approaches. God's plan has always been for the church to be led by a united plurality of shepherding elders in each city, who themselves are ruled over by the Chief Shepherd, the Lord Jesus Christ (Acts 20:17, 28; I Pet. 5: 1-4).

Genesis 10 (NAS)
10. **"And the beginning of his kingdom was Babel [Babylon] and Erech and Accad and Calneh, in the land of Shinar.**
11. **From that land he went forth into Assyria, and built Nineveh and Rehoboth-Ir and Calah,**
12. **and Resen between Nineveh and Calah; that is the great city."**

"**And the beginning of his kingdom was Babel [Babylon]**." When the carnal man gets power over others, he begins to build himself a kingdom, and it is then only the beginning. Nimrod the rebel was the first builder of the kingdoms of men. And notice, this first kingdom ever mentioned in the Bible was Babel or Babylon, meaning in Hebrew "confusion or mixture"; but in the language of Babylon, it means the "gate of god." They actually believed this was truly the way to get to God! And doesn't every false religion as well as every sect of Christianity believe the same thing about themselves? How pathetic! And how we need an understanding of Babylon and its confusing mixture of the carnal and satanic ways of man. God hates our Babylonish ways and He hates a mixture! God demands and deserves pure, undefiled, and undeviled religion!

Next Nimrod built **Erech**, 100 miles S.E. of Babylon, and 40 miles N.W. of Ur where Abraham would soon be born. Here excavations have shown that it was occupied continually for the next 4000 years. Amazingly, in Erech "was discovered the first ziggurat, or sacred temple tower, and evidence of the first cylinder seals [of writing]," dating about 3300 B.C. (UBD, pg. 320). Religion and literature always go together!

Communism, the religion of atheism, has spread around the world very rapidly primarily because of literature. And it is very significant that after the Christian missionaries taught the people to read, the communists filled their hands with their own written propaganda. Not only has the free world not taken advantage of the need for good reading materials, the church has allowed the false religions and cults to flood the world with their false theologies, while to a large degree ignoring the need for godly literature themselves. Literature is so very important to true religion. We would not have our Bible except the Lord had many men write down over hundreds of years what He wanted us to know. The printing press was invented by Gutenberg in Mainz, Germany in the mid-1400's for the express purpose of printing the Bible so that God's Holy Word could be easily disseminated into the hands of the common man in their own language, just as it had originally been written!

I, myself, was saved while reading the life story of a Christian missionary. What had prepared me were the prophecies that my father had taught me from his reading of books and literature at home. I was taught prayer through a book, and then fasting through a tract. It was through literature that I was inspired to go to the mission field as a dental missionary. There I was brought into the reality of the gifts of the Holy Spirit by being challenged to read a book that the Lord had a woman missionary leave on a desk where I was invited to stay. She had been led of the Lord to go to the mission field to work in a Christian book store disseminating literature through Christian Literature Crusade. After my return, it was through a booklet that I came into an understanding of the fivefold ministry; and it was through my study of books on Greek that I came to understand proper interpretation of many scriptural doctrines. And the list goes on and on. Literature, my friend, is very, very important, and both God and the devil know it! Do you? And if you do, stop, and ask yourself, "What am I doing about it?"

The sacred temple tower in Erech is evidence to us that man has always been religious, but the religion of Babylon is the religion of rebellion. Here in Babylon their hair was worn long, a significant sign of rebellion, as it is today! It reminds us of Absalom who because of open, flagrant rebellion against David (who was both his father and his King, and was easily proven to anyone spiritually minded to be God's chosen leader of His people) was killed as he hung in a tree, caught by his hair that he had been so ungodly proud of. It is just as true today that anyone riding the mule of stubbornness will eventually run in fear and be found dangling to death by the cords of pride, unbelief, rebellion, and self-will, having followed the devil by willfully going against God and His Word!

After Erech we have **Accad** which means "to strengthen" or "fortress." And what a revelation it is when we start to understand how the kingdoms of men are strong fortresses, whether worldly kingdoms, false religious kingdoms, or the kingdoms of men within the church itself! Fortresses are strongholds which restrict people; they keep people in and they keep others out. God is our protection, but men love to invent carnal ways "to protect their sheep" when actually they are only protecting their own kingdoms. God's sheep hear His voice, and also hear Him through the Word and the voice of anyone who speaks the truth; they do not need and should not be intimidated by the fear and the carnal tactics and the false teachings that bind so much of the church in disunity and disarray. Disorder in the church will not be changed to God's order until God's leaders repent and come to the Lord and start meeting together to build His kingdom in the earth and not their own.

Jesus is the door and the sheep are to be able to go in and out and find pasture; but too often (in fact the great majority of the time) the sheep are prevented from grazing under the Chief Shepherd's care and are restricted to the oversight of only one shepherd. Consequently they are either famished or prevented from feeding on the balanced and more complete diet that the multiple ministries of plural shepherding elders and others of the fivefold ministry would feed them with (Jn. 10:9; Eph. 4:11-16). In particular, Babylonian administration hates and despises the holy apostles and prophets because their teaching and understanding of the way the church is to live and function in unity is always a threat to the carnal kingdoms of men, the so called "local churches." Sectarianism, whether denominationalism or congregationalism, is always a carnal strong high tower, a substitute for God, and a fortress against the invasion of the Spirit of God and His troops who bring release and freedom to the people of God.

Also, far too often the brick and mortar buildings that men call churches are spiritual fortresses where the saints are guarded or bound and never equipped and led out to battle in order to defeat the forces of Satan, and to take captive his prisoners for the kingdom of God! That job is left to the king of the castle who is unable to defeat the enemy alone, or is too busy administrating the daily affairs of his kingdom. The church is to be a moving flock, not a fixed fortress! God is our fortress! The Chief Shepherd is well able to protect us by His rod and staff. Of course the world says, "Keep religion in your buildings and leave politics to us!" and all the while it subverts and perverts true religious faith and practice, and godly government, under the vigorous leadership of Satan himself! How much wiser are the children of this world in their generation than the children of light! (Lk. 16:8).

It is very significant and important to realize that the forces of evil and the doctrines of atheism, communism, secular humanism, and new-age religion have been spread and are ruining our country and the world without building buildings on every corner which are used but a few hours per week. Instead, they have been spread historically through literature, and most recently by radio and television, and the wicked and godless have now subverted control of the school systems and are using the school buildings to teach our youth five days a week throughout all of their formative years! While we have used God's tithes to build buildings instead of using it for literature, and financing those who would spread the gospel full time, the enemy has used our tax money (not their own) to build schools to teach godlessness and subvert the faith that we are to earnestly contend for (Jude v. 3).

51

I'm afraid the only contention of ours is too often with each other rather than the enemy's troops and teachings.

Genesis 10 (NAS)
10. "**And the beginning of his kingdom was Babel [Babylon] and Erech and Accad and Calneh, in the land of Shinar.**
11. **From that land he went forth into Assyria, and built Nineveh and Rehoboth-Ir and Calah,**
12. **and Resen between Nineveh and Calah; that is the great city.**"

After Nimrod began his kingdom building by lording it over men, he built his first city in which to rule over and from which to extend his dominion. After Babylon, he built three other cities in order to extend his kingdom. Then after gaining control of the land of Shinar, he went into the land of Assyria and built four more cities, over which to rule. Since they were built very close together, just 60 miles around, they were often called by the principal city, "**Nineveh, the great city,**" which Jonah would later write took three days to go through (Jon. 1:2-3; 3:2-4; 4:11). By building these four cities very close together, Nimrod doubled his expanding kingdom, and made it more defendable. (The same thing which is true with so many men today!) You see, the spirits of pride, unbelief, rebellion, and selfish ambition are never satisfied, and they will not stop until forced to, as they have world wide ambitions ever before them. How easy it is to mistake our world wide vision of spreading the gospel for a world wide ambition of spreading our own carnal kingdom! Please note, that as these carnal kingdoms spread, they always require a chief city and central headquarters from which to work, not the "**Jerusalem above**" from which the Lord Jesus speaks and heads His church in direct revelation and instruction through the Holy Spirit! Notice also, that as a kingdom grows, other cities become great; and as this is a carnal kingdom, not taught and sustained by godly means, it leads to competition and eventually division, unless more restrictive carnal methods are instituted to maintain the ways of men in forming and sustaining their kingdoms. These ways are respectable ways in the eyes of the carnal man, the time honored ways of religious institutionalism which are an abomination in the sight of a holy and unifying God. Jesus said "**that which is highly esteemed among men is detestable in the sight of God!**" and then immediately followed that with the statement, "**the kingdom of**

God is preached [brought as good news], and every man presseth into it" (Lk. 16:15, 16 NAS, KJV). Truly, God's kingdom and His ways are truly the "**good news**"! However, unless men's sole ambition is to build the kingdom of God and not any of their own, and they are vigorously praying and fasting to obtain the kingdom and subdue the flesh in true faith, they will always be competing with one another in pride and the carnal ways of deceitful rebellion.

Egyptian history records what is believed to be an accurate account of Nimrod's death. Shem, the godly son of Noah, together with seventy-two judges, had Nimrod put to death for his apostasy. They cut up his body into pieces and then sent them to various cities as a warning as to what divine justice befalls anyone who commits such a dreadful offence as leading others astray from the true and living God. Scripture records similar justice against high offences (Judg. 19:22 - 21:1; I Sam. 11:6-7). Certainly, eternal death and eternal shame befalls all throughout the ages who are guilty of the same horrendous offence.

In conclusion of this section on the beginning of Babylon, let us remind ourselves that whether we are dealing with godless philosophies, or all false religions, or the dozens of false cults that claim to be Christian, or the hundreds of sects within Christianity itself, or the millions of divisions between individual believers, the root causes of all false religious attitudes are all expressed so richly and simply here in these beginning chapters of Genesis — namely idolatry, unbelief, rebellion, pride, selfish ambition, and fears. Whether we go from "**Babel [Babylon]**" to "**Nineveh . . . the great city**" (which are the last recorded words of Nimrod's kingdom building), or whether we go on through the centuries and all around the world to the final conclusion of what was started at the tower of Babel to "**Babylon the great**," "**the great city which reigns over the kings of the earth**," we shall always find that the root causes of any kingdom building, other than building the kingdom of God, are idolatry, pride, rebellion, unbelief, fears, and that devilish selfish ambition that together grip and control not only all of unregenerate mankind but all of carnal Christianity as well (Gen. 10:11-12; Rev. 17:5, 18 NAS; Jam. 3:13 - 4:10; Gal. 5:14-26; II Cor. 12:20). Therefore, we need to stop right now and consider what we are doing about these sins in our own lives, and to reflect upon how we can change our ways to align ourselves with Him and His life.

Having studied Babylon as it is revealed to us in the beginning, let us go on to understand its manifestation immediately following and later during the period of the Old Testament.

Babylon: After the beginning and through out the time of the Old Testament.

Throughout the entire period of the Old Testament we find Babylon mentioned repeatedly. It usually appears as the enemy of Israel, and later as the nation into which God sent His people into captivity because of their sin — their unbelief, pride, rebellion, fears, and self indulgent ways, and their yielding to Babylonish idolatry.

But, before we consider Babylon as a land of captivity, let us consider some of the religious aspects of the city of Babylon. We read from secular history as well as various scriptures how the sin of Nimrod began the foundation of all false religion and spread from Babylon all around the world. [For reference work concerning this, which I consider must reading, the finest book that I've found available is the classic, *The Two Babylons* by Alexander Hislop, published originally in 1853.]

After Nimrod's death, his wife, Queen Semiramis (referred to in the Hebrew scriptures as Ashtoreth or Ashtaroth), deified Nimrod as the Sun-god (later to be known as Baal), as if he was the one through whom all things live and grow. Then she gave birth to an illegitimate son (which was only the first of many children from her dissolute life "for whom no ostensible father on earth would be alleged") due to her licentious practices, which she claimed was a supernatural conception; and that through the child Tammuz, Nimrod had actually been reborn and given new life (The Two Babylons).

Semiramis, because of the danger of openly worshipping her late husband, Nimrod, as the first deified mortal, and her living son, Tammuz, secretly began what has become known throughout history as the Babylonian "Mysteries," and later as the Greek "mystery cults."

Soon Semiramis, the very beautiful but abandoned queen of Babylon with the "son of God" in her arms in supposed fulfillment of the prophetic scripture of a promised Messiah, "became the favorite object of worship. To justify this worship, the mother was raised to divinity as well as her son, and she was looked upon as destined to complete that bruising of the serpents head . . . which Nimrod, the great Son, in his mortal life had only begun" (The Two Babylons, pg. 75).

Together Nimrod, Semiramis, and Tammuz were worshipped as gods by many nations, including Aram, Sidon, Moab, Ammon, and Philistia. But after Semiramis and her son Tammuz became the focal personages and objects of worship, this began what has been called "mother and child worship," which spread throughout the world and became known by different names in each language. In classical Greek writings, Nimrod is known as Ninus, his wife Rhea, and her son as Baccus; while in Hebrew they are most often known as Baal, Ashtaroth, and Tammuz (Judg. 2:13; 10:6; Eze. 8:14-16). In Canaan or Phoenicia, which later became part of Israel, we find this mother and child worship also by the names of Ashtoreth and Tammuz (I Ki. 11:5, 33). In Persia, the mother was known as Aditi (the goddess of infinity), and her son as Mithra (the sun-god), while in India he was known as Mitra. In Egypt they were known as Isis and Horus; in Greece as Aphrodite and Eros, as well as Irene and Plutus; in Rome Venus and Cupid, as well as Fortuna and Jupiter. In nearby Etrusca the mother-goddess was called Nutria, up in Germany Hertha, in Scandinavia Disa, among the Druids Virgo-Paritura. She was also known in Rome as Cybele, by the Greeks and Syrians as Astarte, and Ishtar by the Assyrians. As this cult moved east of Babylon the goddess was also called Indrani in India; and the mother and child were known also as Isi and her child Iswara, as well as Devaki and Crishna. Moving on to China she was known as Shing Moo and also Ma Tsoopo; and she and her child have been found on the American continents among primitive Indian tribes here. So truly, the words of the heathen in Ephesus later rang out, "**Great is Diana** [translated from Latin, but the Greek is Artemis] **of the Ephesians,**" "**whom all Asia and the world worshippeth**" (Acts 19:28, 27 KJV).

Another aspect of Babylonish worship is that it became polytheistic; it had over 5000 additional gods and goddesses who the people believed had once been living heroes on the earth and had then moved to a higher plane. They had a god for each month and each day of every month, for every problem and purpose, for every occupation and aspect of life. But, even though they developed many lesser gods and goddesses, they maintained a belief in the one supreme God who existed in three persons. However, the doctrine of the Triune God was perverted as it came to be "the Eternal Father, the Spirit of God incarnate in a human mother, and a Divine Son, the fruit of that incarnation" (The Two Babylons). Then the first person of the Godhead became overlooked, and the mother and child became the grand objects of worship. Such is the case in Hinduism today; "Brahma, according to the sacred books, is the first person of the Hindoo Triad, and the religion of Hindostan [the name of the northern part of India] is called by his name [Brahmanism], yet he is never worshipped, and there is scarcely a single temple in all India now in existence of those that were formerly erected to his honour" (The Two Babylons, pp. 19 & 20). Therefore the lustful and licentious Semiramis was worshipped as the "Mother of God"; and Babylon's Mysteries (as her secret religious practices were known by) became the foundation of idolatry and consecrated prostitution; this was the original "**Mystery Babylon . . . the mother of harlots and abominations of the earth**" (Rev. 17:5 KJV).

Semiramis, who was Queen of Babylon, after her husband's death reigned as sole ruler of both the state and religion. Consequently another practice and belief of ancient Babylon, and the cult which spread around the world, was to worship her also as the "**queen of heaven**," as the prophet Jeremiah tells us (Jer. 7:18; 44:17-19, 25). Archaeology reveals to us that many centuries before Christ, the Phoenicians worshipped her under the name of Astarte by the use of a chain of beads. In ancient Greece, India, Tibet, China, Japan, and Rome, as well as in modern Islam, the "prayer beads" have been found repeatedly to be used in the repetition of "vain prayers" as warned against by our Lord himself (Mt. 6:7-15). After her death this Babylonian mother was claimed to have been raised from the dead and taken bodily up into heaven where she now sits as a divine "Mediatrix" with her son.

It is very significant as we follow this false cult around the world and throughout the centuries, and how it will become mixed with true Christianity later, that we mention several other important facts for further understanding and investigation. The story was told and retold, and we read that after Nimrod was killed, Semiramis gave birth to Tammuz because of her licentious practices, and eventually an evergreen tree (the palm tree was used in Egypt, the fir tree in Rome where it was decorated with red berries) was used as a symbol of his birth in winter. The ever green tree symbolized Semiramis' claim that everlasting life came through her son, and that after Nimrod was killed he came back to life in the person of her son — the beginning of reincarnation. Centuries later in Rome, before Christ was born, a feast was celebrated in one cult of sun worshippers from December 17-21, for five days before the winter solstice on December 22, the shortest day light day of the year. It is one of the two times of the year when the sun is at its greatest distance from the celestial equator. After the winter solstice the day light time is measurably longer, thus indicating the beginning of the return, the reviving, or rebirth of the sun. This feast in Rome, shortly after the time of Christ, was extended two more days and was called the Saturnalia, Feast of Saturn (the Roman harvest god), another name for Nimrod, when "many families offered sacrifices of young pigs [precursor of the Christmas ham]" (World Book Encyclopedia, WBE). It was a gay, seven day festival when schools were closed and businesses stopped. Drunkenness and revelry abounded. "Families held banquets. . . . The last days of the festival were spent visiting and exchanging presents," some of which were little clay images (WBE). Since December 25th was the celebration of the birth of Mithras, the Babylonian Messiah and Persian sun-god, which would reach Rome later in about A.D. 69, the Roman Emperor Aurelian who had come to worship the sun, in A.D. 274 declared the sun-god as the official deity of the Roman Empire and set December 25 as *natalis invicti solis,* the day for the celebration of the "Nativity of the Invincible Sun." Thus the Saturnalia, the birthday of the sun, and the chief feast of Mithras, whose feast consisted of chickens and geese, with pine-cones providing aromatic fuel for the altar, were all united by the Roman Emperor on December 25.

The Yule Log comes from the Chaldee (Babylonian) name for "infant" or "little child," and was burned on December 25th by our Pagan Anglo-Saxon ancestors as "Yule-day" or "Child's-day." It represented "the dead stock of Nimrod, deified as the sun-god, but cut down by his enemies; the Christmas-tree is Nimrod *redivivus* — the slain god come to life again" (The Two Babylons).

"Kissing under the mistletoe" was started by the Babylonians while the Jews were in captivity there. The mistletoe (which is a tree parasite, meaning it will eventually kill the host tree) was regarded as a representation of the Babylonian Messiah, the counterfeit of the divine "**Branch**" (Zec. 3:8; 6:12), and the kiss being a token of pardon and reconciliation (Gen. 33:1-4; 45:1-15; Lk. 15:20) or greeting (Rom. 16:16; I Cor. 16:20; II Cor. 13:12; I Thes. 5:26; I Pet. 5:14).

"Thus the very customs of Christmas [Christ's Mass] still existent cast surprising light at once on the revelations of grace made to all the earth, and the efforts made by Satan and his emissaries to materialise [materialize], carnalise [carnalize], and degrade them" (The Two Babylons, pg. 99); and how they counterfeit the one who is the "**Truth**" and the "**Word of God**," and create a deceptive and deadly mixture.

It was further taught that Semiramis had been miraculously born also, as having come down from heaven in a huge egg. Later, the rabbit, as well as the egg, became a symbol of fertility; and so we have the Easter rabbit and eggs. It was also taught that after her son Tammuz was killed at forty years of age, she mourned and fasted for him for forty days and nights in the spring of the year (Lent means "spring"), one day for each year he had lived. Consequently in the spring when vegetation springs forth, it was taught that this was a sign that Tammuz was restored to life again from the underworld in answer to their prayers, which period ended with a great Spring Festival and feast; and an egg was used again as a symbol of his life out of death. A worship service at sunrise became part of the celebration in honor of Tammuz because Semiramis taught that the sun, the source of light, heat, and fire, had been incarnate (in flesh) as Nimrod, who had been reincarnated as Tammuz, the source of spiritual light and salvation. The period of weeping for the false Messiah to come forth in spring is what the prophet Ezekiel saw many years later when this paganism of Baal (sun & fire) worship was mixed with the true religion of Jehovah, when the Israelites were shown to the prophet in a vision as being at the temple of God with women "**weeping for Tammuz**" while men "**worshipped the sun toward the east**" (Eze. 8:14, 16 KJV).

The name of this mother-goddess in Babylon and Assyria later was Ishtar (which is akin to the Hebrew Ashtoreth mentioned in the scriptures), the goddess of love and fertility, identified with the Phoenician Astarte (American Heritage Dictionary). Astarte is believed to be the same as "Eostre, the goddess of love or Venus of the north, in honor of whom a festival was celebrated by our pagan ancestors, in April; whence this month was called Ostermonath" (Noah Webster's 1828 Amer. Dict.; see also TTB). This celebration in German was called Ostern, and in Saxon, Easter. Easter only appears once in the King James Version of the Bible, but is an erroneous translation of the Greek word πασχα, *pascha*, which means Passover (Acts 12:4). As it is the custom of Babylonians to eat the flesh of unclean things, this became also the practice of the backslidden Israelites who worshipped Babylonian deities. This is referred to by the prophet Isaiah when he wrote, "**Those who sanctify and purify themselves to go to the** [idol] **gardens, following one in the center [after the rites of Achad** ("The Only One")]**, who eat swine's flesh, detestable things, and mice, shall come to an end altogether, declares the Lord [Jehovah]**" (Isa. 66:17 NAS, ref. The Two Babylons, pg. 16). (Achad, whose name means "The Only One," was a deity consisting of three persons, and from which as this religion spread eastward is the source of the three headed Buddha many years later.) And so we have the Easter ham.

From the tower of Babel spread the practice of building elaborate buildings, temples and towers; images and later obelisks were erected. Although immorality was an intricate part of Semiramis' religious practices, absolute authoritarian rule controlled the masses, and secret rituals controlled the celibate priests. Elaborate ceremonies developed, and very quickly horrible sacrifices. Abraham, who was living during the lifetimes of Noah and his son Shem, came from Babylon where he was both very familiar with what happened at the Tower of Babel, and also with human sacrifice as we can understand from his testing with Isaac. Later, during the time of the Old Covenant, it is recorded that children were sacrificed to pagan gods such as Moleck and Baal as sons and daughters were made to "**pass through the fire**" to them (Lev. 20:1-3; Deut. 12:31; II Ki. 16:3, 17:30-31, 23:10; Jer. 32:35); and eventually the practice of eating the flesh of human sacrifices developed. Baal, we remember, was the main god of the Babylonish heathen in Israel referred to dozens of times throughout the scriptures.

Other significant facts concerning Babylon and the type of culture that developed is that at first they used the rich mud deposits from the Euphrates river to make clay brick temples known as ziggurats. This is from the Babylonian word "ziqquratu" and "denotes a sacred temple tower and means a 'pinnacle' or 'mountain top'" (UBD). What some believe to be the remains of the oldest ziggurat in existence is at Biblical Erech, the city built by Nimrod after Babel (Gen. 10:10). However, the ziggurat called Birs Nimrud is six miles SW of ancient Babylon, and others believe this is the site of the original tower of Babel. It is built on a square base of paved brick that is 500 feet on each side. Then there are seven square stages of brick built up into a huge terraced pyramid; the largest at the bottom being 272 feet on each side and 26 feet high, and the top level being only 20 feet square and 15 feet high. It is therefore approximately 138 feet to the top of the seventh stage which has the remains of an ancient chapel building nearly covering the top which is an additional 15 feet high. The entire ziggurat is a solid mass of clay built with buttressed walls and each paved level of sun dried brick and slime (bitumen). It is interesting to note that in support of their religious astrology, each of the seven levels is painted with a different color in honor of gods, represented by planets; five major planets plus the sun and the moon. There are no interior rooms except for the chapel on top, which is reached by exterior stairways winding up the sides of the ziggurat. History records how the kings of Babylon "greatly prided themselves upon the height of their temples and boasted of having their tops as high as heaven" (UBD). [It is also interesting to note what looks like a miniature Babylonian ziggurat, approximately 30 feet high, that was recently built and now stands so proudly on the campus of my alma mater, Ohio State University, between walled mounds of dirt with wild looking tall grass on top which also look like these ruins of ancient Babylon.]

Later in Babylonian history, additional shapes were used and the temples and palaces were among the most splendid buildings of the ancient world. The "Hanging Gardens of Babylon" built by Nebuchadnezzar with the Euphrates River flowing through the city of Babylon was considered one of the "Seven Wonders of the Ancient World." This same great king built a huge image of gold, 90 feet high, in honor of himself, as a result of a dream that he had. When Daniel's godly interpretation was mixed with Nebuchadnezzar's Babylonian idolatry, the king demanded everyone to bow down and worship the golden image that he had made; but Shadrach, Meshach, and Abed-nego obeyed God's Word in refusing to worship anything or anyone but God Himself (Dan. 2-4). Although Nebuchadnezzar witnessed the miraculous saving power for the Hebrew children of the true and living God, it was not long before the same spirits of pride, selfish ambition, rebellion, and unbelief which were in Nimrod manifested themselves openly when Nebuchadnezzar boasted as he looked out from his palace, **"Is this not Babylon the great, which I myself have built as a royal residence by the might of my power and for the glory of my majesty?"** But, **"While the word was in the king's mouth, a voice came from heaven, saying, 'King Nebuchadnezzar, to you it is declared: sovereignty has been removed from you . . . [for] seven periods of time** [seasons; years]'"; and immediately the word was fulfilled (Dan. 4:30-33 NAS). A similar word of judgment is being spoken today from the same God to the present ruler of

Babylon, Saddam Hussein, possessed with the very same spirits. Amazingly, men of God who build their idolatrous kingdoms, and who may then even discover the miraculous power of the true God, often find themselves judged and removed from their "church kingdoms" because of these very same spirits today. We are in the very last of the last days now! The coming of the Lord Jesus Christ in power and great glory draws near! Soon, before this great event, many in and out of "Babylon" all over the world will say with Nebuchadnezzar of old, after the dealings of God, "**Now I . . . praise, exalt, and honor the King of heaven, for all His works are true and His ways just, and He is able to humble those who walk in pride**" (Dan. 4:37 NAS).

Additional facts concerning the land of Babylon which we need to know in order to more thoroughly understand this religious and political system are as follows: It had various classes of society. "The aristocracy included government officials, priests, and large landowners. The common people worked as traders, craftsmen, clerks, and farmers. Slaves made up the lowest class.

"The Babylonian economy depended largely on farming. The king and nobles owned much of the land. Temples also controlled large acreages.

"Babylonian religions had many gods, elaborate temple rituals, and colorful religious festivals. Every important city had its own special god or goddess. The king represented the deity on earth.

"There was much literary work and huge libraries. Stone statuettes were carved about 3000 B.C. with hands clasped in worship. Pottery, gold and silver jewelry were works of art. Since it was a land without stones or trees, the people used baked or sun-dried bricks for building. Industry and commerce were remarkably well developed and they exported agricultural products and native crafts throughout the Middle East" (WBE).

In 539 B.C., Belshazzar, king of Babylon, saw the handwriting on the wall for which Daniel gave the interpretation, and his Babylonian kingdom fell to Darius the Mede who then ruled as king over the land of Babylon under Cyrus the Great in the expanded Medo-Persian Empire. Prior to this, Hammurabi, one of the great kings of Babylonia in the 1700's B.C., had given the famous law code known as "The Code of Hammurabi." Then there developed what seems to be a perverse love of law-making. Now with Darius the Mede in control of Babylon, the enemies of God tried to use the law of the Medes and Persians which could not be revoked to destroy Daniel by deceiving the king and having him pass a law against prayer to God; this resulted in legally forcing him to have Daniel thrown into a den of lions. But God intervened with a miracle and saved Daniel; and instead, all of the wicked who plotted against him were destroyed by the lions.

With its conquest by the Medes and Persians, the destruction of Babylon began as prophesied by Isaiah (13; 14; 21; 47) and Jeremiah (50; 51), never to rise again!

Now that we have considered some of the aspects of the religion and culture of ancient Babylon, let us consider why it became a land of captivity for God to send His people into.

Babel, Babylon, being the beginning and center from which all false religion started and spread, was made by God a "land of captivity" for His people as they were influenced by and then gradually given over to Babylon's idolatrous, iniquitous system. The reason is that the same sins that initiated Babylon's creation — namely, rebellion, pride, selfish ambition, fear and unbelief — were not repented of by God's people, and God had to judge and chasten them also.

We see these sins in Israel continually and they were so very evident at the time that Israel cried out to become like all the other nations, and to be led by a man as king instead of God as king. God had been their judge, lawgiver, and king for many centuries, and had given them the law through Moses and appointed judges to represent Him to the people. When Israel was obedient they were blessed, and when they were disobedient they were chastened. But then as the people continued to forsake the Lord and serve Babylonish gods as they had done since they had been brought forth from Egypt, the elders of the people came to the prophet of God, Samuel, and said to him, "**Behold, you have grown old, and your sons do not walk in your ways. Now appoint a king for us to judge us like all the nations**" (I Sam. 8:1-8 NAS). They should have requested better judges, but since they demanded a king, a king the Lord would give them; but He warned them that they would not like the result. The king would take the best of everything for himself and his servants; take a tenth of all their produce, vineyards, and flocks (a tithe for his kingdom, not the Lord's servants); bring the people into servitude for himself; and the Lord would not listen to their cry when they became distressed because of it (I Sam. 8:9-22). But the people would not listen to the prophet of God, rebelled against having Jehovah as King, refused to believe in His ways, and were lifted up in pride; they thought they knew what was best, as they were determined to have their own way (I Sam. 10:19; 12:16-19). They got it — in a king just like themselves, Saul. Although not proud at first, he rebelled against the word of the Lord that came repeatedly through God's prophet (I Sam. 15:17-26). He did not believe and wait on the prophet to do the ministry, but presumptuously did the work of God on his own (I Sam. 10:8; 13:8-14). He feared the enemy, and he feared his own people, more than he feared God (I Sam. 13:11-12; 15:24). One of the most graphic examples of Saul's rebellion is recorded in the fifteenth chapter of First Samuel where the prophet of God reprimands him for his rebellion and tells him that God has rejected him from being king over His people. Contained in Samuel's words of rebuke to Saul are insights we need if we are to properly understand the nature of all false religion, Babylonish worship, and the supernatural demonic aspects of it. Samuel said, "**For the sin of witchcraft is rebellion. Idolatry and iniquity are both insolent willfulness**" (I Sam. 15:23 lit.). Here God is revealing to us that the principal reasons that people become involved in witchcraft and occult activities, or the idolatrous ways of Babylonish type religious practices, and open themselves up to the deceitful schemes of the devil, are the sins of rebellion and self will! And add to these sins, the involvement of spirits of rebellion and other types of demonic spirits, and we can better understand religious history and the state of spiritual conditions today and in the future.

Now, after Saul was rejected as king and David was anointed to replace him, Saul was not dethroned in the natural for many years because God used him in the preparation of David and the nation of Israel. This preparation took many years before God brought David to the throne.

Also, when Israel rejected God as King and built its first kingdom of a man, with a man as king making the rules, they did not keep the year long Sabbaths for the land as God had commanded them. And they lived this way for 490 years, so God sent them into the Babylonian captivity for 70 years, one year for each of the seventh year Sabbaths that the nation of Israel had not kept according to the word of the Lord (Lev. 25:3-4; 26:33-35; II Chr. 36:20-21; Jer. 25:8-14; 29:10-14).

The story of Israel in Babylonian captivity is one of sorrow, as they hung their harps upon the willows and said, "**How shall we sing the Lord's song in a strange land?**" (Psa. 137:4 KJV). Although they planted gardens and built houses in Babylon, they were not building God's kingdom but someone else's (Jer. 29:5, 28). They did not enjoy the freedom that they had experienced in Israel, nor bring God's victory over the evils of the land, but were under harsh servitude; and those who were left in Jerusalem suffered great persecution and poverty (Lam. 1:1-5, 11; 5:1-18). Nebuchadnezzar, king of Babylon, was of course under attack by the same spirits that had captured Nimrod; and when he was lifted up in pride he was dramatically humbled by the God of heaven (Dan. 4). His selfish ambition was allowed by God to build one of the wonders of the world, and then God dealt with him and brought him out of unbelief and into the faith of who was really on the throne in heaven and in earth.

The final destruction of the Babylonian Empire came in 539 B.C. when one of the generals under Cyrus the Great, ruler of the Medes and Persians, conquered the capital city of Babylon in one night; and the decay of that great city began (Dan. 5:30-31). For a very short time Darius the Mede ruled there as part of the Medo-Persian Empire under Cyrus the Persian (Dan. 6:28, 9:1; 10:1). In 514 B.C. King Darius Hystaspes, the third king of Persia after Cyrus, subdued a rebellion at Babylon and tore down its walls (Ezra 4:5; Hag. 1:1; Zec. 1:1). The last king of Persia was defeated in 331 B.C. by Alexander the Great, who came to Babylon while establishing the third world empire prophesied by Daniel — Greek (Dan. 2:39; 7:6; 8:21; 11:2-3). He attempted to make Babylon, which lay mainly in ruins, the capital of his empire by rebuilding it, but the cost was prohibitive. God had said that Babylon would never be rebuilt (Isa. 13:19-22; 14:22-23; Jer. 25:12; 50:13, 39-40; 51:26), and so soon Alexander died at only 33 years of age, after his brilliant military conquest of the world. After his death four of his ruling generals eventually succeeded in dividing the empire into four kingdoms as prophesied, each setting up a royal house with themselves as king (Dan. 8:22; 11:4). Seleucus, one of the four, conquered Babylon in 312 B.C. and ruled over the eastern area known as the Syrian kingdom. He soon founded Seleucia as his capital not too far from Babylon, but on the Tigris river, and gradually Babylon was abandoned, its buildings fell into complete ruins, and it became a desert, the home of unclean creatures as prophesied (Isa. 13; 14; 21; Jer. 50; 51). Thus we have the end of the greatest world city of antiquity, queenly Babylon, which has laid in ruins for two millennia until this day.

Now that we have seen Babylon as it was principally during

the time of the Old Testament, and its influence on God's people and the result, and then its final destruction, let us look at Babylon in the time of the writing of the New Testament.

Babylon: In the time of the writing of the New Testament.

Since the city of Babylon had been destroyed and had lain in ruins for several hundred years by the time of the writing of the New Testament, the Babylon that is mentioned in the New Testament scriptures is not the original physical city of Babylon but refers to either the land of Babylon or the next world empire's ruling city that had taken on all the spiritual characteristics of the original city of Babylon from which it had gotten them. That city is, of course, none other than Rome, the fourth and last world empire prophesied by Daniel which he wrote would kill the Messiah, and destroy Jerusalem and the temple (Dan. 9:26).

The name Babylon is mentioned twelve times in the New Testament. The first five times, it is clearly in reference to the historical land of Babylon which was the name of the land when the Jews were brought to it in captivity (Mt. 1:11-17; Acts 7:43).

The next time Babylon is mentioned is when Peter includes a closing greeting to the Christians he was writing to in what is known today as Asia Minor or Turkey. At the end of his letter he indicates that Silvanus (Latin form of the name Silas) was the one through whom his letter was written; and he also indicates where he is writing from: "**She who is in Babylon, chosen together with you, sends you greetings, and so does my son, Mark**" (I Pet. 5:13 NAS). All scholars agree that the "she" in this passage refers to the church of the Lord Jesus, not an individual woman. In fact, the King James Version translates the literal "she" as, "the church"; which is also according to the reading in some early manuscripts. Also, Mark was not Peter's son naturally, but spiritually. And so as Peter is referring to the church in a figurative sense, and to Mark in a spiritual sense, he refers to Rome in the figurative-spiritual sense that both the Christian church and the Jewish rabbis of the day understood so very well. Also, I believe there is good scriptural evidence to believe that it is Rome, the same city meant in the remaining six references to Babylon in the New Testament, all in the book of The Revelation. First, Peter had founded the church of Rome on the day of Pentecost when he preached to the devout Jews that had been gathered in Jerusalem **"from every nation under heaven"** (Acts 2:5). Some of these we are expressly told were **"visitors from Rome, both Jews and proselytes"** (Acts 2:10 NAS). Peter had been chosen by the Lord Jesus to have the keys of the kingdom and thus be the first to open the doors to both the Jews and the Gentiles (Mt. 16:18-19; Acts 15:7). This he did on the day of Pentecost to the Jews, and again to the Gentiles — more Italians — Cornelius, his relatives and some friends; which were living at Caesarea, the port city to Italy from which they would spread the gospel and from which also Paul would later embark for Rome (Acts 2; 10; 11; 23:11, 23, 33; 27:1). Also, the area of ancient Babylon was known principally in the time of the New Testament writers as Mesopotamia, meaning "the land between the rivers" — the Tigris and Euphrates. When Luke records the different peoples gathered from all over the world on the day of Pentecost, he mentions the **"Parthians and Medes and Elamites, and residents of Mesopotamia"** together, all peoples from this same general area; and quite importantly he does not call this land Babylon (Acts 2:9 NAS). Neither does he when referring to where Abraham lived, but stated it was **"in Mesopotamia"**; originally called **"Ur of the Chaldees"** (Acts 7:2; Gen. 11:31 KJV).

Again, the last six references to Babylon are about the city which then ruled over the kings of the earth, where Christians were taken captive and killed: Rome — and its future development (Rev. 14:8; 16:19; 17:5; 18:2, 10, 21). Both of the great apostles, Peter and Paul, were martyred at Rome, as were tens of thousands of other faithful witnesses for Jesus. The historical literary and archaeological evidence is overwhelming that Peter was executed in Rome. Nero opened his gardens on the Vatican hill and executed a great multitude of Christians there in A.D. 64 and Paul was martyred in Rome on the Ostian way. Within less than 150 years we have records by the Roman presbyter Gaius that memorials had been erected at both of these spots to each of these great founders of the church in Rome. Later, in A.D. 335 the Emperor Constantine had the bones of the two apostles transferred from the catacombs, where they had been taken and kept for many years, to the basilica of St. Peter on the Vatican hill constructed over the tomb of Peter, and to the Church of "St. Paul Outside the Walls" on the Ostian road where Paul was martyred, both of which he had built.

Rome and her empire were persecuting Christians when The Revelation was written in approximately A.D. 95, and she continued to do so for another 200 years. Then the Spirit of Jesus conquered pagan Rome, so Satan changed his strategy.

What happened was that in A.D. 306 Constantine I (c. 280-337 A.D.) was declared Emperor of the West Roman Empire by both his own and his father's armies after his father, who was the emperor, died. Then in A.D. 312 Constantine was dramatically converted in an historical moment when he and his army faced Maxentius and his army, his strongest rival. This confrontation would determine his destiny and that of the empire, and actually that of the civilized world. He marched from France into Italy with his troops, agonizing in prayer to the gods; and the true and living God revealed Himself by a vision in the heavens, brighter than the sun, the day before the battle. It was visible to both him and his soldiers, that they would be victorious if he went forth in the name of Christ. He pondered upon the vision, and then the Lord confirmed His instructions in a dream that night. The next day, Constantine (in his new faith and with the Spirit of the Lord going with him) and his army who was also energized in spirit, defeated Maxentius at the famous "Battle of Milvian Bridge."

And so Christianity began to receive favored treatment among all the different religions in the western empire. A year later in A.D. 313 Constantine, along with Licinius, the emperor of the East Roman Empire, issued the Edict of Milan which declared Christianity "legal" and thus gave Christians the freedom of religion. In A.D. 324 after Licinius had turned and started persecuting the Christians, Constantine initiated a virtual crusade against him and defeated him in battle, and Constantine became sole ruler over the entire Roman Empire, both the East and the West. Thus, Christianity grew in numbers and political power. A year later he called a council of churchmen at Nicaea in Asia Minor concerning the dispute over the Trinity, and consequently in A.D. 325 the famous Nicene Creed was formulated by this council. It was then in A.D. 330 that Constantine officially moved the capitol from Rome to ancient Byzantium and named it New Rome. But it was soon renamed Constantinople, meaning the "City of Constantine"; today we know the city in modern Turkey as Istanbul since the name was officially changed in 1930. Although Constantine was baptized a Christian shortly before he died in A.D. 337, it wasn't until about A.D. 380 that Christianity became the official state religion under the emperor Theodosius I.

Emperors became the supreme rulers over the church and the state, and thus corruption within the church was increased because of their immaturity and of the leaders of the church at that time. Because of the power and influence of the emperors and the carnality of church leadership, often pagans were baptized in mass without the true baptism into Christ in the Holy Spirit. The mixture that resulted, allowed the wicked spirits of Babylon influencing and controlling Rome, to at first influence and then control the professing institutionalized church that arose. But more of this later.

First, let us realize here that the early church, and later the Roman Catholic and Protestant leaders, have all agreed that the Babylon of the book of The Revelation is the city of Rome! Only in recent years as false spirits proliferate, has the meaning of Babylon begun to be substantially referenced to other entities such as other cities like New York, or countries like the United States of America, or most recently to the city or the land that was physically (literally) ancient Babylon itself. However, as we look at the book of The Revelation we see clearly that it is first a literal city. In the first reference we read, "**Babylon is fallen, is fallen, that great city, because she made all nations drink of the wine of the wrath of her fornication**" (Rev. 14:8 KJV). Although the best manuscripts do not place here the word city, we see that in six other occurrences Babylon is not only called a city but a "**great city**" (Rev. 17:18; 18:10, 16, 18, 19, 21). In one she is additionally called "**that mighty city**," and in one is conclusively defined as being "**that great city, which reigneth over the kings of the earth**" (Rev. 18:10; 17:18 KJV).

In addition to being a literal city, the next point we need to see from this first reference in verse 14:8 is that Babylon is a city ruled by idolatry. The meaning of the word "fornication" has always been in both the Old and New Testaments "idolatry" when used in a spiritual sense (Isa. 23:15-17; Eze. 16:15-43; 23:37). This fits perfectly with what Isaiah said, "**Babylon is fallen, is fallen; and all the graven images of her gods he hath broken unto the ground**" (Isa. 21:9 KJV). Throughout the Old and New Testaments, God's people are spoken of as married to the Lord; therefore having affairs with other entities and worshipping and serving them, whether idols, false Gods, or materialism, is marital unfaithfulness; and this is spoken of as adultery in a spiritual sense, with fornication being a broader term including all types of this sin, whether adultery or various perversions (Isa. 54:5; Hos. 1 - 3; II Cor. 11:2). Here in Revelation 14:8 we have the term fornication used because every conceivable type of illicit, perverse relationship with the world is practiced.

The next thing we want to understand is the phrase how Babylon has "**made all nations drink of the wine of the wrath of her fornication**" (Rev. 14:8 KJV). This emphasizes to us that idolatry intoxicates a person; their spirit, soul, and body are all effected. As "**Harlotry, wine, and new wine take away the understanding** [lit. **heart**]" (Hos. 4:11 NAS), so too does idolatry, spiritual harlotry! It is the worship and service of things other than God; and takes away the reasoning and heart of man, and makes him to compromise his beliefs. Jeremiah said it so beautifully, "**Babylon has been a golden cup in the hand of the Lord, intoxicating all the earth. The nations have drunk of her wine; therefore the nations are going mad**" (Jer. 51:7 NAS). As nations partook of Rome's idolatry, they were intoxicated by her pleasures and debauched by her corruptions. Those who resisted were destroyed by her brutality and passionate fury upon all who would not swear supreme allegiance to the emperor and worship him as God. In fact the followers of Caesar who later were forced to worship him were called in the Greek Καισαριανοι, *Caesarianoi;* and they called the Lord's disciples, followers and worshippers of Christ who would bow the knee only to King Jesus, Χριστιανοι, *Christianoi,* or Christians. This took place first in Antioch (Acts 11:26). The party that did homage to King Herod the Great and later bowed to his ruling descendents were called Ηρωδιανοι, *Herodianoi,* or Herodians (Mt. 22:16; Mk. 3:6; 12:13).

It is most interesting to note that the context of this reference in Revelation 14:8 is an angel saying (with a loud voice for all who live on earth) to worship God the creator, then a second angel reporting how the nations had worshiped Babylon the great whom God has judged, and then a third angel warning everyone not to worship the beast and his image or this time they will drink of the wine of God's wrath forever and ever! (Rev. 14:6-11). I believe that there is a natural progression of sin here. If someone will not honor God by putting Him first in everything they do, then whatever they put first is an idol; and they will be intoxicated by their idolatry, whether of men or ministry or whatever; and if they steadfastly refuse to flee from their idolatry, worshipping and serving it, they will ultimately lose the Spirit of God and worship the Antichrist when he moves in his satanic power and deception.

The next reference to Babylon the great is Revelation 16:19 where we find that she is a city that is judged when the other cities of the world are judged. Then we have chapter seventeen where we are told symbolically that Babylon the great is a great whore (harlot, prostitute) that sits on many waters, and fornicates all over the world with kings and the inhabitants of the earth, and also sits on a beast of seven heads (Rev. 17:1-3). Then it is explained to us the meaning of all this symbolism. From the literal meaning of the Greek words used, Babylon is actually an idolatrous city of seven mountains or hills, and reigns (literally has kingship) over the kings of the earth at the time this was written in approximately A.D. 95; which city has dominion over nations, multitudes of them, and over races or ethnic groups, and the peoples who speak different languages (thus a description of world-wide power and influence) (Rev. 17:2, 9, 15, 18). Rome had been, was then, and would continue for several hundred more years to be the city from which a world empire ruled over the earth. This was the kingdom revealed through Daniel over 600 years earlier. No other ruling city in the history of the world is known as the city of seven hills as Rome, known far and wide as the *Urbs Septicollis,* "the city of the seven hills." Only Rome was "**the great city, which reigns over the kings of the earth**" (Rev. 17:18 NAS).

In the next reference to Babylon we learn that this city lived so sensuously, luxuriously, that all who had relationships with her were affected. The wholesale traders became rich because of her extravagance. And her own people and the kings of the earth were captivated by her excessive indulgence of the physical senses, making that which is of the flesh exalted rather than that which is of the spirit; consequently the spirits of evil prevailed rather than the Spirit of God (Rev. 18:3, 7, 9, 2).

Next, we are told that she is "**the strong city**" whom God will judge, reminding all that God rules supreme over the earth; and no people, even the strongest city that ever ruled the earth, Rome, will escape His righteous judgment (Rev. 18:8, 10 NAS). As a consequence of God's judgment, the merchants of the earth mourn because of their loss in business: the sale of all kinds of jewels, fabrics, furniture, food, animals, and interestingly, the bodies and souls of mankind (vv. 11-12, & 13 lit.). These last things are in reference to the merchandising of Rome in both the slavery of people and in their very lives as well. The spectacle of men fighting to the death to entertain the multitudes in the arena as gladiators (from the Roman word *gladius,* meaning sword) over many centuries is a sad reminder of the depraved nature of fallen man. In profound contrast to this, the Roman Colosseum still stands today in ruins in modern Rome also as a memorial to the faith of the early Christians who partook of the divine nature; many of whom were also bought as slaves, and were thrown to the lions or burned as torches there, and yet went to their deaths in peace, singing the praises of Almighty God!

In the final reference to Babylon, it is revealed that her judgment will be a sudden, violent destruction just as she had tormented and killed multitudes, especially the innocent holy people of God, including His apostles and prophets (Rev. 18:20-24). As the bricks of Babylon were burned by man in the beginning to make her strong and lasting, this time the fires of God's wrath and divine justice will burn, and it will be everlasting! And the saints of the Most High will be heard to say, "**Hallelujah! Her smoke rises up forever and ever**" (Rev. 19:1-3 NAS).

As we have seen that this Babylon of Revelation is Rome, let me give a few objections to this truth and the explanation as to why they are incorrect. Some say that Babylon is not a city because in Revelation 17:10 the seven heads are given meaning as seven kings. However, a careful examination of the text in both the English and Greek will give us the truth that John is saying that the seven heads of the beast have a double meaning; one is to the city of seven hills (v. 9), "**and**" the other is to the fact that there are seven kings (v. 10), both interpretations to the vision of a woman sitting upon a beast of seven heads (v. 3). Again, the woman is the city that sits on seven hills (vv. 9, 18), and this city is seen riding the beast that has seven kings, one of which is the final beast. Kings that are beasts are men who rule like brute beasts without the heart of God; they rule out of the unregenerate nature of man while being possessed with demonic spirits. This final ruler will be given power and great authority and his throne from the old dragon himself, Satan (Rev. 12:9; 13:2-4); and another beast, the "**False Prophet**," will cause all upon the earth to worship "**the first beast**" which we commonly call the Antichrist (Rev. 13:11-12; 19:19-20). The Antichrist, or "**the Beast**," is the final embodiment of all that is of Satan; and he is the one whom Satan forces all to worship instead of God's true Christ, the Lord Jesus! (Rev. 13:4; 16:13; 20:2, 10).

Another error concerning "Babylon the great" is when God tells someone by the Holy Spirit that something is "Babylon" they think He is referring to the original or final manifestation rather than to an entity that is perhaps a daughter of Babylon, or something that is Babylonish in its character. We will see this more clearly as we proceed.

71

Now let us look more clearly at the city of Rome, or Roma as it is in Latin. Amazingly, it was founded on a site where originally on the Capitoline hill a temple of the Babylonian Messiah had been erected in what was then called Saturnia, "the city of Saturn," another name for Nimrod, therefore, "The City of Nimrod." Rome's beginning is a mixture of truth and error which is as we have seen a chief characteristic of "Babylon." Romulus, Rome's founder and first king in 753 B.C. and the one from whom we get the name, was according to tradition the twin son of Mars and was preserved when outcast by his cruel relatives through the kind attention of a wolf and a shepherd's wife. Romulus killed his brother Remus over a dispute regarding the founding borders of Rome. So we can see that the historical and mythological origins of Rome are exactly what we would expect as we see the history of this world famous city revealed throughout the centuries until now. Satan of course is the wolf and the church is the true shepherd's wife, and we shall see this continual attempt to mix and accommodate truth with error, Christianity with paganism, true religion and false, throughout the long history of Rome. First, idolatrous Babylonian worship, then leaders who have murdered one another to gain dominance from its very inception, is the foundation of Rome. The roots of selfish ambition, pride, rebellion and unbelief concerning the true and living God, have been with violence and demonic inspiration from the beginning.

Rome's location is in central Italy on the western coast, just 17 miles up the Tiber River which empties into the Tyrrhenian Sea, an arm of the Mediterranean Sea. Built originally on marshy ground, again it is a mixture of land and water. At first the settlement included only the Palatine hill, but as the years went on other hills were added; and legend tell us that a later ruler, Servius Tullius, enclosed seven hills within a wall on the east side of the Tiber River during his reign of 578-534 B.C. Later, there is evidence that a wall which is still partially in existence was built around the seven hills in 378 B.C., and this wall is named the Servian Wall in honor of Servius Tullius. The historic Seven Hills are the Palatine, Capitoline, Quirinal, Caelian, Aventine, Esquiline, and the Viminal Hills. Hence Rome has been called in Latin the "Urbs Septicollis," "the city of the seven hills." Many centuries later, after the time of Christ and the writing of the New Testament, more hills (such as the Vatican Hill on the west side of the Tiber) were enclosed within another larger wall by the Emperor Aurelian in A.D. 270, which wall also still partially stands today and is called the Aurelian Wall.

Now, modern Rome today includes not only the historic *Septemontium*, the "Seven Hills" of ancient Rome, and the additional hills within the Aurelian Wall, but also a much larger area in order to accommodate the present population.

Interestingly, when Romulus started the settlement on the ruins of Saturnia, he induced fugitives, criminals, and foreigners to live there, and so Rome was started as an "asylum for outlaws." Consequently respectable people shunned the inhabitants of Rome, who then obtained their wives by strategy. They put on a show which attracted a neighboring group of people called Sabines, and then captured for themselves wives from among them by force. Later a compromise was worked out with the Sabines who then became joint occupants of the city. In 714 B.C. Romulus suddenly disappeared and was reported to have been taken up to heaven. The city then gave him divine honors under the name of Quirinus, built a temple in his honor, and ranked him among the twelve great deities; a priest, called Flamen Quirinalis (Breather of Quirinus, a priest who bestows the spirit by breathing upon), was then appointed to offer him sacrifices. And thus we have the origins of the world famous city of Rome, worshipping man in flaming idolatry, building temples in vainglorious exaltation of its leaders — Rome, corrupt with Babylonish traditions and spirits from the beginning, destined to be as ancient Babylon, "a synonym for political power and territorial expansion" (original Unger's Bible Dictionary).

Another error being taught today in order to try and disprove Rome from being the Babylon of Revelation, and therefore all that this involves, is that Rome is situated on more than seven mountains; and that actually they are not mountains at all, as the scripture records, but simply hills. First, we have amply shown how the historic Seven Hills of Rome were originally enclosed within a wall that surrounded the city for over 500 years, and that wall was the wall of the city during the writing of the book of The Revelation. Secondly, the Greek word used in scripture is the word, *oρη, ore,* a plural form of the noun *oρoσ, oros,* and means "a rising" and can refer to either a hill or a mountain as can be clearly seen by its use in the scriptures. For instance, "The Sermon on the Mount" was given on an *oros* (Mt. 5:1), and anyone who has been there by the Sea of Galilee can tell you that the traditional spot is a gradual sloping hill, and that all the area around there is similar. When Jesus said, "**A city that is set on a <u>hill</u> cannot be hid**" the same word is used, *oros* (Mt. 5:14 KJV)! Also, the "**Mount of Olives**"

73

which most people have seen in pictures if not in fact is not a high mountain, but a large hill overlooking the Kidron valley and across to the Eastern Wall of Jerusalem. I've personally walked from the Wailing Wall down through the valley, past the Garden of Gethsemane, and up the hill to the summit in a few minutes, and the same word is used in scripture, *oros* (Mt. 21:1; 24:3; 26:30)!

We have also seen how no other city in history is known as the "City of Seven Hills" as Rome has been for over 2500 years. One can look at encyclopedias, reference books (both religious and secular), bible handbooks, and this truth is readily found. And let me give one concluding remark from the official English Bible of the Roman Catholic Church since A.D. 1609, the Douay Version's reference to The Apocalypse (The Revelation), Chapter 17, Verse 5: "*A mystery.* That is, a secret; because what follows of the name and title of the great harlot is to be taken in a mystical sense.— Ibid. [Ibidem: *Latin*, meaning "in the same book, chapter, page, etc."] *Babylon*. Either the city of the devil in general; or, if this place be to be understood of any particular city, *pagan Rome*, which then and for three hundred years persecuted the church; and was the principal seat of empire and idolatry."

Now, concerning calling cities by other names, and revealing mysteries, as John does in Revelation 17:5, 9, 18, he had just referred to Jerusalem in a spiritual, or as some call it a mystical sense. He wrote concerning the two witnesses which will be killed during the reign of the Antichrist, "**And their dead bodies will lie in the street of the great city which mystically** [πνευματικοσ, *pneumatikos,* **spiritually**] **is called Sodom and Egypt, where also their Lord was crucified**" (Rev. 11:8 NAS).

So we can see clearly that when John writes concerning a "**great harlot**" "**woman**" (Rev. 17:1-18 NAS), interpreted as a great idolatrous city (v. 18), who "**sits on many waters**" (v. 1; interpreted as "**peoples and multitudes and nations and tongues**," v. 15), "**clothed in purple and scarlet**" (v. 4)

[The purple color represents royalty and rulership (Dan. 5:7, 16, 29 lit.); and the scarlet represents salvation, the sanctuary, high priest, and priesthood (Isa. 1:18); but there is no mention of the deep blue of heaven, specifically the color reminding us that we are to follow the spoken and revealed Word of God to us, and not to follow our "**own heart**" and "**eyes**" and play "**the harlot!**" But God says "**blue . . . to look at . . . in order**

74

that you may remember to do all My commandments, and be holy to your God." Because "I am the Lord your God who brought you out from the land of Egypt {the world and its religious systems} to be your God; I am the Lord your God!" (Num. 15:37-41 NAS). The three colors of blue and purple and scarlet are given together 26 times (Ex. 25:4-39:29), and the blue more times by itself (Num. 4:6-12; 15:38); therefore the purple and scarlet of Babylon without the blue represents a counterfeit, false authority, false salvation, false church, false high priest, false priesthood; usurping the place of our Lord Jesus Christ and counterfeiting His kingdom, high priesthood, and priests; it is a harlot and not the bride!],

"and adorned with gold and precious stones and pearls" (v. 4; extremely wealthy), and committing acts of "fornication" (vv. 2, 4; 18:3; idolatry), and who sits "on a scarlet beast, full of blasphemous names" (v. 3; a wicked governmental power against God and His kingdom), and on "seven mountains" (v. 9; the historical, world-wide reputation of Rome), who kills "the witnesses of Jesus [v. 6; true Christians]," and is called "Mystery, Babylon" (v. 5; a mystery, a hidden secret, v. 7, interpreted spiritually as a city which in worship holds on to the demons and doctrines of the Mystery Cults of ancient Babylon which had been destroyed), and he concludes by writing, "And the woman whom you saw is the great city, which reigns [Gk.: εχουσα βασιλειαν, exousa basileian, has kingship, royal dominion; present active tense when this was written] over the kings of the earth" (v. 18), identifying this woman as the ruling city of the world at that time, John therefore positively identifies this city as none other than ROME! And this city which was the seat of the idolatrous Roman Empire which persecuted Christians was not only at that time Pagan Rome, but later its Babylonian spirits and doctrines invaded the church here and continued the idolatrous empire which has ever since been called Papal Rome!

And only the spiritually blind, such as the uneducated, the willfully ignorant, or those hanging onto the same spirits and doctrines will not understand this! The amazing thing is that even some who once saw the truth and even taught it are now denying the truth! But the scripture is true and being fulfilled, "The lamp of the body is the eye; if therefore your eye is clear, your whole body will be full of light. **But if your eye is bad, your whole body will be full of darkness. If therefore the light that is in you is** [or, has become] **darkness, <u>how great is the darkness</u>!"** (Mt. 6:22-23 NAS)

Therefore, let us briefly continue our look at early Roman culture during the beginning of the New Testament period.

Out of the city state of Rome had grown the Republic from 509-27 B.C., and then Augustus declared himself emperor. Now we have the beginning of the mighty Roman Empire, supreme authority residing in one man, aided and advised by the senate, called the *Curia.*

In 31 B.C. Augustus had "proceeded to make the city of Rome a city of marble rather than of brick — though the marble was a veneer over the structural brick or concrete. . . . The public buildings of Rome were magnificent, more than worthy of the emperors who erected them. The houses of the rich, usually on the various hills of the city, were sumptuous. But most Romans lived in tenements. . . . Admission to the games was free, and such games, including chariot racing, gladiatorial contests, and theatrical performances, attracted huge crowds. . . . The existence of slavery made unnecessary a quest for labor-saving devices" (The Interpreter's Dictionary of the Bible, IDB).

Under Roman education, literary criticism flourished. Roman poems and philosophical opinions "were used by Jewish and Christian apologists." The literary criticism which flourished was "chiefly as a part of rhetorical education. The student would learn to analyze grammar, composition, and style; he would also be trained to judge the authenticity of documents and of narratives regarded as historical. Such judgments are later reflected in early Christian and anti-Christian criticism of the Bible" (IDB).

There were many religious beliefs in Rome, but chief among them were the foreign cults or "Mystery religions" which had come primarily from the Orient, Babylon. "The most important were the Egyptian Isis, [and] the Great Mother from Asia Minor [Diana], and the Persian Mithras." "Her [Isis] public rites, together with testimonies to her miraculous powers, made her cultus attractive. Similarly the Great Mother was publicly advertised. Both Isis and the Mother had begging priests who went everywhere." "Her [Ephesian Artemis, Roman Diana] temple was a huge landholding corporation served by eunuch-priests called *Megabuzoi* (a Persian title); by other attendants called Essenes, who were subject to rigid rules of purity and abstinence; and by thousands of female slaves, hierodules." One of the fourteen districts or regions of Rome was named after the goddess Isis, there were many private chapels built for her, and eventually "temples of Isis could be described as 'everywhere'" (IDB).

The other very popular "Mystery religion" (with similarities such as baptism), the Persian cult of Mithras, had spread over the empire of Alexander the Great. This was another name for the sun-god, Tammuz, the false Christ, which under the name Mithras was worshipped as the "Mediator"; and in Israel had been known as Baal-berith, "Lord of the Covenant," and El-berith, "God of the Covenant" (Judg. 8:33; 9:46). "In India, under the name Vishnu, the Preserver or Saviour of men, though a god, he was worshipped as the great "Victim-Man," who before the worlds were, because there was nothing else to offer, offered himself as a sacrifice. The Hindu sacred writings teach that this mysterious offering before all creation is the foundation of all the sacrifices that have ever been offered since" (The Two Babylons). This "saviour" "guaranteed a blessed immortality to those who had been initiated into his mysteries — by baptism, purification by honey, and the use of bread, water, and wine consecrated by priests, called 'fathers', who enjoined a high moral code" (Oxford Dictionary of the Christian Church). Thus Mithras, as well as the cult of Isis, two of the popular cults of "the son" and "the mother," perpetuated another Babylonish doctrine — Baptismal Regeneration.

Dionysus, or Bacchus, was a god of fertility in nature, notably of the vine. He was the god of wine in Greek and Roman religion. Great feasts, called Dionysia or Bacchanalia, were held in his honor in Athens and Rome, and celebration with much dancing, drinking, and revelry. The art form of Greek tragedy developed from the ceremonies that took place during the Dionysia at Athens.

In Rome "Jews and Christians were conspicuous because of their denial that their God was known by non-biblical names. It should be added that as far as we know, the adherents of non-biblical religions never had any difficulties in coming to terms with Emperor-worship; they might advocate monotheism, but it was not an exclusive monotheism.

"Civil theology consisted of their analysis of the twelve gods officially recognized by the state and served by a college of sixteen pontiffs, chief of whom was the Pontifex Maximus" (IDB). This was a religious position that had been purchased by Julius Caesar in 63 B.C. on his way up the political ladder. By violence and bribery he was elected in 59 B.C. with Crassus and Pompey, two powerful generals, as a consul and member of the First Triumvirate that ruled Rome. He then obtained governorship of Gaul where he began a brilliant military career to gain more power. After Pompey's wife Julia, Caesar's daughter, died, and then Crassus died in a battle, Pompey, a military hero, became jealous. In 49 B.C. Pompey persuaded the Senate to order Caesar to give up his army and return to Rome. Caesar had no intention of becoming defenseless, and thus "crossed the Rubicon" into Italy with his army and took control of Rome. He defeated Pompey and his army in Greece, and when Pompey fled to Egypt, Caesar followed. When he reached Egypt, he found that Pompey had been assassinated by the Roman controlled Egyptian government, but there he met Cleopatra and fell in love with her. He fought and won a civil war to restore her as ruler of Egypt, and then brought her to Rome. These were the last days of the weakened republican form of government, and in 46 B.C. Caesar, his family name, having supreme military power was made dictator for ten years by the Senate. But in 44 B.C. he assumed absolute power, and entered upon a perpetual dictatorship for which he was assassinated within a month by a group of aristocrats who believed he wanted to be a king. The next year a temple was erected to the "divine Julius" by vote of the Senate, and this event marked the beginning of Roman Emperor-worship (Emperor-worship having been a part of Babylonian and then Egyptian and Greek culture for centuries).

In 44 B.C. the Second Triumvirate was formed consisting of Gaius Octavianus, Marcus Lepidus, and Mark Antony. Just as the First Triumvirate had resulted in political and armed struggles and civil war between three leaders for absolute power, so too did the Second. After victory in the civil wars, Gaius Julius Caesar Octavianus, grandnephew and heir of Julius Caesar, was voted in 27 B.C. by the Senate of Rome the name Augustus, which means "Reverend" or "Exalted One," and given authority over religious, civil, and military affairs. As his great uncle Julius Caesar had become the Father of the Roman Empire, Augustus thus became the first emperor and Founder of the great Roman Empire, and was the ruler when Jesus was born. He became the Pontifex Maximus and received worship. He died in A.D. 14, and "when Augustus' 'mind' had ascended to heaven, prayer could be addressed to it" (IDB).

"Rome tolerated other religions, at least as long as they were not regarded as threatening either the established religion or traditional morality.

"They regarded foreign religions as 'superstition,' meaning that they were brought to Rome by unenlightened members of the lower class. Just as the Jews believed that idolatry led to adultery, so Romans believed that foreign superstitions led inevitably to sexual promiscuity or cannibalism, or to both.

"In Roman eyes Christianity was a superstition since it was obviously foreign; it had arisen in Judaea. It was a superstition because it involved the worship of a criminal condemned by a Roman governor, and its adherents were (therefore?) suspected of immorality. Its missionary zeal, its eschatological emphasis, and its unwillingness to relate itself either to Judaism (a religion tolerated in the Empire) or to the state cults meant that it could only be regarded as at least potentially subversive" (IDB).

The primitive religion of Rome was prehistoric, as we have written, made up of rites and practices belonging to ancestral custom. The rites were usually some form of sacrifice, and there were many other kinds such as: supplications, lustrations (purifications), lectisterniums (banquets set before the gods), circumambulations (walking around properties, etc.), processions, and other symbolic acts. It was essentially a system of ritual.

"Cicero defined religion as the 'cult of the gods'; this term meant more than worship and included care, devotion, and constant attention to their needs and demands.

"Hence Roman religion was legalistic, with specific requirements which men must meet if they hoped for specific responses on the part of the higher powers." Divine guidance was given by various means including "divination (especially the 'reading' of the markings observed on the liver of the sacrificial animal)." This could be traced back to Babylonia (Eze. 21:21).

It was believed that certain "sacred" places or things possessed supernatural power. In dealing with the supernatural, it was of paramount importance that the correct formula be used.

There was a "deep feeling of the 'numinosity' [the presiding of a spirit] of the Palatine, which was the real center of Roman religion throughout its long history. . . . Officially the Capitol was the religious center of the Roman Empire; in reality the Palatine was the sacred hill which enshrined the deepest religious loyalties" (IDB).

"Ambarvalia, or lustration of the fields, consisted in a circumambulation of the farm by its owner [acting as priest of his family] and his *familia* (which included the slaves), all dressed in white, and leading a group of animals for the sacrifice — viz., a sow, a sheep, and a young bull . . . that the last named was originally a male lamb. . . .

"The offering of a young lamb to the spirit resident in a spring; a few beans or flowers offered to a tree nymph or to the family ghosts; the pious observance of ancestral customs," were practiced for much longer on the farms and in the country towns. The word for farmer is *Pagani* and thus later the word "pagan" came to be used for those who were not Christians because the farmers were the last to accept Christianity.

"On the other hand, the public religion of the Roman state (especially as observed in Rome itself) was thoroughly organized. At its head was the pontifical college, which included the several pontiffs later increased to sixteen, with the presiding officer of the college, the Pontifex Maximus. Next to him was the Rex sacorum (king of rites, who inherited the ancient priestly functions of the early kings). It was the duty of the pontifical college to oversee all public rites and religious ceremonies, to ascertain the will of the gods either through divination (by augurs) or through consultation and interpretation of the Sibylline books. But in time the whole system fell into disrepute, especially when, under the later Republic, commanders and magistrates did not hesitate to manipulate the auspices or the calendar or the interpretation of signs and portents in furtherance of their own purposes" (IDB).

As Rome grew in political importance, conquering vast territories, syncretistic tendencies arose. These tendencies to reconcile or unite opposing religions altered the whole character of Rome. "The gods of the conquered had flocked into the city, brought there by the *invocatio* or the invitation or the vows of conquering generals and by their now enslaved votaries [those bound by vows to a religious life; devoted worshipers]" (IDB).

However, the early Christian church did not incline "to adopt or adapt ancient Roman religious customs — the whole outlook of the church was too Hebraic, too biblical, to find values in primitive pagan rites; above all, the hope of redemption through Christ and the eschatological expectation of the coming kingdom of God found little contact or support in Roman religion — save only where, as in Vergil, Roman religious thought had already been influenced by similar ideas" (IDB).

The church of the first century "met the greatest threat to its existence when it confronted the imperial cultus (the worship of *Roma* and the emperor). . . . Emperor-worship was one more importation from the East." Its spirit was political, commercial, and religious as it "celebrated the establishment of world peace under Augustus, and was meant to be a 'religion of all good men'" (IDB). Yet we see arising emperors like Nero, a prime example of all that is evil, perverse, and demonic, martyring the saints and the finest of apostles, Paul and Peter, and consequently judged by God as he committed suicide approximately four years later and entered the torments of an eternal hell. And so with Emperor-worship, Christians were not able to participate, and thus the result was many years of persecution and martyrdom.

It is most interesting to note that in the church of Rome in Paul's day, earthly, soulish, and demonic wisdom was very much at work already as evidenced by the fact that there were those men in the church who were preaching Christ out of such envy and selfish ambitions that they were wanting to cause an apostle further distress in his imprisonment for the gospel, which they were proclaiming themselves (Phil. 1:12-20; Jam. 3:13-18; Rom. 16:17-19). This seed of impure motives of worldliness and of persecution of an outstanding apostle gradually grew and grew until finally mixed with pure unbelief as we shall see in the centuries that follow.

Babylon: From the New Testament until now.

In the preceding section we saw Babylon in all its paganism outside the church. Rome was ruling the world, and it was the chief seat of all that was the development of historic Babylon. Now we shall see how the true church of the Lord Jesus Christ divided; and the larger portion slowly changed from a spiritual body, as built by the early apostles with Christ as its head, into a carnal organism, without His headship; and then it changed into an organization which contains both the true church, which is the true believers, and unbelievers. The next development is when carnal leadership so persecutes the true believers, who are wanting to be spiritual, that portions of the true church leave the organization to attempt to be the church as the Lord intended. Then the carnal organization becomes institutionalized to the point that unbelievers actually take control and it becomes a horrible mixture of truth and error, believers and unbelievers, and develops into a Babylonish type kingdom not representative at all of the kingdom of God. It becomes worse as it is influenced and driven by the ruling spirits of Babylon, which we remember are idolatry, pride, rebellion, selfish ambition, fear, and unbelief; and it is gradually transformed, as it picks up the doctrines of ancient Babylon, into "Babylon" on its way to becoming "**Babylon the great**" (Rev. 14:8; 16:19; 17:5; 18:2, 10, 21). Along the way, as true believers see light and depart from the institution, they take with them characteristics and practices from their Babylonish mother. A few will see their errors, and will repent and seek to return to the original way of the Lord in expressing His life as a body; and a few will join them. But the vast majority will see the various errors, and because they are still ruled by the spirits of Babylon, they will go on in the various ways of Babylon. Some may even go on and develop more Babylonish ways themselves, and may even become worse as Babylon's daughters than the original from which they departed. Since the original organization is not the true bride of Christ, but committing spiritual fornication as she practices different types of idolatry, God calls her a whore. And her daughters who are practicing many of the same kinds of idolatry are called by God "harlots" as well. We shall better understand this now as we follow the history of the church of the Lord after the New Testament church was first established.

One of the first and I believe the most important practice that the church discontinued was in the second century when she departed from the direct headship of the Lord Jesus Christ. The early church is described in many ways in the scripture, and one of the most important is as a body, the very body of Jesus Christ with the Lord Himself as its present and immediate head (Ro. 12:5; I Cor. 10:16-17; 12:12-28; Eph. 1:22-23; 4:12, 15-16; 5:23-24, 30; Col. 1:18, 24; 2:19; 3:15). What happened was that in each city which had been ruled by a plurality of elders who were also called bishops (who were responsible for shepherding the one flock in that city under the Chief Shepherd, the Lord Jesus, who was always in their midst as their Head and Leader), soon one man of the ruling elders was selected who became known as the bishop of that city, and the rest of his ruling brethren retained the title of elders, but not bishops (in contrast to this practice, see: Phil. 1:1; Acts 20:17, 28; Tit. 1:5-7; I Pet. 5:1-4). This of course usurped the headship of the Lord Jesus Christ with His Spirit in control, the infinite "**Spirit of Wisdom and Understanding, the Spirit of Counsel and Strength, the Spirit of Knowledge and the Fear of the Lord**" (Isa. 11:1-5 NAS), and placed a mere finite man in all of his incomparable deficiencies, his weaknesses, ignorance, and fallibility as head of the local church, and of course consequently started the gradual degeneration and eventual division and sometimes destruction of the local church in each city. But this took some time. This loss of the Lord Jesus Christ being head of the local church in each locality, as planned and structured by God Himself, was simultaneous with the loss of the office of apostle (with its authority and function of oversight, establishing doctrine and ordaining elders [bishops] in every city) and with this the apostolic doctrine of the Lord Jesus being the one and only head, the Chief Shepherd. The Lord was replaced by the singular bishop of each city with the other elders subordinate to him, and this bishop then became the one to ordain elders. Eventually the bishops of surrounding cities were the ones recognized to ordain a bishop of another city. If we have a group of elders of a city functioning as bishops, that is, taking the oversight by looking to the Lord Jesus in their midst as their only corporate head, it is quite different than if we look to only one fallible man attempting to be the head. The head is the member of the body from which we have origination of thought and understanding, function and action, and the seat of creativity and memory. The mind of Christ is perfect; the mind of any man is imperfect, and subject to all the fallibility, weakness, and proneness to listen to one's wife (both one's spouse as well as the bride of Christ, the church) as was the mind of the first man, Adam. Adam knew the truth, but chose to listen to his wife rather than to the Word of God. (And I might add here that the weakness of hearkening unto one's wife rather than to God is one of the most common sins that results in men losing their spiritual standing, place, and ministries in God.) Losing the headship of Christ over the church in any locality and recognizing one fallible man as head is devastating, the results of which very few people today realize. This ungodly hierarchical development began in the second century, and then in the fourth century there was rapid deterioration. In the second and third century there had been conferences in which the leaders of neighboring cities gathered to discuss doctrine and solve problems that arose as people moved from place to place, but it was the fourth century that brought about the hierarchical structure that finalized in one man at the top, and that in Rome — and so we see it today in most every individual church government.

To understand how this happened, let us look more closely at Constantine's conversion and the events that followed. Constantine had been declared Emperor of the West Roman Empire by his army after his father, who was the emperor, died in A.D. 306. To secure that position Constantine marched his army from France toward Rome to confront Maxentius, his chief rival, in an expedition which was destined to either exalt or ruin him. Oppressed with anxiety, he prayed earnestly as a pagan to the gods. He respected the God of the Christians, but wanted some satisfactory proof of His real existence and power. The testimony of Lactantius, the tutor of Constantine's son Crispus is precious in this regard as to how God answered his prayer. He writes, "Constantine was warned in a dream to make the celestial sign of God upon his soldiers' shields, and so to join battle. He did as he was bid, and with the transverse letter X circumflecting the head of it, he marks Christ on their shields. Equipped with this sign, his army takes the sword" (The Two Babylons). The author, Alexander Hislop, goes on to say, "Now, the letter X was just the initial of the *name* of Christ, being equivalent in Greek to CH. If, therefore, Constantine did as he was bid, when he made 'the celestial sign of God' in the form of 'the letter X,' it was that 'letter X,' as the symbol of 'Christ,' and not the sign of the cross, which he saw in the heavens." This is also the case according to Ambrose, the well known Bishop of Milan, when he mentions, "The Labarum, that is, the ensign consecrated by the NAME of Christ" in reporting about the standard of Constantine that was borne before his troops. There is no mention of the cross, which was taken from the letter "T" as the symbol of Tammuz, the false Messiah, but it was the letter "X," the sign of the true Messiah, our Lord Jesus Christ, which was actually seen. However, what has been repeated down through our Babylonish church history, is that Constantine saw a vision in the sky of a cross with the words, "In this sign conquer." But this story is refuted also by two other testimonies. One, an inscription at the head of a Christian monument found in the catacombs of Rome which reads, "In this thou shalt overcome" with the letter "X" immediately beneath the words. The other, the very standard of Constantine, as handed down to us on medals struck at that time, confirming the testimonies of both Lactantius and Ambrose, bearing on it these words, "In this sign thou shalt be a conqueror" with the letter "X." This is according to the scripture found in the Psalms, "In the name of our God we will set up our banners" (Psa. 20:5 NAS).

An so Constantine, and I believe as a new creature in Christ, engaged Maxentius in battle in the name of our Lord Jesus Christ, at the famous "Battle of Milvian Bridge" outside of Rome. He defeated Maxentius, who was drowned in the Tiber River, and won a history changing victory with his forces in the year A.D. 312.

With this victory Constantine became sole ruler in the western Empire, and then met with Lucinius, who was ruler in the east, in the city of Milan and ordered cessation of the persecution of Christians by what is known as "the Edict of Milan" in A.D. 313. Then after this official recognition of Christianity, Constantine called a conference at Arles in A.D. 314 of all the bishops of Christendom, "each with representative presbyters [elders] from his Church" to discuss the matter of the ordination of bishops. Not all of the bishops would come, but nevertheless, thus began the spiritual fornication of the church with the "**kings of the earth**" (Rev. 17:1-2; 18:2-3, 9); and this insured the gradual degradation of the church, and the creation of Babylon from within Christendom, and its eventual participation with non-Christian Babylonish religions, and its inevitable development into becoming "**Babylon the great!**"

When the emperor, as the chief authority of the Roman Empire, engaged himself in the affairs of the church, also as a Christian but under the influence of the spirits of Babylon as he was also Pontifex Maximus, and it was accepted by leading bishops of Christendom, a mutual covenant was established between church and state. Consequently the Babylonish Roman governmental spirit of authority entered the churches (cities) which participated and they became organized into a confederacy along the lines of the government of that empire. As the bishops of a Roman province met, the bishop of that area's leading city, known as a metropolis, became appointed as their leader; he was then known by the same title as his civilian counterpart, a metropolitan. And just as civil provinces were grouped into dioceses, and the governors (metropolitans) of each province were subordinated to the governor (exarch or patriarch) of a diocese, the bishop of the chief city of a diocese became known as an exarch or patriarch, the titles of the secular government being retained for this hierarchy of new leadership roles in the confederated churches. Some cities did not submit to this growing confederation and so the bishop of those cities was known as an "*autokephaloi*," which means "self-headed"; which of course they were, since they had already usurped the headship of Christ. These individual bishops were no match for the carnal power plays that were to come when the bishop of Rome, the ruling city of all the dioceses of the empire, would soon become the dominate man in the man-made church confederation inspired by the spirits of Babylon.

It was then that world ruling pagan Rome, noted for its persecution of those holy and spiritual, especially of apostles and prophets, became the world center of the enslaving form of spiritual Babylon within universal Christendom, which would become noted for its carnally minded persecution of those holy and spiritual, especially of apostles and prophets (Rev. 18:20, 24; Rom. 8:6-7; Jam. 3:14-16). Christianity, officially sanctioned by the state first under Constantine, then became the official state religion under the emperor Theodosius I about A.D. 380. Thus the majority of the church which was (and is now) "holy" and "catholic" (meaning universal) was transformed into what would become known as the "Roman Catholic Church" of the "Holy Roman Empire." "Babylon the great" was thus born within Christendom! And consequently we shall now see how more of the spirits and doctrines of ancient Babylon entered into this great world-wide organization gradually over the following centuries until we have what is so evident today.

To understand how a body of spiritual men could allow such horribly false teachings as we see today in the mother and daughters of Babylon, we must see how the spiritual purity of the church first was corrupted.

First, we have seen how spiritual men cease to seek the mind of the head of the church His way, and start the way of the world in replacing Jesus with a man as head of each city. This of course was done after first replacing Jesus as the head over each gathering of believers, whether of a few, or of hundreds. Jesus had said, "**For where two or three have gathered together in My name, there I am in their midst**" (Mt. 18:20 NAS). And He is there as head, and to be looked to as such, not as a helper to our plans and programs. Whenever we have a self-willed person or leader, they usurp the headship of Christ, and the mind and will of God is lost. That is why one of the scriptural qualifications of an elder is that they be "**not self-willed**" (Tit. 1:5-7).

Also, we see from the scriptures that in the beginning it is revealed that we are in fellowship with God and His son, our Lord Jesus Christ, and consequently with one another, and are the church of God because we "**are sanctified in Christ Jesus,**" and made "**holy**" (I Cor. 1:2; 3:17). We have been justified by His grace, redeemed by His blood, saved by His mercy through the washing of regeneration and made new by the Holy Spirit that we might become faithful in Christ Jesus, holy and blameless before God (Tit. 3:5-7; Eph. 1:1-7).

However, G. H. Lang, in his excellent book, *The Churches of God,* shares with us how the purity of the church was corrupted after the loss of the true headship of the Lord Jesus by a change in the understanding of Christian unity. He states that there were three forms which the conception of unity had taken during three periods of time. "In the earliest period the basis of Christian fellowship was a changed life," he writes, a life made holy by God's indwelling Spirit through faith in Jesus. This is the result of being "born from above," and becoming a new creature in Christ Jesus. John describes this as walking "in the light," which he explains is walking in God, His love and obedience to His Word, just as Jesus walked — walking in truth (I Jn. 1:5-7; 2:3-11; II Jn. vv. 4-6).

However, in a second period the idea of a "definite belief" became the basis of union and dominated over that of a holy life. For example, the official baptismal creed of the church of Rome, believed to have originated around A.D.150, which has come to be known as the Old Roman Creed, was used. [It had evolved from earlier simpler texts based on the Lord's threefold baptismal command as found in Matthew 28:19. As the Roman creed was used, more truth was added, and it developed into the Apostles' Creed, which was destined to be used by Christians in the West ever since that time. Later this Apostles' Creed was used by Roman Catholics to express faith in "the Holy Catholic Church" (capitalized because they see the church as an institution — theirs); and much later by Protestants in "the holy catholic Church" (partially not capitalized because they see the church as the spiritual body of Christ, both holy and universal, made up of many institutions); but which would be accurately written if understood, "the holy catholic church" (never an institution of man!).]

But then in a third period, insistence on set beliefs known as the "Catholic faith," led to an insistence on "Catholic order." After Constantine officially recognized Christianity and masses of pagans were marched into the rivers for baptism, the purity of the church really became corrupted. Christians were no longer persecuted, and the faith became popular. In A.D. 324, Constantine defeated Lucinius, emperor of the East, and became sole ruler of the Roman Empire. Then Constantine called another conference in A.D. 325 called the Council of Nicaea which was brought about over the doctrinal dispute concerning the nature of the godhead, and the doctrine of the Trinity was then formalized in the Nicene Creed still used today. Then in this third period the idea of unity took the form of unity of organization. It was superimposed over the idea of unity of belief. It was not enough for a man to be living a good life and hold to the "Catholic faith," but one must belong to an association under the leadership of a recognized bishop, which in turn was part of a larger confederation of churches, the sum of which was the Catholic Church.

However, in the scriptures we see first an individual unity with God Himself through Jesus Christ and the person of the Holy Spirit (Jn. 17). Then we are exhorted to "**keep the unity of the Spirit in the bond of peace**" and endeavor to attain to the "**unity of the faith**" (Eph. 4:3, 13 KJV). This unity is built upon individuals who are in union with God, but this unity is lost by sin. Purity is a prerequisite to union with God! "**Who shall ascend into the hill of the Lord?**" and "**Lord, who shall abide in thy tabernacle?**" but the pure in heart and those who hate not only sin but hate those who insist upon it (Psa. 24:3-6; 15 KJV). This is where the early church failed. They started to allow people to remain in their midst who were not living as they should, then to even allow men to be appointed to leadership positions who were not living holy before the Lord. No wonder then that when pagans were brought into the church in mass, that the impurity brought so much corruption that interference from the state was not only tolerated but called upon. This was precipitated between two major factions, those who insisted upon purity for participation in church fellowship and those who opposed it. And when the Catholic party invoked the secular power, "the secular power made ecclesiastical puritanism a capital crime" (*The Churches of God*, by G. H. Lang).

It is interesting that the puritan party realized that impurity was a capital crime with God, and thus, those living in sin should be put out of the church in demonstrating this truth. Also, putting the impure out keeps the church pure, and free from sin and judgment; and it is the loving discipline for those who refuse to repent of their sins (I Cor. 5). The puritan's way was under the direction of Christ the head, to call upon God to purify His church; then we could have fellowship in love. The Catholic's way was under the headship of man, to call upon the State for unity first, with its accompanying fellowship in fear, and then work for purity secondarily. The scripture was wrested then as it is today by those who allow sin in either their lives or others. "**The field is the world**," they said, "and the good and the bad **grow together until the harvest**." But the puritans said, "**the field is the world**, and not the Church: it is in the world and not in the Church that the good and the bad are to grow together" (Mt. 13:24-30, 36-43). And they practiced the teachings of God's Word which tells us that the church must be cultivated, pruned, and purged, and we are responsible in working with the Holy Spirit to accomplish this task! (Jn. 15:1-6; Mt. 15:13-14; I Cor. 5:7-13; II Thes. 3:6, 14-15; Psa. 101: 7-8).

And so it is today! I have been involved with many Christian leaders in seeking unity among all believers, but these issues have not changed. When purity is sacrificed for unity, a work comes to naught. When peace is sought before purity, it brings failure, and sin continues and grows. "**But**," James says, "**the wisdom that is from above is first pure, then peaceable**," not the other way around! (Jam. 3:17 KJV). Please hear me on this, and what the Spirit is saying!

Now that we have seen how the early church went astray, losing the practical headship of Christ and seeking unity first and purity secondarily, thus becoming Babylon in its infancy, let us follow the course of organized hierarchical Christianity and observe the introduction of more of Babylon's abominable teachings and practices into it.

No sooner had the Roman "king of the earth" entered into an adulterous affair with the church, but about A.D. 330 prayers for the dead were instituted, which had been one of the practices of the Babylonian religion of Rome. This is not just false and a waste of time, but alters tragically in the minds of people the understanding of the Biblical truth concerning the finality of this life before eternal judgment, and so gives them false hope beyond the grave in which they think they can alter their own destiny after they die. This is a lie from the father of all lies, who is the real author of all the false teachings that we shall discuss. God says, "**it is appointed unto men once to die, but after this the judgment**," and no amount of prayers will alter one thing for a person after they die (Heb. 9:27 KJV). It is over! And they go before God for judgment for their lives as lived here and nothing can change it. Our prayers for the living are what counts, if of course they are done properly, which we shall see in a moment.

But, before we give a list of many of these false Babylonish teachings that entered into organized Christianity, let us look at those which are the most important and abominable.

First, Christ is not head of His church on earth, but a man. Roman Catholic doctrine stresses the fact that the Pope is head of Christ's church on earth, and Christ is the head in heaven. That means Christ is head in heaven only, and not on earth. But we read in scripture, "**All authority has been given to Me in heaven and on earth**" (Mt. 28:18 NAS). And, "**by Him all things were created, both in the heavens and on earth, visible and invisible, whether thrones or dominions or rulers or authorities — all things have been created by Him and for Him. And He is before all things, and in Him all things hold together. He is also head of the body, the church; and He is the beginning, the first-born from the dead; so that He Himself might come to have first place in everything. For it was the Father's good pleasure for all the fulness to dwell in Him, and through Him to reconcile all things to Himself, having made peace through the blood of His cross; through Him, I say, whether things <u>on earth</u> <u>or</u> things in heaven</u>**" (Col. 1:16-20 NAS).

Again, Paul intercedes for the Ephesians to the Father that they know "**the working of the strength of His might which He brought about in Christ, when He raised Him from the dead, and seated Him at His right hand in the heavenly places, far above all rule and authority and power and dominion, and every name that is named, not only in this age, but also in the one to come. And He put all things in subjection under His feet, and gave Him as head over all things to the church, which is His body, the fulness of Him who fills all in all**" (Eph. 1:19-23 NAS).

These scriptures plainly and clearly reveal, if we have "**the spirit of wisdom and revelation in the knowledge of Him: the eyes of your** [our] **understanding** [heart] **being enlightened**" (Eph. 1:17-18 KJV), that Paul prays for Christians to understand that Christ is head over everyone on this earth as well as in heaven, both now and forever! Everywhere, all the time, forever! The Pope is not the head of Christ's church on earth, but neither is a president of some denominational daughter of Babylon, or a pastor of some local assembly! Christ says, "**where two or three have gathered together in My name, there I am in their midst,**" and He is present there as head! (Mt. 18:20 NAS). When these scriptures were written — now — and forever He shall be! Anyone usurping His place is an imposter, a thief, and a robber, and will be disciplined or destroyed as He sees fit! (Jn. 10:1-13; Heb. 10:30-31). There never was a Pope until A.D. 610, but there are thousands of them today, Protestant and independent! And many just as dictatorial and deceived as any that ever existed. Christ is not present in our midst as some on-looker from heaven, hoping that we will do His will; but He is here as head to be looked unto for His mind, His direction, His very life to be brought to us and poured out through us as His body. We are not just His representatives, but He is Himself in us, representing Himself through us to a lost and dying world! Oh, may God help us to see Him as He really is, in truth, and what it is for Him to be head over our lives and especially our gatherings unto Him! (Gen. 49:10 KJV).

It is significant to note that in the Greek the word "ανη, anti," means either "against" or "for, instead of, in place of"; for example: **"Suppose one of you fathers is asked by his son for a fish; he will not give him a snake instead of [anti] a fish, will he?"** (Lk. 11:11 NAS). Therefore, an antichrist system is one in which someone other than Jesus Christ is head!

Another tremendously false teaching is one in which our prayers are made ineffectual and useless. Jesus taught us to pray to the Father in His name, but the mother and child worship exalts the mother and in practice denies the rightful place of the Son of God, Jesus our Lord (Jn. 15:16; 16:23-26). The worship of Mary is evident in literature and practice. It involves serving her first, praying to her, and exalting her far beyond the correct teaching of the scriptures and spiritual reality.

I believe the practice of praying to her in worship is very tragic. The scripture says **"there is one God, and <u>one mediator</u> between God and men, the man, Christ Jesus; who gave Himself a ransom for all"** (I Tim. 2:5-6 KJV). That means what it says, <u>one</u>, not two which includes Mary, or even hundreds, which involves the practice of praying to "the saints," many of whom have recently been declared not to have ever even existed. Well, the prayers to Mary are wrong and a waste, the same as those to non-existent saints. For anyone to hear the prayers of literally millions of people all over the world at the same time, one would have to be God, and Mary is not God. There is only one God, as the scripture which we just quoted states so plainly. And only Christ Jesus died for our sins as a ransom, not Mary, nor anyone else!

The worship of Mary is from a false spirit, it is a doctrine of the devil, and it is costing millions of people their eternal souls, as well as the millions of dollars associated with this false worship. The rosaries, shrines, trips to them, and literature and statues are an enormous expense, all for worse than naught — for the deception of mankind, and the eternal damnation of poor souls. We are told to worship God alone, and bowing down before any man or woman, dead or alive, is spiritual deception, idolatry, forbidden and condemned in the scriptures (Acts 10:25-26; 14:11-18; Rev. 19:10; 22:8-9; I Cor. 6:9-10).

It is significant that in the religion of ancient Babylon the practice of using prayer beads in worshipping the mother-goddess was extensive, and they are also used today by Hindus, Buddhists, Moslems, and other pagans around the world, as well as by Roman Catholics. Nimrod, in deified form, became known as Baal, and his wife was worshipped as "Baalti," meaning in English, "My Lady." In Latin it is *Mea Domina*, and in Italian it is corrupted into the well known *Madonna*. This exaltation of Mary over her son, our Lord Jesus Christ, is constantly portrayed in this fashion, and she is worshipped by such titles as the "Mother of God," "Queen of Heaven," and "Mediatrix," the female mediator between God and man. It all originally came from, and now also comes from Babylonian demons.

When Paul came to Ephesus he had a dramatic encounter with the mother and child worship, where the worship of the mother predominated in the massive and exuberant worship of Diana, the Latin form of the name Artemis (Acts 19:23-41). Silver shrines were big business, and repetitious shouts of "**Great is Diana of the Ephesians**" were inspired by the demons possessing those so enraged by Paul preaching the truth to them (Acts 19:28, 34 KJV).

Since we learn from the scriptures of this demonic center for the worship of the Babylonian mother-goddess, Diana, and from history that this included the means of prayer beads, it is of no coincidence that it was here at the Council of Ephesus in A.D. 425, held in the famous Church of the Virgin Mary, that the Roman Catholic Church was demonically influenced to give the title of "The Mother of God" to Mary (My Catholic Faith).

It was soon after these demon spirits entered into the Roman Church that they gave recognition to Mary as having supposedly remained a virgin throughout her life, and it was considered heresy to teach that Mary had other children by Joseph after Jesus' birth. This was made official at the Council of Chalcedon in A.D. 451 by the doctrine of the "Perpetual Virginity of Mary." But Mary had other children after Jesus, and was not a perpetual virgin for we read that Joseph "**took her as his wife and kept her a virgin until she gave birth to a Son**" (Mt. 1:25 NAS). And concerning His natural brothers and sisters we read, "**Is not this the carpenter, the son of Mary, and brother of James, and Joses, and Judas, and Simon? Are not His sisters here with us?**" (Mk. 6:3 NAS; Mt. 13:55-56). Mary was not without sin according to the church fathers of the first five centuries. Then from the sixth to the twelfth centuries she was regarded as having original sin but divinely protected from personal sin, this view being maintained by earlier "infallible" Popes and about two hundred theologians. In the twelfth century on December 8th, the Roman Church first observed the "Feast of the Immaculate Conception," and then later on that date in A.D. 1854 the Pope promulgated the doctrine of the "Immaculate Conception" as an Article of Faith to be received and believed by all. This doctrine which claims that Mary was born without original sin from Adam and never committed any sin from the time of her birth until her death is again contrary to scripture and Mary herself. Mary said, **"My soul doth magnify the Lord, and my spirit hath rejoiced in God <u>my Saviour</u>"** (Lk. 1:46-47 KJV). Mary would have needed no Saviour unless she had sin, neither would she have gone to the temple and offered sacrifices for her own purification according to the law, which she did (Lk. 2:22-24).

The teaching that Mary was taken bodily up to heaven has existed since soon after the Council of Ephesus, but this "Assumption of Mary" was officially declared only recently, in A.D.1950; and she was declared "Mother of the Church" in A.D.1965. Since 1969 the Roman Catholic Church has observed January 1 as the "Solemnity of Holy Mary, the Mother of God" (an extremely important holy day observance), replacing the "Circumcision of Jesus" (eight days after His birth). And today the worship of Mary is proliferating like a fragrant but noxious weed as never before.

The worship of Mary with all the associated false teachings about her (such as attributing miraculous powers to her as they were to the Egyptian Isis), is indeed not just idolatry and clear evidence of the spirits of ancient Babylon never having ceased their seductive working, but the gradual development of this worship throughout the centuries is God's undeniable revelation to all who have eyes to see and hearts to understand what the **"Mystery, Babylon the great, the mother of the harlots"** <u>is</u> within Christendom.

"Papal Infallibility" is another gross error and tragic teaching, and also is the result of years of the evil spirits of Babylon working. Like the pagan god Janus, the Pope was finally declared "Infallible in matters of faith and morals" in A.D.1870 at the First Vatican Council, by an adulterous Pope who had several mistresses, three of them nuns, by whom he had children. Along with this sin is the horrible usurping of the place of God, the Lord Jesus Christ, and the Holy Spirit upon this earth. This is readily observed in the many titles given to the Pope, meaning "father," the word coming from the Roman word in their language of Latin, "papa." He usurps the place of our heavenly Father when he is called "Our Holy Father," contrary to the plain teaching of Jesus when He said, **"Do not call <u>anyone</u> on earth your father; for One is your Father, <u>He who is in heaven</u>"** (Mt. 23:9 NAS). He usurps the place of the Holy Spirit when he assumes the title "Vicar of Christ," which means the one representing Christ upon the earth, contrary to what Jesus said, for example, in John's gospel, **"And I will ask the Father, and He will give you another Helper, that He may be with you forever; that is the Spirit of truth. . . . But the Helper, the Holy Spirit, whom the Father will send in My name, He will teach you all things, and bring to your remembrance all that I said to you"** (Jn. 14:16-17, 26 NAS). Also, Jesus said, **"He will bear witness of Me,"** and He will be the one to speak for Jesus, and speak to the churches (Jn. 15:26; 16:13-14; Acts 13:2; Rev. 2:11, 17, 29). He usurps the place of Christ upon the earth when he is called "Supreme Pontiff of the Universal Church," and "Our Most Holy Lord," and as such is considered head of the church on earth. Jesus taught us **"Do not be called Rabbi; for One is your Teacher, and you are all brothers. . . . And do not be called leaders; for One is your Leader, that is, Christ"** (Mt. 23:8, 10 NAS). And the Father raised Christ from the dead, **"and gave Him to be the head over all things to the church," "so that He Himself might come to have first place in everything," "both in the heavens <u>and on earth</u>"** (Eph. 1:22 KJV; Col. 1:18, 16 NAS).

Compare this to the Pope's title of "Pontifex Maximus." This was the title given originally to the head of the principal college of pagan priests in ancient Rome, and later given to Julius Caesar in 63 B.C. It was continually used by the Roman emperors until abdicated by the emperor Gratian in A.D. 376 because of his Christian convictions that it was idolatrous and blasphemous. But, it was then quickly taken up by the Bishop of Rome in A.D. 378 when Damasus was elected to that office. And so the Pontifex Maximus, the official High Priest of the Mysteries, was now "The Pope," "Most Holy Father," "Father of Christendom," "the High Priest," "The Bishop of bishops," "The chief teacher and ruler of all Christians," who is to be addressed formally as "Your Holiness," and whose full title is: "Bishop of Rome and Vicar of Jesus Christ, Successor of St. Peter, Prince of the Apostles, Supreme Pontiff of the Universal Church, Patriarch of the West, Primate of Italy, Archbishop and Metropolitan of the Roman Province, and Sovereign of the State of Vatican City" (My Catholic Faith, MCF; WBE). It is significant that after his political election to become the

Pope, a new Pope is carried on a portable <u>throne in regal dress</u> from the Vatican to St. Peter's Church, where at his <u>coronation</u> the cardinals pay homage to him by bowing before him and kissing his foot; after which he says Mass. The senior cardinal deacon places the three-tiered gold <u>papal crown</u> (the tiara, which is modeled after the head-dresses of the spiritual rulers in ancient Babylon, Assyria, and then pagan Rome, is actually <u>three crowns in one</u> representing "his preeminence in the threefold office of Teacher, Priest, and Pastor," with a little gold cross on top) upon his head and announces that the Pope is now "<u>Father of princes and kings, Ruler of the world on earth, and Vicar of our Saviour Jesus Christ</u>" (WBE; MCF). As such he is clearly the Babylonish King of Christendom!

Another interesting example of the spirits of ancient Babylon that ruled the rulers of the Roman Empire in Rome (being manifested and later possessing the rulers there in the Vatican) is that after Romulus (the first ruler of Rome who had supposedly introduced the first Roman calendar), Julius Caesar, with the aid of an astronomer, changed the Roman calendar by developing a new one; he named the month of July after himself and added a day, making it a 31 day month. After that, Augustus named the month of August after himself and took one day from February and added it to his month. Later, Pope Gregory XIII, also by the advice of the astronomers, in A.D.1582 had the Julian calendar (which was named after Julius Caesar and used since his time) corrected by developing the calendar which we now use today all over the world; and it is of course named after himself, the Gregorian Calendar.

It is interesting to note, concerning calendars and dating, that it was a monk, Dionysius Exiguus, who in A.D. 532 started the system of dating events beginning with the year he believed Christ was born. A.D. is the abbreviation for "ANNO DOMINI," which is Latin for "in the year of our Lord." B.C. stands of course for "BEFORE CHRIST."

And so it should not be surprising when we see that the ones who have usurped the titles and places of God in the lives of millions of people world-wide are in confusing contradiction to each other. Such is the case, for example, when one Pope condemned Joan of Arc to be burned alive as "a witch," and later another declared her to be "a saint." When many Popes had denied the teaching of papal infallibility, it is difficult to comprehend how later it could become an official doctrine of the church unless one

95

understands the deceitfulness of the human heart, the working of the spirits of ancient Babylon, and the judgment of Almighty God upon a system so corrupt and apostate.

Although there are many dangerous and false doctrines that have come into the Roman Church because of these spirits of Babylon, another very important one to discuss briefly is the Mass. This doctrine of the Roman Church holds that the actual physical body and blood of our Lord Jesus Christ is present in the Communion Supper, which is called "The Eucharist," after the Greek word meaning "thanksgiving." Again, its origin is in the counterfeit religion of ancient Babylon. In Egypt the priest would consecrate small, thin, round (symbolizing the sun god) cakes or wafers, which were supposed to become the flesh of Osiris. The predominate form of Babylonish religion in Rome at the time of Christ was known as Mithra. It also taught the doctrine of transubstantiation and used the sacraments of cakes and "Haoma" drink which closely parallels the Catholic Eucharistic rite.

The progressive degeneration of the Lord's Supper as taught in the scriptures was over many years. Although Constantine was instrumental in introducing many of the pagan practices of Rome into the professing church when he embraced Christianity, it was not until A.D. 394 that the daily ritual of the Mass began in its infant form. In the New Testament scriptures, Communion was an actual supper meal patterned after the Passover in which all brought food and wine as they could afford; which often meant the poor had nothing to bring but were assured participation with everyone else in this "Agape," meaning "Love Feast," as it was called (Mt. 26:17-30; I Cor. 10:15-24; 11:17-34; Jude v. 12). During the supper meal, bread and wine which were normally used for meals were prayed over and thus sanctified in remembering **the Lord's death until He comes**" (I Cor. 11:24-26 NAS). Although Paul makes it plain that it is an actual participation in the body and blood of the Lord Jesus Christ, it remains bread and wine (I Cor. 10:16-17; 11:26-28). It does not become physically the flesh and blood of Jesus, but when done in faith it is true spiritually (I Cor. 10:3-4, 16). However, the spirits behind the pagan teaching, that their religious rites were the eating of the actual flesh of their god, were eventually successful in deceiving the leaders of the Catholic Church, but not without a struggle with the truth. A Benedictine monk named Radbertus published a treatise openly advocating transubstantiation in A.D. 831, but for the next four hundred years theological war was waged over this teaching by bishops and people alike. Finally in A.D.

1215 at the Fourth Lateran Council it became part of their dogma when Transubstantiation was officially defined by the Pope. Soon thereafter in A.D.1220 adoration of the wafer, or Host as it is called, was decreed, and the actual worship of the elements became official. At the Council of Constance in A.D. 1414 the cup was forbidden to the laity, and then soon after the beginning of the Protestant Reformation the Roman Church met to define and confirm this doctrine and did so at length at the Council of Trent in A.D. 1545-46. It was at this Council in A.D. 1545 when the Church also declared that tradition was of equal authority with the scriptures, and in A.D. 1546 that the Apocryphal books were added to the Bible. All that was done at the Council of Trent was again upheld officially by the Pope at the commencement of the Second Vatican Council in A.D. 1962, which lasted for three years. Soon the Pope issued an encyclical (a letter addressed by the Pope to all the bishops of the world in communion with the Holy See) concerning Transubstantiation entitled, Mysterium Fidei, which reads in part: "During the Second Vatican Council the Church has made a new and most solemn profession of her faith in and <u>worship</u> of this mystery. . . . For if the sacred liturgy holds the first place in the life of the Church, the mystery of the Eucharist stands as the heart and center. . . . Those who partake of this sacrament in Holy Communion eat the Flesh of Christ and drink the Blood of Christ, receiving both grace, the beginning of eternal life, and the 'medicine of immortality'." This is idolatry! Making anything into an image that either represents or is claimed to be God and then worshipping that image is idolatry. We are to worship God alone, and not images of God. God said, **"You shall not make for yourself an idol** [man-made image], **or any <u>likeness of what is in heaven above</u>** [Christ] **or on the earth beneath or in the water under the earth. You shall not worship them or serve them"** (Ex. 20:4-5 NAS). Jesus said that true worshippers must worship the Father, **"in spirit and truth"** (Jn. 4:21-24 NAS). That is, we worship in our spirits after receiving His Holy Spirit by being born of His Spirit, and in accordance with His Word which is the truth — not the contradictory traditions of men.

The sacrifice of the Lord Jesus Christ on the cross at Calvary was a once and for all event, never to be repeated ever! However, Transubstantiation teaches that the Lord Jesus Christ is sacrificed in an unbloody sacrifice and is offered up to God every time a Catholic priest offers Mass, meaning He is sacrificed continually hundreds of thousands of times every day on their altars. But, it is written, Jesus is "a high priest, holy, innocent, undefiled, separated from sinners and exalted above the heavens; who does not need daily, like those high priests, to offer up sacrifices, first for His own sins, and then for the sins of the people, because this He did once for all when He offered up Himself" (Heb. 7:26-27 NAS). "He entered the holy place once for all" (9:12 NAS). "All things are cleansed with blood, and without shedding of blood there is no forgiveness" (9:22 NAS). "Nor was it that He should offer Himself often, as the high priest enters the holy place year by year with blood not his own. Otherwise, He would have needed to suffer often since the foundation of the world; but now once at the consummation of the ages He has been manifested to put away sin by the sacrifice of Himself. And inasmuch as it is appointed for men to die once and after this comes judgment, so Christ also, having been offered once to bear the sins of many, shall appear a second time for salvation without reference to sin, to those who eagerly await Him" (9:25-28 NAS). "We have been sanctified through the offering of the body of Jesus Christ once for all. And every priest stands daily ministering and offering time after time the same sacrifices, which can never take away sins; but He, having offered one sacrifice for sins for all time, sat down at the right hand of God, waiting from that time onward until His enemies be made a footstool for His feet. For by one offering He has perfected for all time those who are sanctified. And the Holy Spirit also bears witness" (10:10-15 NAS).

Beloved, Jesus is our High Priest, and we are all priests unto God, to offer up the sacrifices of praise and thanksgiving for what Christ has done, once! and for all of us (I Pet. 2:5; Heb. 13:15-16). If we are doing this by the faith of God that the Holy Spirit gives, we understand and are resting in Him; however, if we are not born of His Spirit or do not have this assurance in our hearts because of the false traditions of men, we are unsure of our salvation and will look to another person to offer up sacrifices, as the pagans do, for our sins, hoping that they will be able to help us. Never!

By now, beloved, anyone ought to be able to understand clearly that the spirits of Babylon invaded Christianity and began the creation of Babylon the great within the professing church. But before we go on to look then at her daughters, let us look at one more very significant aspect of Babylon that is a source of idolatry throughout the true church world-wide.

One of the original characteristics of Babylon was, as we

remember, to build a city, buildings, and a religious tower. The New Testament reveals to us that the true church of the Lord Jesus Christ never built physical buildings, but taught that they, the people of God, were the true building; and by the example set down in the scriptures that they gave us, it obviously was not the plan of God to spend time or money building buildings for worship, but rather all efforts and finances were spent building people, the true temple of the Holy Spirit, the true house of worship that God seeks.

Now, when Constantine recognized Christianity, he then opened up the huge Roman buildings used for courtrooms and other civic activities, basilicas, for Christian worship; and many of the pagans flocked into the organized church, now that it was acceptable politically and socially.

The Vatican received its name because originally the Vatican Hill had been a "Vaticinia," meaning, "a place of divination," and it is said that the hill was the headquarters of the divination-deity named Vaticanus. At a later period the hill was used for the annual worship of Tammuz, who we've read of in the Bible is the son of the Babylonian mother-goddess, at which time a pine tree was felled and an effigy of the god was fixed to it.

On this very spot now stands the Vatican City, the chief city of "Babylon," and for centuries the largest building in Christendom, St. Peter's Cathedral. It was constructed over the ruins of St. Peter's Basilica which had been patterned originally after the Pantheon of pagan Rome. It is the most elaborate and expensive "Church" building ever erected! In the center of the court yard entrance of St. Peter's is the actual pagan obelisk taken there by Caligula, a Roman Caesar from A.D. 37-41, from Heliopolis, the Greek name for Bethshemesh, Egypt, specifically mentioned in the scriptures (Jer. 43:13). The name of the town means "the House of the Sun" and was the center for the worship of Baal, the sun god, and the mother-goddess. The first obelisk ever erected was by Queen Semiramis at Babylon, and was a symbol for the worship of both the sun and sex, hence its erect nature as a phallic symbol. Is it not amazing that the very same obelisk (a standing image began by Nimrod's wife at the place of the original city and tower of Babel) that stood at the center of this pagan worship exposed in the Old Testament (Jer. 43:13), is now erect at the center before St. Peter's in the city which is the center of Babylonish Christianity in the New Testament (Rev. 17:18)? And that the obelisk, a sacred pillar, was always an important image in the worship of Babylonish religion? (Ex. 23:24; Lev. 26:1; Deut. 7:5-6; 16:22; I Ki. 14:23; II Ki.

10:26-27; 18:4; 23:14; Eze. 26:11). The Vatican City is an independent political kingdom of itself with its own government and Swiss Guard and now reigns over much of Christendom; and it is in fact an exact representation of pagan Rome (taken from ancient Babylon) with its leader having the same titles, mitre headdress (patterned after Dagon the ancient fish-god Judg. 16:23; I Sam. 5:2-7; I Chr. 10:10), garments, and customs; and the operating principles of its system include the very same rituals, practices, doctrines, accomplishments, and ambitions as pagan Rome! And its end will be the same also!

With this all in mind, let us now look more closely at the traditional church building of the Roman Church. It is patterned after the synagogue which was developed while the Jews were in captivity in the land of ancient Babylon. The law is our school master to bring us to Christ, and if someone does not see and enter into the grace of our Lord, he only sees and understands aspects of the Old Testament law. During the Old Testament we see for centuries that the people did not have multiple buildings all over to worship in, but had one tabernacle, made of linen curtains and transported from place to place as they moved, which we are told in the New Testament was a pattern of the true tabernacle which is in heaven and to which we as New Testament believers are to <u>now</u> come regularly for worship; a spiritual worship in which we come directly into the heavens before Jesus our Lord and Head, our Judge, Lawgiver, and King, our great High Priest (Isa. 33:22; Heb. 7-10). But when one does not see the spiritual, heavenly realities, one is absorbed with the things of this world; and here we have man patterning after the world's systems or the law which is to bring us to Christ (Gal. 3:24). When Israel rejected God as King and demanded a man as king like all the other nations, interestingly it was only then that God also allowed a national temple to be built by their king (Solomon); they wanted to emulate in a similar way the Babylonish worshipping people around them which had their kings build temples to their gods. But there was to be only one temple for the entire nation, in Jerusalem; and it was to be a type in this New Testament era of the temple in heaven, where the new Jerusalem is (Heb. 8:1-5; 9:1-24; Rev. 4:1-11; 11:19; 15:5; 21:2). However, after they were sent to Babylon because of their Babylonish ways, they returned to build many "temples" to their God as they had seen and copied in Babylon, but they called them synagogues.

The synagogue, which began in Babylon, is essentially a

rectangle, with an altar central at one end. This is where, in the tabernacle, continual sacrifices were offered, but in the synagogue buildings the end platform was elevated and the Torah, the Law, was placed, with two pulpits on either side. There were, and still are today, rows of pews in which the people not called to the Old Testament priesthood sat and listened to that special class of men called for this purpose. There were elders of the synagogue, with a chief ruler who determined who could speak, read the scriptures, and pray. He summoned fit persons to preach, and was the overseer of the physical care of the building as well. It had a main entrance at the opposite end, with smaller doors on each side; and was so very important in the life of the Jewish community that there were numerous synagogue buildings in each city. The order of worship was set: with prayer, the reading of a portion of both the law and the prophets, the blessing of the priest, a translation in the known language of the people of the scripture that had been read, a discourse, and then a benediction which was more a confession of faith than a prayer. The lesson from the Torah was so arranged that the Pentateuch, the five books of Moses, was completely read in a cycle of three years, and then there followed a chosen portion from the prophets; but it is significant that the preaching could be done by any competent member of the congregation.

One has only to enter a Roman Catholic Church building today to see the similarities in structure, procedure, and customs. The physical layout in older buildings is identical, and basically the same in all the rest. The separated clergy of garbed "priests," the split elevated pulpits, the altar at one end with pews for "lay" members who do not basically participate in the procedures except on cue from the ruler, the reading of the Old and New Testaments scriptures in three year cycles, having their own language (Latin instead of Hebrew), and many of the doctrines and other customs are a mixture of both Old Testament and Babylonish ways; other similarities are such things as idols, candles, icons, and towers (steeples) toward heaven. [The word "clergy" is from the Middle English *clergie,* from Old French *clerc* (influenced by *clerge,* "body of clerks"), which is from the Late Latin *clericus,* a cleric, from the Greek *klerikos,* "belonging to inheritance, cleric" (with reference to the Levites whose only inheritance was the Lord); the word "laity" as opposed to the "clergy" is from the word "lay," and means "common man," and comes from the Middle English *laie,* from Old French *lai,* from Late Latin *laicus,* from Greek *laikos,* from *laos,* "the people" (The American Heritage Dictionary).] And, unlike

101

the one national temple with the High Priest in Jerusalem, a type of Christ our High Priest now in the one temple in heaven, there are many Babylonish church buildings located throughout different areas of a city just like the many synagogues in each city, patterned after the many pagan temples in the city of Babylon.

It was not until Constantine, as a king committing fornication with Mystery Babylon, that buildings began to proliferate for Christian worship; and very quickly then in that fourth century there is reported that at least forty church buildings were in existence in Rome. The most prominent among them were the three great basilicas built by Constantine: St. Peter's built on the steep slope of the Vatican hill in the midst of a pagan cemetery, St. Paul's outside the walls, and St. John Lateran.

Now that we have looked at each of the major doctrines of ancient Babylon that have been brought into Christianity, let us consider a list of a number of others also and the estimated time at which these teachings were gradually introduced.

Prayers for the dead	A.D. 330
Making the sign of the cross	A.D. 330
Baptismal Regeneration promulgated	A.D. 360
The veneration of angels, dead saints, and images	A.D. 375
Title of Pontifex Maximus taken by Bishop of Rome	A.D. 378
The celibacy of priests introduced	A.D. 385
Communion adopted as a daily ritual	A.D. 394
The worship of Mary	A.D. 431
Priests began to wear special clothing	A.D. 500
The doctrine of Purgatory introduced	A.D. 593
Worship in Latin mandated (repealed in Vatican II)	A.D. 600
First man to be proclaimed Pope	A.D. 610
The custom of kissing the Pope's foot	A.D. 709
Communion proposed as a sacrifice by Radbertus	A.D. 831
The dogma of Papal infallibility announced	A.D. 1076
Marriage of Priests forbidden	A.D. 1079
Rosary beads adopted	A.D. 1090
Mandatory attendance at Communion	11th c.
First Crusade ("Holy War") initiated by the Pope	A.D. 1095
Transubstantiation of the Mass defined officially	A.D. 1215
Adoration of the wafer, called the Host	A.D. 1220
Bible forbidden to laymen (repealed in Vatican II)	A.D. 1229
The cup forbidden to laity at communion	A.D. 1414
The doctrine of Purgatory became official	A.D. 1439

Protest of Ninety-Five Theses by Martin Luther	A.D. 1517
Tradition declared of equal authority with Bible	A.D. 1545
Apocryphal books added to the Bible	A.D. 1546
The Immaculate Conception of Mary	A.D. 1854
Infallibility of the Pope in faith and morals	A.D. 1870
Assumption of Mary bodily into heaven	A.D. 1950
Mary proclaimed "Mother of the Church"	A.D. 1965
Official: "Solemnity of Holy Mary, the Mother of God"	A.D. 1969

Now, let us follow this Babylonish woman into motherhood, for she is as the scripture rightly says, "**THE MOTHER OF THE HARLOTS AND OF THE ABOMINATIONS OF THE EARTH**" (Rev. 17:5 lit.).

As we have reported, after Constantine became sole ruler of the Roman Empire, he moved his capital officially in A.D. 330 from Rome to the site of the ancient city of Byzantium where he had built a new city which he named "Nova Roma," New Rome; but soon it was renamed Constantinople, meaning the "City of Constantine." Two of the reasons reported as to why he did this are: One, because the eastern half of the empire had become more important than the western half, and as the eastern half grew stronger, the western grew weaker. Two, Constantine wanted to get away from the powerful pagan influences of Pagan Rome. The Empire was again split in A.D. 395 after the death of Emperor Theodosius I, and the West Roman Empire ceased to exist in A.D. 476 when the German chief Odoacer deposed the last emperor of Rome, Romulus Augustulus, whose name reminds us of Rome's first king and first emperor. The East Roman Empire, also called the Later Roman, or Greek, or Byzantine Empire continued until A.D. 1453 when Constantinople fell to the Turks and became part of the Ottoman Empire.

It is significant to note how Constantinople was captured, as "this event is considered one of the most significant occurrences in the history of the Western world, for it brought to an end the Byzantine Empire, under which much of Eastern Europe was Christianized"; and "it also gave to the Ottoman Turks a new capital for their own empire" (The Catholic Encyclopedia for School and Home, TCESH). The Sultan Mohammed II, called the Great, had great ambitions of territorial expansion, and his strategy was that since the Ottomans had already conquered most of Asia Minor he would next conquer the Balkan Peninsula so as to completely surround the city of Constantinople. The city was highly fortified and had repulsed all attempts for centuries by various forces to capture it except when the Latins successfully took the city with the armies of the Fourth Crusade in 1204 A.D. and pillaged it for three days, after which it was recaptured by the Byzantines in 1261 A.D. and the Greeks again had control. The Sultan was successful in taking most of the Balkans, and so now Constantinople had become "a Christian island in a Moslem sea" (WBE). The strategic position of Constantinople can best be realized by looking on a map and seeing that the city lies partly in Europe and partly in Asia, and therefore connects not only the land trade route between the two but also controls the entrance to the Black Sea. After the Sultan began the siege, the Latin pope in Rome refused to send aid to the Greek emperor in Constantinople, and it was finally captured by the Janizaries, the elite of the standing army of the Ottoman Empire which were almost all from the children taken from their previously captured Christian parents, children who were then instructed in the Islamic religion and trained under iron discipline. "Their religious fanaticism added to their military valor because they believed death in warfare against the unbeliever gained them Mohammedan paradise" (TCESH). The name Janizary came from the Turkish word *yenicheri* meaning "new troops," but the corp existed from A.D.1330-1826. It is also significant that Janizary music was "Crude, noisy music produced by shrill wood instruments, various drums, triangles and other percussion instruments (Webster's New International Dictionary, Second Edition, Unabridged). How meaningful this is for us today as Christians who have been brought under Babylonian bondage have their children taken "**captive through philosophy and empty deception, according to the tradition of men, according to the elementary principles of the world, rather than according to Christ**" (Col. 2:8 NAS). The evolutionary, humanistic, sexually, ethically, and musically perverted, socialistic and Marxist teachings of the godless, unionized, government schools, and even many religious (or formerly religious) colleges and seminaries, is destroying our children and society. I know! I was quickly captured during my university training! But, praise God, I was recaptured very soon after by Christ! "**Hallelujah!**"

After A.D. 1517 Constantinople "was the seat of the Caliph, the Orthodox (Sunni) Muslim leader, and thus the center of most of the Muslim world" (Collier's Encyclopedia, CE). Prior to the Muslim invasion the people of the city had called it Stanbul, meaning "The City," but it was not until 1930 that the name of

Constantinople was officially changed to Istanbul, believed to have been taken from an old Greek phrase, εισ την πολιν, *eis ten polin*, meaning to go "Into The City" (The Catholic Encyclopedia, TCE). As old Rome had been the center of the world's power, now New Rome became that center. It has been important to many peoples for centuries as shown by more of the different names by which it has been called. The Persians and Arabs know it as Deri-Seadet, the Italians and Levantines as Cospoli, the Bulgars as Tsarigrad, and the Greeks as Constantinopolis. It has one of the best locations of any city in the world as it is well situated for defense, and as we have stated before, lies at the trade crossroads of Europe and Asia. "The land and sea routes that pass through Istanbul have been main streets of history" (WBE). Or as another historian has put it, "Constantinople was to become one of the great world capitals, a font of imperial and religious power, a city of vast wealth and beauty, and the chief city of the Western world" (CE).

When Constantine built his new capital city he planned it exactly like old Rome, the first capital of the Empire, by incorporating it on seven hills and dividing it into fourteen regions with privileges similar to Rome. He built it with new public buildings such as the senate house, forums, a capital, circuses, porticoes, and many church buildings such as the Church of the Holy Apostles, destined to be the burial place of the emperors, and thus of course Constantine himself. The oldest section of the city is still known as Stamboul today, and here we find many great buildings from the past including Saint Sophia, meaning Holy Wisdom, which was originally built as a Christian cathedral by the emperor Justinian the Great (the last emperor to speak Latin) between A.D. 532 and 537. When built, it was the <u>largest</u> church building in Christendom, and remained so <u>until</u> St. Peter's Basilica in Rome was <u>purposefully rebuilt</u> into St. Peter's Cathedral. In 1506 A.D. the pope started the rebuilding of St. Peter's and it took 150 years. The cathedral was first designed in the shape of the Greek cross (a cross with four arms of equal length), but before it was completed the nave was lengthened and St. Peter's took the form of the Latin cross. During the reign of Heraclius, the Church of Saint Sophia in Constantinople owned 365 estates, and he established 625 clerics as the number necessary for its service. It is the finest and most famous example of Byzantine architecture in the world, but when the Turks overthrew the city they turned it into a mosque, as they did most other church buildings, covered its mosaics, and it became the pride of Islam. However, in 1933 it became a museum and many beautiful pictures, including Christ and the "Virgin Mary," were uncovered.

"In A.D. 625 Heraclius added the famous quarter of Blachernae with its venerated Church of the Blessed Virgin, whose image was considered as the palladium [protecting idol] of the city" (TCE). With this spirit of idolatry ruling over the city, one can readily see how the worship of icons (a picture or image representation in painting of some sacred personage, as Christ or a saint or angel, itself venerated as sacred; taken from the Greek word ειҡων, *eikon,* meaning image or likeness) is so much an important part of the Eastern Church headquartered there, and why iconoclasts (breakers of icons), who arose with such vigor from time to time, met with such fierce opposition. For instance, in A.D. 726 the Emperor Leo III issued an order that all images and paintings in churches should be covered or destroyed, but many monks and people opposed it. Shortly, "after the second Nicene Council met in A.D. 787, the Empress Irene permitted images to be worshiped, as long as the worship had a different quality from that owed to God. Finally, in A.D. 842, the Eastern Church reached a settlement which permitted pictures but not complete statues or images" (WBE). In the Roman Catholic Church, it is stated that images are venerated only as symbols, but one has only to read the writings of the Church, or watch the people bow, kiss, and worship (meaning to bow down and do homage) images and leaders themselves to refute the hypocrisy of trying to change reality by changing the meaning or use of words. But this is only to be expected in the mixtures of modern Babylon, following ancient Babylon, and its religious daughter, ancient Egypt and its similar emphasis on idols (the Israelites had just left Egypt when the commandment was given to them forbidding such practice). It is the breaking of the Second Commandment which says, "**You shall not make for yourself an idol** [lit. **a graven image], or any likeness of what is in heaven above or on the earth beneath or in the water under the earth. You shall not worship them or serve them; for I, the Lord your God, am a jealous God, visiting the iniquity of the fathers on the children, on the third and the fourth generations of those who hate Me, but showing lovingkindness to thousands, to those who love Me and keep My commandments**" (Ex. 20: 4-6 NAS). This is why the Roman Catholic Church has deleted this Second Commandment in the Decalogue and split the last one in order to maintain the Commandments with ten in number (MCF).

In following then this continuation of Babylonish idolatry, it is important to note that after Constantine recognized Christianity in A.D. 313 and inaugurated New Rome in A.D. 330 in honor of the Christian martyrs, he completed the hippodrome there, a large open air public arena started by Emperor Septimius in A.D. 203, and placed on its site the Serpentine Column that he had brought from Delphi, Greece. And then later Emperor Theodosius I erected in the center of the entrance of this Constantinople Hippodrome an obelisk removed from Heliopolis in Egypt, the same exact type as had been brought from there to the Circus Maxima in old Rome and which was later to be moved a short distance in A.D. 1586 by order of the Pope to stand erect and center before St. Peter's Cathedral.

As Constantine "believed that he was God's chosen servant, he regarded himself as responsible to God for the good government of the church." Consequently, it was in Constantinople that "the divine right of kings, rulers who were defenders of the faith — as opposed to the king as divine himself — was evolved" (CE).

Therefore, this new center of Christianity, New Rome (as Constantine had originally called it, with so many identical features as old Rome) after years of bitter hatred, conflict, and war with old Rome, became the headquarters of the main daughter of Babylon when in A.D. 1054 the institutional Church was split into Roman Catholic and Eastern Orthodox Church denominations. As the Eastern Orthodox Church spread, it has maintained biblical truths still held in A.D.1054 that the Roman Catholic Church hasn't. However, although two of the main issues used in splitting the church were doctrinal, division is a work of the flesh, and is always the result of jealousy, selfish ambition, and the other spirits of Babylon at work (Gal. 5:20; Jam. 3:13 - 4:12).

One of the two doctrines where the East and West Churches differed was over whether the bread used at the Eucharist was to be leavened or unleavened. The Roman Catholic Church used unleavened bread (although they permitted leavened bread) as it was the continuance of the Passover Feast in which only unleavened bread was used by the Jews and thus by Jesus (Ex. 12:8, 15-21; 13:6-7; Mt. 26:17; Mk. 14:12; Lk. 22:1, 7-8). The Orthodox, however, claimed that Christians were to be different from the Jews, and that the bread is to be a sign of new life and vitality, not deadness as unleavened bread. However, not only the Passover Feast would have us use unleavened bread, but Paul's writings on the Lord's Supper would also have us realize that we are to be without leaven, which is given as a type of sin, and therefore we are to "**celebrate the feast, not with old leaven, nor with the leaven of malice and wickedness, but with the <u>unleavened bread</u> of sincerity and truth**" (I Cor. 5:6-8 NAS).

The other major doctrine of disagreement was the "Filioque." That word stands for the phrase "and from the Son" which was added by the Latins in A.D. 589 to the Nicene Creed in reference to the Holy Spirit coming forth "from the Father and the Son." The Catholic Encyclopedia states, "Filioque is a theological formula of great dogmatic and historical importance. On the one hand, it expresses the Procession of the Holy Ghost from both the Father and the Son as one Principle; on the other, it was the occasion of the Greek schism." The Greeks objected and said that the Holy Spirit came forth "from the Father only"; but after much debate their position became twofold, either "from the Father only" or "from the Father through the Son" (TCE). The Greeks said in A.D. 1054, "If the Latins would renounce the Filioque, peace could be restored," as it was the chief grievance against the West (The Catholic Encyclopedia for School and Home, TCESH).

Now Jesus said, "**If you love Me, you will keep My commandments. And I will ask the Father, and He will give you another Helper, that He may be with you forever; that is the Spirit of truth**" (Jn. 14:15-17). "**But the Helper, the Holy Spirit, whom the Father will send in My name, He will teach you all things, and bring to your remembrance all that I said to you**" (Jn. 14:26). "**When the Helper comes, whom I will send to you from the Father, that is the Spirit of truth, who proceeds from the Father, He will bear witness of Me**" (Jn. 15:26). "**But I tell you the truth, it is to your advantage that I go away; for if I do not go away, the Helper shall not come to you; but if I go, I will send Him to you**" (Jn. 16:7). "**Therefore having been exalted to the right hand of God, and having received from the Father the promise of the Holy Spirit, He has poured forth this which you both see and hear**" (Acts 2:33)(all ref. NAS).

Now it seems clear from the scriptures that Jesus received the promised Holy Spirit from the Father and gives Him to us. And it can be said further that after we receive the Holy Spirit, others can receive the Holy Spirit from and through us as the scripture says, "**He therefore that ministereth to you the Spirit, and worketh miracles among you, doeth he it by the works of the law, or by the hearing of faith?**" (Gal. 3:5 KJV). This was the experience of Peter and John when they were ministering to the Samaritans after they had accepted the gospel and been baptized by Philip and **"they began laying their hands on them, and they were receiving the Holy Spirit"** (Acts 8:17 NAS). And it was Paul who laid hands upon the Ephesians and they received (Acts 19:6). This was years after a disciple, not an apostle, named Ananias had done the same for Paul, and also healed him (Acts 9:10-17).

I bring this matter of the "Filioque" before you, one which has been used to divide millions of professing and some "possessing" Christians for centuries, to help illustrate how fighting and causing schism over doctrines as petty as this are not only works of the flesh, but initiated and maintained by people who themselves are devoid of the Spirit of God, people who only have a doctrine of reality, and not reality itself! For centuries, empty men have been laying empty hands on empty heads, and people have been receiving a ritual, not reality.

But, praise God, in the present revival taking place, men who have been ordained in both divisions are now receiving the true Holy Spirit, being ordained of the Lord Jesus, and ministering the Spirit of God to those who are hungry and thirsty. Empty people are being filled!

What a shame it is that practices and doctrines that are at the very heart of the gospel, the Communion, reminding us of the One who died to make us one, and the receiving of the Holy Spirit, the only One who can make us one, are perverted and twisted and made to divide us!

Jesus said, **"A new commandment I give to you, that you love one another, even as I have loved you, that you also love one another. By this all men will know that you are My disciples, if you have love for one another"** (Jn. 13:34-35 NAS).

It is being filled with the Spirit of God, and thus with the love of God, that gives us the power to be true children of God and what He wants us to be. So many are caught up in religion and ritual, and not true godly reality in Jesus Christ our Lord!

True disciples will not divide over doctrinal differences such as these, but will be **"endeavouring to keep"** (KJV), **"diligent to preserve the unity of the Spirit in the bond of peace"** until reaching **"the unity of the faith"** (Eph. 4:3, 13 NAS).

Continuing now with this daughter of Babylon, the Eastern Orthodox Church, it has need like all organizations to return to the biblical truths practiced in the first century as found in God's Holy Word. But of course, this would mean the end of itself as a sectarian, non-scriptural entity, the product of losing the headship of Christ and developing in Babylonish hierarchical ways. It is the major Christian Church in Greece, the old Soviet Union (now known as the Commonwealth of Independent States), eastern Europe, and western Asia. Rather than being under a Pope, and although the patriarch of Constantinople is given greatest honor, it has been divided by strife and carnal politics into many independent "self-governing" Churches. The two largest daughters of Babylon having branches in the United States are the Greek Orthodox Church and the Russian Orthodox Church, but there are also the lesser known ones such as the Syrian, Serbian, Bulgarian, Romanian, Ukrainian, and Albanian Orthodox Churches. Some of the other major differences between the Orthodox and the Roman Catholic are that the Orthodox have a married priesthood, they do not hold to the Pope nor papal infallibility, and they make more use of icons. However, there are a number of Churches that are a mixture of the two. They put themselves under the Pope of Rome, but have a married priesthood; the largest Rite of which is the Byzantine Catholic Church, which has nearly all of its church buildings modelled after the Basilica of Holy Wisdom in Constantinople.

Before the split between Roman Catholic and Eastern Orthodox, there was another major division that occurred earlier in A.D. 451 when the Council of Chalcedon condemned as heresy the doctrine of only a single nature of Christ Jesus. Alexandria, Egypt, one of the most powerful patriarchates (meaning ruling divisions) in Christendom then broke away from both Rome and Constantinople, and the Coptic Orthodox Church became independent. Consequently, many of its ancient traditions are very similar to the Roman Catholic and Eastern Orthodox. Most of the "Copts," as they are called (the word taken from the Greek word *Aegyptios* meaning "Egyptians"), are located mostly in Egypt and Ethiopia, and are under the patriarch of Alexandria.

As the Roman Church spread mainly north and west, it's power and influence grew. This advance was mainly due to the military conquests of Charlemagne, meaning "Charles the Great" in French, king of the Franks, who had conquered all of western Europe except Spain. Charlemagne believed his mission was to conquer these lands in order to convert the waring pagan tribes living there to Christianity, which meant bringing them under the control and teaching of the Church of Rome. Near the completion of his effort, a remarkable event occurred when on Christmas day in A.D. 800 Charlemagne was crowned at St. Peter's in Rome as "Emperor of the Roman Empire" by the Pope; and thus he became the supreme ruler of the western half of organized Christendom, and an extender and protector of Roman Catholicism throughout the lands of western Europe. He sometimes referred to his palace at Aachen, which lies just east of the boundaries of Germany, Belgium, and The Netherlands, as the "New Rome"; where later 28 Holy Roman Emperors were crowned as rulers of what became known as the "Holy Roman Empire." Charlemagne believed himself to be the Vicar of Christ on the earth, the ruler of Christ's earthly kingdom, and a reflection of the Lord's rulership in heaven. This word vicar means "the one who represents the authority of another" and thus, as has happened before, this title has been taken from an emperor of the Roman Empire and claimed by the "Bishop of Rome." But as such he is an imposter and has, in the minds and lives of millions, usurped the position of "**head of the church**" (Eph. 5:23) from the Lord Jesus Christ who has "**all authority . . . in heaven and on earth**" (Mt. 28:18), and is the true "**head over all things to the [true] church, which is His body, the fulness of Him who fills all in all**" in heaven and on this earth! (Eph. 1:22-23 NAS). The empire Charlemagne "revived" lasted in one form or another for a thousand years, and both civilized and established the control of Roman Catholicism in the area until the Protestant Reformation brought Lutheranism to Germany, the Anglican Church to England, and the Dutch Reform Church to Holland.

After the beginning of the Orthodox Church with its headquarters in New Rome, Constantinople, it spread into Greece, and north into Russia. After the fall of the Byzantine Empire in A.D. 1453, all of its lands except Russia were in Muslim control. Soon the claim was made that Russia was the only successor to the Byzantine Empire and was the "Third Rome," so Ivan IV crowned himself "Czar of all Russia" in A.D. 1547 (the title of Czar being taken from the Roman title of Caesar, because he believed himself to be the true ruler of the Roman Empire). It is most interesting that the last Czar, Nicholas II, was overthrown by the Russian Revolution in 1917 and was executed by the Soviets in 1918; thus the last leader of the "Roman Empire" was destroyed by modern communism, the most godless, antichrist system ever to seek and gain such world wide domination. It in turn has been overthrown by the sovereign moving of the Spirit of the Lord in establishing the kingdom of God within people of the old Soviet Empire. And we shall see Babylon the great of the old Roman Empire destroyed by the godless Antichrist who will in turn be totally destroyed in the physical and glorious return of our Lord Jesus Christ in establishing His kingdom openly upon the earth! Hallelujah!

Another important historical fact that is worthy of our consideration before we go on is that of the Crusades, which lasted for several hundred years. In July of A.D.1054, after long and sharp disputes, the Pope ordered his legates to lay on the altar of St. Sophia in Constantinople the Bull of excommunication against the patriarch there (the leader of the Greek realm of the church). This act resulted in a popular revolution, and five days later the Patriarch of Constantinople replied by excommunicating the Pope and the "Azymite" [ones who use unleavened bread in Communion] Latins (The Catholic Encyclopedia, TCE). Then in November A.D.1095, not long after this formal split between the Church of Rome and the church at Constantinople, a new Pope announced at a Church council at Clermont in southern France his project for a Holy War against the Moslems who had gained control of the Holy Land and were also capturing territory from the emperor in Constantinople who had asked for his help. The Pope felt that this would "be favorable to a reunion of the Greek and Roman Churches, in schism since A.D.1054" (TCE).

Although previous Popes had promised absolution (forgiveness) of their sins to troops who died defending Christians against Moslems who had been invading Italy, now the Pope promised a plenary indulgence to all who would "take up the cross." This scriptural term by Jesus was "wrested" and redefined as meaning to make a solemn vow to fight in this Holy War against the Moslems, and a white cross was worn as a badge on the outer garment of those who took part. The Latin word for cross is crux, and thus what became known as the Holy Wars of the Middle Ages has become better known as The Crusades.

"In Catholic terminology, the word 'indulgence' means remission of the temporal punishment due for sin which has already been forgiven . . . which must be fulfilled either in this life or the next" (The Catholic Encyclopedia for School and Home, TCESH). When going to confession, there is a "penance," a satisfaction imposed by the confessor. Thus, "the forgiven sinner, by means of indulgences, has an excellent means of paying this debt during his life on earth" (TCESH).

Concerning the Crusades, many became "Crusaders" for different reasons. "Some hoped to win military glory or get new lands. Others were looking for adventure. Merchants joined the ranks in search of new markets. Criminals joined to run away from justice. The preaching of Pope Urban II, which prompted the First

Crusade, appealed to men's political and economic ambitions, as well as to their religious fervor" (WBE). The essential spiritual privilege of the indulgence given by the Pope was: "Crusaders who had confessed their sins were freed of the penance they had to perform either in this world or the next, even if they were prevented by death from actually going on the Crusade" (TCESH). Since the Crusaders were freed from arrest for debt, and from usury, and the Pope became "guardian of their wives, and families" as they became "soldiers of the Church," and feudal Barons were enticed to lead the fight for the Church instead of fighting one another as they had been doing, the power of the Papacy increased greatly (TCE/TCESH).

It is most interesting that in A.D.1009 before the Crusades started, the Moslem Caliph of Egypt, in a fit of madness, ordered the destruction of the Holy Sepulchre and all the Christian establishments in Jerusalem. Thus the reconstruction of the Holy Sepulchre in A.D.1027 by the Byzantine emperor left not the original to possess for which the Crusades were started, and for which people still go on pilgrimage today. But since it was taught, and is yet believed, that "where the image is, there is the Spirit," it still gave rise to powerful motives, both to the pilgrimages to the "Holy Places" and to the Crusades themselves. Thus we find that in the Fourth Crusade, European Crusaders under Rome attacked the Greeks in Constantinople, and we read, "The holy relics especially excited the covetousness of the Latin clerics . . . and there were few cities in the West that received no sacred booty from the pillage" (TCE). Many Orthodox were slaughtered then, and since then down through the centuries many others on both sides have died in countless battles of bitter hatred between these two divisions in Christendom (which remains today and can be seen in the conflicts in Bosnia), as well as battles with the Moslems (also in Bosnia, the Middle East, Africa, Eastern Europe, and Southern Russia).

Then, there were the courts of Inquisition which were given unlimited powers to eradicate all "heretics" — true Christians, including some godly Roman Catholics because of their wealth or position, Jews, and Moslems — anyone who would not support the superstitions and idolatries of "the Catholic faith." And history reported, "a defence in the Inquisition is of little use to the prisoner, for a suspicion only is deemed sufficient cause of condemnation, and the greater his wealth the greater his danger." And, those "who read the Bible in the common language, the Talmud of the Jews, or the Alcoran [Koran] of the Mahometans [Moslems]" were accused

113

(Fox's Book of Martyrs, FBM).

By the deliberate design of fear, the most horrible diabolical tortures, and executions of burning people alive at the stake (accomplished at grand public ceremonies called by the persecuting Church an "auto da fé," an "act of faith"), the Inquisitions wrote one of the most shameful and sordid chapters in the history of Christendom from A.D.1229-1834. They were instituted by a fiendish Pope, and then maintained and praised by many succeeding Popes of like diabolical disposition. They were initiated for the religious, political, and economic power of Rome, but were the dread fear of kings everywhere. They were an excuse for plunder and rape, by both priests and people, and lasted officially for over 600 years. They were truly the darkness of the Dark Ages! And the consequential judgment by God upon the nations that participated is still evident today!

One's education is not complete without reading the horrid account of the most inhumane cruelties and barbarous slaughter of hundreds of thousands of humble, innocent, and faithful Christians, who rather than confess to the superstitions and idolatry of Papal religion, were willing to be burned alive in the martyr's flame, and "prove the power of faith over the flesh" (FBM).

These are they "**of whom the world was not worthy**" (Heb. 11: 35-38). They knew well the fallibility of the "infallible Church," and chose to submit to the eternal rather than the "infernal." The scriptural knowledge that they had come to know and understand can be aptly testified to in the words of an illiterate woman, who had been accused by her Roman Catholic husband and children, as she was teased with questions by Catholic priests and friars before her burning. "'Nay,' said she, 'you have more need to weep than to laugh, and to be sorry that ever you were born, [than] to be the chaplains of that whore of Babylon. I defy him and all his falsehood'" (FBM, Forbush edition, pg. 277). Since she could neither read nor write, but had an unusual memory of the scriptures, to read four pages of her shining testimony reveals the wisdom of the preaching of her day. She spoke out boldly for the truth for many days, whereas many were led to go very quietly to the stake, simply trusting in the One who would strengthen them in the trial, and would greet them "on the other side." As multitudes stood calmly without crying out, or bewailing their fate, or even flinching in the fire, but welcoming their deaths as the entrance to that better world which awaited them, the sacrifices of the martyrs of Jesus give abundant proof of the reality of the true gospel, and the truth of who was and is right concerning the issues for which they gave their all. Following their Master, they were led as He, as "lambs to the slaughter" by the institution which had the scriptures but would not obey nor believe them, except selectively; and we would do well in light of what is going on now and especially of what is to come (Rev. 20:4), to remember His words to the church in Smyrna, **"Do not fear what you are about to suffer. Behold, the devil is about to cast some of you into prison, that you may be tested, and you will have tribulation ten days. Be faithful until death, and I will give you the crown of life"** (Rev. 2:10 NAS)!

Today, many tens of thousands are still being martyred for their Christian faith, but they have overcome Satan **"because of the blood of the Lamb and because of the word of their testimony, and they did** [and do] **not love their life even to death"** (Rev. 12:11 NAS).

With the Crusades, the Inquisitions, the idolatry, the corruption of selling indulgences (sins were forgiven by payments instead of by grace and repentance), the bitter fighting between divisions within Christendom, and all the persecutions against God's true believers by Babylonish institutionalized Christianity, is it any wonder then that it was necessary for God to send a major reformation?

Although the Reformation which started in A.D. 1517 by Catholic priest, Martin Luther, as he protested mainly the selling of indulgences in order to build the Babylonian St. Peter's Cathedral in Rome, brought home fundamental truths to millions ("salvation by faith" and "the priesthood of all believers"), the idolatrous structures of Babylon were never completely abandoned, and consequently most religious activity within Christianity today involves idolatry of many kinds. The daughters of Babylon are still worshipping, meaning holding to and serving, not only icons and images, but also the denominations' hierarchical structures and doctrines and names and buildings and traditions. Independent groups do much the same, idolizing themselves, their leaders, preachers, pastors, congregations, callings, and ministries. An idol is anything that we hold as more important than God, or which we serve before looking to God and serving Him in His way — and idolatry in this regard is rampant. God's people listen more to the preaching and words of men than they do to the true words of God because they are not true disciples of the Lord, searching to understand and obey the true Word of God. They

115

yield to the spirit of the world, rather than praying, fasting, giving, and living in the living Word of God, as interpreted by the Spirit of God.

The spirit of ancient Babylon, whereby people worshipped their leaders, and which spread from there to Egypt, to Greece, and then into Pagan Rome in Emperor-worship, and then into Papal Rome in worshipping the Pope, in bowing down and kissing his toe, and doing homage to Cardinals and other high officials, is also rampant throughout Christendom, in exalting leaders beyond scriptural positions and serving leaders over and beyond one's allegiance to God Himself. Homage originally meant the reverence that a vassal showed "in owing faith and service" to his feudal lord. And this is just what many leaders expect today of those who have submitted to their authority and false church structures. When God's Word is denied in order to honor man, and make a man the head of the church, whether the world-wide Roman Catholic Church or a local church congregation, this spirit is being manifested; it is a spirit of Babylon.

We might add here, for additional clarity and insight concerning buildings, that a basilica was originally the name for a public building used in the Roman Empire for civil courts and meetings, and later, as would be expected, was used in giving honor in the naming of Roman Catholic church buildings. "There are two kinds of Roman Catholic basilicas, major and minor. Major basilicas have a special altar that can only be used by the pope or those he delegates," such as St. Peter's and St. John Lateran in Rome. "A Cathedral is the main church of a bishop's province. His throne stands in this church. The word *cathedral* comes from the Greek word *kathedra*, meaning *seat* or *bench* [*throne*, Am. Coll. Dict.] (WBE)." "The cathedral in Mexico City is the oldest church in North America. St. Patrick's Cathedral and the Cathedral of St. John the Divine in New York City are built in the Gothic style. The latter was designed as the largest Gothic cathedral in the world" (WBE). St. Patrick's is Roman Catholic; Saint Paul's Cathedral in London belongs to her daughter, the Church of England; and St. John the Divine, as well as The Cathedral of Saints Peter and Paul in Washington, D.C., also known as The National Cathedral, are part of the Episcopal Church, a granddaughter of the Roman Catholic Church. It is significant to note, in reference to Revelation 18:11-15, that Saint Mark's Cathedral in Venice, Italy, built in the shape of a cross like most cathedrals, has among other things four bronze horses in front, brought from Constantinople, because "<u>By law,</u>

every merchant who traveled to the Orient had to bring back some object for the church. This built an art collection" (WBE).

Before concluding this section on Babylon, I would like us to consider how the cultural and religious structure of ancient Babylon was the same as what was developed later in ancient Rome, and from there is the same as what has been developed in the various countries that have been colonialized by Roman Catholicism, such as in Latin America and elsewhere. The difference in North and South America is the presentation of the gospel of Jesus Christ. One in a freedom of expression brought here by those of the Protestant Reformation, and the other by Roman Catholicism. The natural resources, water, minerals, climates, and so forth, of both the North and South American continents are very similar, but the resulting type societies are very different.

Let me quote another item from a historian before any further comment.

"The real impact of Roman religion upon Christianity was seen long after the persecutions had ended, when the political ideas and ideals of responsible world government, of the universal maintenance of law and order, and of a <u>hierarchical</u> organization of society came to expression and fulfillment in Latin Catholicism." [After the third century the language of the Western church was changed from the biblical Hebrew and Greek to the Roman Latin.] "Its conception of sainthood was tinged with the ancient ideal of sobriety, seriousness, even solemnity (*gravitas*), which had been characteristic of the earliest type of religious feeling in Italy. Its conception of worship and devotion was formed on the ancient Roman appreciation of piety (*pietas*), with its strong attachment to family and especially filial duties; its great virtues of humility (*humilitas*), as contrasted with pride or arrogance (*superbia*); and of loyalty (*fiducia*), which came to include the church's theology as well as its ethics, so that men spoke of the duty of belief and of unquestioning acceptance of theological definitions and of ecclesiastical authority — all these basic characteristics of Latin Catholicism, which placed a stamp on the whole of Western Christianity for many centuries (including that of modern times), were a legacy from the best elements [the quoted author's opinion] in the ancient Roman character, now combined [I would say mixed], sweetened, and inspired by the ethics of the gospel, but also modified by new circumstances and conditions" (IDB).

Might I suggest to the reader, that after reading this chapter on Babylon, that you go back and read the history again that I have given of ancient Babylon, to understand how the predominate national religion determines not only the type of faith of a nation, but its economic system, and consequently the degree of prosperity or economic bondage that prevails. This is true whether that religion is atheism, Islam, Buddhism, Hinduism, Shintoism, Confucianism, Judaism, Roman Catholicism, Protestantism, or pure Christianity, and this can be readily seen as we look at various countries of the world.

In North America, the freedom of religious worship was used by God to found the greatest Christian nation the world has ever known, but of course, unfortunately, some of the Babylonish traditions were retained, and now the ever increasing yielding to the same spirits of Babylon (pride, unbelief, rebellion, selfish ambition, and fears) are now reducing us and bringing upon us judgments similar to those the Lord brought upon Israel and Judah in the past. May God give us the grace to repent and return to Him before it is too late! I believe He will, but not without very severe chastening and judgment!

In concluding this section on Babylon, let us understand that Babylon is a religious system composed of a mixture of demonic spirits and their doctrines; and it is not just the system of ancient Babylon, nor in this New Testament era of the mother church, the system of Roman Catholicism, but it includes all of the denominations and groups that have come out of that system and held on to its basic spirits, practices, and teachings. It is gathering as Christians and not gathering under the headship of Jesus Christ. It is any gathering where men have a pre-planned agenda, a church tradition of order that is not one in which God's people gather to wait upon Him, to allow the Holy Spirit to inspire and anoint whosoever He chooses, to function in any way that He chooses, to manifest the life of Christ through. All of the callings, ministries, gifts, talents, and anointings (all called charismata) of the Holy Spirit are to be allowed, and be under His direction. No pre-planned agenda except that which has been given by Him! And we can soon tell where an agenda is from, by how men function and by the fruit of what is accomplished. One has only to read the accounts of revival to realize the freedom, grace, and power of God's way, and that the scriptures are clear on these points. A concluding statement could well be the scripture itself where Paul wrote, "**What is the outcome then, brethren? When you assemble, each one has a psalm, has a teaching, has a revelation, has a**

118

tongue, has an interpretation. **Let all things be done for edification**" (I Cor. 14:26 NAS). And then a study of the context of those twelfth through fourteenth chapters of First Corinthians for more understanding of the gifts, ministries, and order when under the order of God!

Babylon: Now!

Now that we have seen what Babylon is, what is it now, how does it affect us?

We have seen that Babylon is an organization of people, not under the headship of Jesus Christ according to the scriptures, but an organization of the unregenerate, or one containing a mixture of the unregenerate and regenerate, or simply one of carnal regenerate Christians, under the headship of man according to the ways of ancient Babylon. We have seen how the doctrines of Babylon, and particularly the organization of Christian people, is most developed in Roman Catholicism; but it is also in the Coptic and Orthodox Churches, and has been continued in the Protestant Churches and independent "Churches" throughout the world. Even in a single, independent congregation, when the leader is not under the headship of Christ, a hierarchy soon develops. The word "hierarch" comes from two words: the first is the Greek word ιεροσ, *hieros,* meaning "sacred," and then the word αρχοσ, *archos,* meaning "ruler, chief, prince, or leader." Hence, it is a hierarchical system where instead of the Lord Jesus Christ being in the midst as the supreme, sacred ruler, the ever present αρχιποιμενοσ, *archipoimenos,* "chief shepherd" (I Pet. 5:4), a man usurps that position. Then he as the only "pastor" usually starts ordaining men under himself as "elders" or leaders of the congregation. As the congregation grows, or as other congregations are started in order to enlarge the ministry but are maintained under the authority of the original "pastor," the hierarchy (a system of persons in a graded order of successive ranks) develops more and more, often using biblical or semi-biblical terms as titles of position, but distorting the scriptural ministries that they represent. No matter how much of "a prince" the man at the top might be, he is no substitute for the Prince of Peace!

The Pope is a political position as well as religious, just as the original Babylon, coming not from divine revelation and origin, but by political vote of the leaders of the church. He rules over an independent civil state, and demands recognition by the heads of state whenever he travels abroad. And so, the leaders of the daughters of Babylon are also political in nature, as are many of the independent congregations of Christendom today. Therefore is it any wonder that the carnality of politics, given to us as a work of the flesh (Gal. 5:20), has resulted in so much of the bondage that exists in the church today? Ερtθεια, eritheia, translated in Galatians 5:20 as "strife" in the KJV, and "disputes" here but most often "selfish ambition" elsewhere in the NAS, means literally "a desire to put one's self forward," an "electioneering or intriguing for office," a "self-seeking pursuit of political office by unfair means," "a partisan and factious spirit which does not disdain low arts." It is derived from ερtθοσ, erithos, "working for hire, a hireling" (Thayer's and Bauer, Arndt, & Gingrich Greek-English Lexicons of the New Testament).

Jesus, while teaching in the temple, spoke His strongest words of condemnation upon the leaders of the Jewish synagogue system that had originated in Babylon; and I must add, they are so appropriate today to the leaders of the "Christian Synagogue System" that has followed in this pattern from them, and Babylon the great within Christendom (Mt. 23:1 - 24:1).

The leaders were seating themselves, not being seated by the Spirit of God, but by their own systems of "seminary" education and ordination. They were so desirous of the admiration of others as they paraded about in their exaggerated religious clothing, loving the places of honor at banquets, and the special seats that they had created in their houses of worship for themselves. They demanded undue respect by creating titles for themselves which Jesus so plainly told us not to do — Rabbi (which is Hebrew, or Doctor which is Latin and means Teacher); or Father; or Leader! And so, is this not to be expected in a Babylonish Christian Synagogue System, I must ask? Pope, Cardinal, Bishop, Monseigneur, Father, Your Holiness, Reverend, Right Reverend, Most Right Reverend, Reverend Doctor, Pastor — they demanded even that men worship them by bowing down and doing homage before their "august persons." Even using a God given ministry of deacon or shepherd as a title is of Babylon. That is why it is translated from the Latin word "pastor," meaning shepherd, instead of from the Greek scriptures. Never in the Word of God do we find an apostle, prophet, evangelist, shepherd, teacher, elder, or deacon using their ministry before their name as a title, never! We see them addressed simply as Paul, Peter, James, and John for example. How about you?

But these blind fools of the old synagogue system were traveling on, all over the world to make followers of and for themselves, all the while praying their way to hell. They could not properly interpret many scriptures because of a system that produced hypocrisy, as it was more interested in the cleanliness of one's outer appearance than the sincerity and purity of one's heart. They were blind guides, preventing men from entering the kingdom of God, and preferring that people serve in the kingdom developed for themselves. Jesus said that they were such snakes that they would go anywhere to persecute, punish in their church services, and even murder the true saints that God would have trained by His system and His anointed ordination. Oh, how this is so applicable of our Christian Synagogue System of the past, as well as of today!

Now, as we take seriously the words of the Lord Jesus in Matthew twenty-three to humble ourselves as servants, let us continue to see how this carnal organization and headship of man is affecting us today.

In the mother and major daughters of Babylon, it will be more obvious and more tragic. The Roman Catholic and Orthodox Churches have so departed from the faith in many places, that even the simple preaching of Christ as Lord and Savior, without anything about baptism or church structure or affiliation, is rejected and actively opposed. Many of their leaders do not know Christ at all, and are so committed to their idolatry that they publicly take a stand against the preaching of Christ as sufficient to save the human soul. Billy Graham, who is the most noted preacher in the world today, who preaches Christ and Him crucified with no signs or wonders, no miraculous manifestations of the Holy Spirit, only the person of Christ, and preaches no church affiliation or structure, nothing about water or Spirit baptism, is often rejected; Catholic and Orthodox leaders oppose the efforts of the simple Gospel, the Good News of Jesus Christ, and tell their people to reject his crusades. This has been done by the Roman Catholic Church in many places throughout the world. In Russia the Russian Orthodox Church actively opposed the Graham crusade in Moscow in attempting to keep the people from attending. They actually paid TV stations to <u>not</u> telecast the crusade. There, also, the infiltration of atheists into the hierarchy of the clergy and their sinister collaboration with the KGB is well known. And now, the Russian

Army has made an alliance with Russian Orthodoxy to literally wage "war against Protestants," and there are photographs and documented reports of "kidnappings, tortures, murders, lynchings" and other "atrocities" (National & International Religion Report, April 18, 1994, pg. 1). In South America the Roman Catholic clergy is notorious for its propagation of Liberation Theology and its deceitful transforming of Jesus into a Marxist revolutionary. Consequently, the tribulation of persecution and martyrdom for one's faith is not infrequent. What wickedness!

In the main-line Protestant churches, moral and theological corruption is rampant. Adultery, fornication, and homosexuality are not only condoned but encouraged by bishops and leaders of these long established man-made organizations. It is no wonder then that their theology is so dead, their churches dying, and some time ago the "God is Dead" crowd was so acceptable. As Jude wrote, they are "**hidden reefs [rocks] in your [our] Love Feasts when they feast with you [us] without fear, caring for** [Greek: **shepherding] themselves; clouds without water, carried along by winds; [waning] autumn trees without fruit, doubly [twice] dead, uprooted [plucked up by the roots]; wild [raging] waves of the sea, casting up their own shame [foaming out their own shame]; wandering stars, for whom the black darkness has been reserved forever [to whom is reserved the blackness of darkness for ever]**" (Jude 1:12-13 NAS, KJV, lit.).

It is indeed amazing that just as the lustful and licentious Semiramis was worshipped as the "Mother of God," and Babylonish worship became the seat of idolatry and consecrated prostitution, this same wickedness exists openly in Hinduism today, a daughter of ancient Babylon; the temple prostitutes become mothers of more harlots as the young girls born to them are consecrated as temple prostitutes also. Although there were times in the past when moral corruption was open within the leadership of the Roman church, most of the immorality for years within the mother and daughters of Babylon was hidden, but today it is continually being uncovered and exposed by the press throughout the world, and is often even being openly proclaimed and advocated.

Now, with the perversion of God's divine order (God, Christ, man, and then woman), women are being ordained within a number of the harlots of Babylon (denominational daughters and granddaughters) within Protestantism who are open, flagrant lesbians who advocate this wicked perverse sin and the worship of the ancient Babylonian goddesses. Recently, in conjunction with the World Council of Churches, four major Protestant denominations, the Presbyterian Church U.S.A., United Methodist Church, Evangelical Lutheran Church in America, and the American Baptist Church, financed a theological conference for women with over 2000 participants in which they recited a liturgy to "our maker Sophia," a Babylonian female deity, and perverted the Lord's Supper by substituting milk and honey in an offering to her. "Working from a basis in feminist theology, conference participants looked to pantheistic religions and the heretical gnostic gospels to 'reimagine' a new god and a new road to salvation." "Many of the 34 major speakers charged that the church and its belief in the incarnation and atonement of Jesus Christ was a patriarchal construct and had caused oppression of women, violence in the streets, child abuse, racism, classism, sexism, and pollution." One feminist theologian said in referring to the Atonement of our Lord Jesus, "I don't think we need folks hanging on crosses and blood dripping and weird stuff" (Christianity Today). Another "urged Christians to adopt a 'new Trinity' composed of Buddhist, Hindu and Filipino goddesses" (Charisma, May 1994). A Presbyterian executive presbyter who attended the conference with his wife who is also a pastor and helped plan it, spoke of it in laudatory terms, and criticized congregations for withholding funds to the denomination in protest (Columbus Dispatch, April 30, 1994).

Such heresy, blasphemy, and apostasy would be unbelievable if it was not for the prophetic word which has warned us that this would happen, and for the wisdom of God to understand what happens to those who rebel against God and His Word! (II Thes. 1:7-10, 2:3, 10-12; I Tim. 4:1-6; II Tim. 3:1-13; II Pet. 2:1 - 3:18; Jude 1:3-19)

But what of those groups that profess to believe God's Word, and even to be filled with His Spirit? They too are rejecting the Word of the Lord as they yield to the spirits of this world. They reject the headship of Christ also, not in theory or confession, but in deed! They are hearers of the Word, but not doers! In most congregations today, man is the head and not Christ. Christ is not looked to for His leading and anointing on whomever He chooses of His body, but He is looked to in order to anoint man's pre-planned agenda and man's selection of order, leadership, and doctrine. No wonder that there is so very little anointing manifested, and so very little real spiritual work accomplished.

Christ, and Christ alone, must be the head! We must submit to His headship in everything — our order, our programs, our doctrine, our lives, and everything about us — both personally and corporately. We must repent of our rebelliously taking it upon ourselves to run our own lives, and especially His kingdom! Repent!!!

It has not been just the Roman Catholics, Orthodox, and main-line Protestants that have rejected the Word of the Lord in so many ways, and persecuted the true saints of the Lord, but many groups — independent Baptists, Fighting Fundamentalists, Holiness, Pentecostals, and now Charismatics — are all doing the same thing, all in the name of the Lord! What an abomination! Whenever men reject the headship of Jesus Christ over their lives, their ministries, or God's church in any way, they deceive themselves and work against the Lord. The tragedy for many who are serving the Lord in various ways, is that they are doing so in such a mixture of the true and false that they regard the true anointing on aspects of their ministries to be a sign that all is well, and it is not! Everyone and everything must come under His divine control, and that means according to His divine Word, and not ours, or the dead traditions of men. Amen? Amen!

It grieves me deeply to see the traditions of men and the spirits of this world dictating to God's people what is the truth and how they should function as Christians. And this is so true in so many ways, both in the congregation and out. Only dedicated disciples, those who are fasting, praying, and seeking God with all their hearts, asking for deliverance from all the work and spirits of the Evil One, can tell the difference, and that only as they mature in the faith themselves sufficiently to be even able to understand the truth as it really is in Christ Jesus! We must come together in prayer and fasting, seeking His will for our lives and the church — His church — seeking His truth for doctrines, what we are to believe, do, and propagate! We must unite under His headship or we will never see or be able to understand His will. I believe God is calling a people out of Babylon who will be what He has desired from the beginning, and we will go on to perfection and tear down the strongholds of the enemy, build up the old waste places, be repairers of the breach and paths to dwell in; and thus, praise God, be used before the coming of the Lord of Glory when He returns to take total control, and put down all rebellion and opposition to His being head over all!

The preparations of the Lord for His soon coming are exciting now as He pours out His Spirit all over the earth. Revival is being experienced all over the world in tremendous ways, and Babylon is not being left out. It thrills me to see Roman Catholics, Orthodox, and others of traditionally dead Churches, and those not so dead, being filled with the Spirit of God as God pours out His Spirit on all flesh; and they are moving in the power and gifts of the Holy Spirit. What is amazing, but is only what should be expected in a fresh outpouring, is to see Roman Catholics and others from dead traditions so excited, and moving in more freedom of the Spirit than even many traditional Pentecostals and Charismatics. But this too has been predicted because this pattern has been repeated. Those who have most recently experienced revival are the ones who oppose the next revival the most vigorously; they have cooled down in their love for the Lord and their missionary zeal of all kinds, and are stubbornly holding on to the Babylonish ways that they have inherited or fallen into, and have resisted the promptings of the Holy Spirit to move on into maturity. Oh, how we still need revival in <u>all</u> our ways, until we become exactly what God wants us to be! Let us continue in prayer for it until it comes!

Another interesting and observable consequence of the spirits of Babylon controlling many of God's people is when a man dies who has had an established ministry, but it was not built on the foundation of apostles and prophets with a plurality of godly shepherds who teach **"the apostles' doctrine"**; the wife then carries on the ministry as the leader. This is exactly what happened when Nimrod died, and Semiramis took over; it is the spirit of Babylon. The scriptures are very clear when not wrested that a woman is not to have authority over a man. Paul writes to Timothy, a young apostle, who is responsible for establishing the church of Jesus Christ in divine order, **"I do not allow a woman to teach or exercise authority over a man"** (I Tim. 2:12 NAS). He then goes on to explain that the reasons are because of the purpose of divine creation, and the proneness to spiritual deception that the woman is given to (I Tim. 2:13-15). He gives many other reasons to the Corinthians (I Cor. 14:34-40; 11:2-16); and the deception of the woman can be clearly seen today, as well as the willful disobedience of the man in hearkening to the words of his wife rather than the words of God (Gen. 3:1-19). For a thorough exposition of this apostolic doctrine, I would refer you to my first book, *The Public Ministry of Women.*

Another significant characteristic of Babylon that we touched on earlier which we need to amplify on slightly because it is so very common now is the practice of putting organizational unity above doctrinal purity, so that the organization (Church or ministry) is maintained at the expense of its doctrine being corrupted. Also, often true doctrine is withheld for the sake of maintaining the organization. Unfortunately, false teachings then circulate freely, and truth may be even opposed vigorously. In addition to putting organizational unity above doctrinal purity, Babylon puts what they call "doctrinal purity" or what they see as the "truth" above moral purity, so that holy living is sacrificed for the sake of maintaining doctrinal positions or what they have chosen to believe. These practices of Babylon result in the grieving, quenching, and denying of the Holy Spirit, so that without the proper ministry of the Holy Spirit and God's appointed ministries, doctrinal positions become false teachings and the dead traditions of the organization. When even true interpretations of scripture, mixed with the traditions of men, become more important than a holy and godly life, the wisdom of God is rejected and replaced with the wisdom of this world which then determines their doctrine, and the demonic energizing of the "**old man**" results in persecution toward those who desire to live the life of Christ obediently and holy according to the true Word of God. When anyone is interested in building the kingdom of God only and not a Babylonish one, they will receive the grace of God to live holy, and will be instructed by the Lord as to what are true teachings, and will not sacrifice moral or doctrinal purity because they also believe "**the gates of hell shall not prevail against**" the church they are building, and God will supply their every need (Mt. 6:33; Tit. 2:11-14; Jn. 7:17; Pro. 23:23; Mt. 16:18 KJV; Phil. 4:19).

In concluding where we are now, a note should be made about this spirit of Babylon that puts more importance on building physical buildings called "The House of the Lord," than building the true "**spiritual house**" of the Lord, the body of Christ (I Pet. 2:5; I Cor. 3:9; Eph. 2:21; Heb. 3:6).

Our word "church" as used in the New Testament is never used for a church building, never! It always and everywhere refers to people, mostly the people of God, but can be any group, such as a civil assembly of citizens for example (Acts 19:32, 39, 41). It is the Greek word εκκλησια, ekklesia, meaning literally "called-out-ones" and can be interchangeable with the word συναγωγη, sunagoge, synagogue, a Greek word meaning "a gathering together." It was not until many centuries after Christ that the word "church" began to be used for a building; and it was taken from the Greek word κυριακοσ, *kuriakos,* meaning "that which belongs to the Lord (*Κυριοσ*)"; but *kuriakos* was used only two times in the scriptures, in referring to either the Lord's supper or the Lord's day (I Cor. 11:20; Rev. 1:10), not a building!

Merrill Unger has given us an interesting note about this spirit of Babylon in conclusion about the Babylonian kings and their zeal for building religious temples (churches). "Following the example of earlier Babylonian kings Nebuchadnezzar [while in his unbelief I might add] has left to us almost exclusively records of his building operations and proofs of his zeal in the worship of the gods and of care in conserving their sanctuaries." And concerning Nabopolassar, his father, he writes, "Nabopolassar followed the ancient Babylonian custom of building temples and attending to the internal affairs of his splendid kingdom. His records have little to say of anything else" (UBD, pp. 781, 782)!

Concerning having this zeal for building buildings of brick and morter, instead of, or more than, the zeal to build only according to God's Word and under the Lord's specific direction to facilitate building the true building of God, the church — it is idolatry and intimately connected with "**covetousness, which is idolatry**" (Col. 3:5 KJV). And we are to be dead to this sin, this "**greed, which amounts to idolatry. For it is on account of these things that the wrath of God will come**" (Col. 3:5-6 NAS). The deceptive twisting of scriptures which men do to justify their idolatrous practices and to try and satisfy or appease their spirits of Babylon is rampant, abominable, pathetic, and a waste and diversion of our time and God's money, and a stench in the flaring nostrils of God!

In summation, let us characterize "Babylon Now" as disorder, confusion, mixture, which is the original definition of Babylon, isn't it? Since God's order is again: God, Christ, man, and then the woman, followed obviously by the children, we see disorder in this authoritative structure. Women and children are running the show in so many ways — in the home, in society, and tragically often even in the church (Isa. 3:12). The rebellion of man against Christ and His teachings is evident as men submit to the spirits of this world, and thus to their wives and their deceptions as Adam did to Eve. The disorder in the home leads to disorder in the church, and the disorder of ordaining women to authoritative positions is one of the biggest contentions within Christendom today. Another disorder of the sexes, not just in family and church order, is Satan's deception to disorder the sexuality of mankind itself! Homosexuality and Lesbianism are other chief points of contention

127

in the church today. But these disorders are to be expected, for as spiritual harlotry increases (participation in Babylonish spirits and doctrines), physical harlotry increases. Men have yielded to the spirits of this world and surrendered their spiritual authority, many becoming spiritually if not physically effeminate, and reversed in their role with women; their succumbing to sexual sins and perversion is a logical result. The perverse ordination of women into leadership and the loss of spiritual discernment will eventually lead to perverse outcomes also if not stopped. We can see the lack of true femininity in women abundantly in mannish manners, attitudes, dress, ministerial methods, and spiritual lesbianism, even when not yet in consummated physical lesbianism.

Now, the most important remedy, if there is to be a return to God's order, is scriptural authority in the church itself, with Christ as the head, and the holy apostles and prophets ministering to the body so that the elders of the true church are united directly under the headship of the head of the church, the Lord Jesus Christ. And this involves an order. First, individually as we seek to order our lives under His headship in every possible way. That means becoming like Him; that means holiness! That means that the crisis of character in the church today must be met with prayer, fasting, repentance, and a return to the true "**apostles' doctrine.**" We must "**contend earnestly for the faith which was once for all delivered to the saints**" (Jude 1:3 NAS). Next, we have had a return among true believers that men must become faithful shepherds. Then the teachers came forth, then the prophets, and now the apostles must come forth in all of the holy power of the Lord Himself. True apostolic power and authority must be restored if we are ever to get out of our Babylonish ways and into the true ways of the Lord, and all of us with the evangelists reap the end-time harvest. A great outpouring of the Spirit of the Living God must be manifested upon His true disciples who are praying, fasting, and seeking Him; waiting, watching, and working for His soon return! When this happens, men will start listening to His holy apostles for truth and not denominational headquarters, each other, or themselves. They will look to the Lord Himself, the anointing, and thus be taught of Him (Jn. 6:45; I Jn. 2:27). Then the Lord will perfect His bride, and she will be ready without spot, or wrinkle, or any such thing! (Eph. 5:27). Hallelujah!

Which brings us to the last phase of Babylon, its soon finish (Latin, *finis*)!

Babylon: In the future, and its soon finish!

If we are to understand as well as experience the fall of Babylon the great, we must realize that we all must be meeting together to pray. We must believe when Jesus said that **"My house shall be called a house of prayer for all the nations"** (Mk. 11:17 NAS) that this is primary, and that we must all be meeting under His headship to pray, not a carnal man's headship, not under authority that rejects the authority and doctrine of God's holy apostles, but under God's authority of true apostles and elders, who are themselves submitted to one another and to the holy Lord Jesus Christ in all areas of their lives.

Then, we must pray for this great end-time revival, for a great outpouring of God's Holy Spirit upon the church, if the church is to become what God wants her to be, and to reach into the world and reap the great end-time harvest!

As this is happening, the true Bride of Christ, the church, will be preparing herself for the Lord's return, and coming into divine order in everything, with Christ as head, His holy apostles in authority under Him, leading the church into truth and victory. While this is occurring, Babylon will be maturing for her finale — destruction as prophesied in the book of The Revelation. Therefore there will be more mergers between man-made organizations until her final state when the Antichrist and the "ten kings" under him are used to judge Babylon and she is destroyed forever!

So, until this great event, expect more confusion, mixture, and disorder among the members of Babylon, but more organizational unity as this great harlot matures. Already we are seeing real advances, not only in unifying the daughters of Babylon within Christendom with themselves, and with the mother of Rome, but also in serious dialogue with all other major religions of the world which are themselves daughters of the original Babylonish mother given to us in Genesis. From private meetings to public symposiums, from the seminaries to the pulpits, people of all religious backgrounds are being taught and prepared for the unification of all religions. The leaders of this movement, coming from within Christendom have of necessity left the uniqueness of our Lord Jesus as being the one and only sinless Son of God, who died for our sins, was buried, and was raised again for our justification. He is merely given place as a great religious leader among others such as Buddha, Confucius, Mohammed, Moses, and others. Thus in this "rapidly shrinking planet" of "one world globalism," as they say, it is becoming increasingly easier for the religions of the world to be united under ethical teaching, moral religious traditions, mutual respect, and the headship of man, and not under the person of our Lord Jesus Christ, the head of the true church.

We can expect this unification to increase and escalate until its fruit is ripened for destruction in that hour when God brings final judgment upon Babylon in all her fleshly, regal splendor. "**The kings of the earth**" and the "**merchants of the earth shall weep and mourn**" as "**Babylon the great**" is judged by our "**Almighty God**" and "**the smoke of her burning . . . rises up forever and ever**" (Rev. 18:2, 9-11, 18; 19:3, 15; KJV, NAS).

As we end this section on Babylon, it would be helpful if we considered how the Lord has judged Babylon in the past and brought about its destruction, as well as destroying the people of Israel for worshipping in idolatrous Babylonian ways.

First, it was Nimrod who built both Nineveh and Babylon, which became for centuries the headquarters of two of the most powerful empires the world has ever known. Although "the Assyrian people were of one family blood with the people of Babylonia" and had "derived their religious ideas from Babylonia, and during all their history had constant contact with the mother country in this matter, as in others," they became rivals (UBD, pp. 101, 102). This conflict and competition between people who worship in Babylonish ways always happens because of the spirits that control them.

In 722 B.C. Assyria invaded the northern kingdom of Israel and took the people away into exile (II Ki. 17:6, 22-23) because they had sinned grievously against the Lord in turning to Babylonish deities and committing abominable idolatries associated with this false religion (II Ki. 17:7-23; Isa. 46:1-3). It is interesting to note that Sennacherib, an Assyrian ruler, sacked Babylon in 689 B.C., but his son Esar-haddon, the next ruler, restored it. At the time of his death, one of his sons, Ashurbanipal reigned in Nineveh and the other son, Shamash-shum-ukin in Babylon. But they quarreled bitterly, and Ashurbanipal attacked and burned Babylon, and killed his brother.

In 612 B.C. the Babylonians, along with the Medes, attacked Nineveh, the capital city of the Assyrian Empire. It was located along the east side of the Tigris River with the Koser River, a tributary, running through it. Nineveh, noted for the beauty of its splendid temples, palaces, and fortifications, but a cruel and wicked enemy of both Israel and Judah, which had been used by God to destroy the northern kingdom of Israel, was destroyed along with her peoples and idols by "releasing the city's water supply and the inundation of the Koser River, dissolving the sun-dried brick of which much of the city was built" (UBD, pg. 796). This judgment of God had been prophesied by the Hebrew prophets, specifically by Nahum when he wrote, "**But with an overflowing flood He will make a complete end of its site,**" and "**The gates of the rivers are opened, and the palace is dissolved**" (Nah. 1:8; 2:6 NAS).

To apply this to spiritual Babylon, we see that many Babylonish organizations and doctrines have been destroyed by the flooding of the river of God over which they have been built, which is the Spirit of God being poured out (Jn. 7:38-39). As this happens the Spirit quickens God's Word, and the true church is then cleansed from its Babylonish ways "**by the washing of water with the word**" (Eph. 5:26 NAS).

Next, we need to see how Babylon herself was destroyed, but first Judah. Remember, Babylon had defeated the capital of Assyria when they took Nineveh in 612 B.C. Then Pharaoh Neco king of Egypt passed through Judah in 609 B.C. on his way to the Euphrates River to battle against Nabopolassar, king of Babylon, at Carchemish. He killed Josiah, the godly king of Judah who came out to fight him on his way, because he said God was with him and wanted him to hurry to battle the Babylonians (II Chr. 35:20-24). With its defeat, Judah came under the control of Egypt, and although the people of Judah placed Josiah's son Jehoahaz on the throne, he only lasted three months and Pharaoh Neco deposed him and had him taken captive and imprisoned in Egypt. Pharaoh Neco placed another son of Josiah on the throne, Eliakim (God establishes), and changed his name to Jehoiakim (Jehovah establishes). Thus the kingdom of Judah was no longer under its own authority, but became a vassal state paying tribute to Egypt, and would soon be under the authority of Babylon. This punishment was due to the sins of Manasseh, Josiah's grandfather, who as king of Judah had seduced the people to worship Babylonian gods and to do evil to an even greater extent than the nations who had occupied the land at the time of the exodus, and whom the Lord had previously destroyed from the land (II Ki. 21:1-16; 23:24-26; 24:3-4).

Now, in 605 B.C., Egypt under Pharaoh Neco together with some remnants of the Assyrian forces is defeated by the Babylonians under crown prince Nebuchadnezzar in the famous history changing battle at Carchemish on the upper Euphrates River as prophesied by Jeremiah (Jer. 46:2). The Egyptians are slaughtered as God avenges "**Himself on His foes**" (Jer. 46:10 NAS), Nabopolassar the ailing king dies, and Nebuchadnezzar, his son, quickly returns to Babylon to claim the throne and be crowned king.

Soon Nebuchadnezzar invades Judah, king Jehoiakim dies a most dishonorable death for his rebellion against him (Jer. 22:18-19), and many of the Jews are led captive to Babylon as prophesied (II Ki. 21:10-15; 24:3-4; Dan. 1:1-6). Nebuchadnezzar places Jehoiachin, Jehoiakim's son, on the throne of Judah, but he does evil in the sight of the Lord in worshipping Babylonish gods as his father had done, and Nebuchadnezzar sends for him and has him taken to Babylon captive also (II Ki. 24:6-16). Nebuchadnezzar then placed Jehoiachin's uncle, Zedekiah, another son of Josiah, as king of Judah, but he also did evil in the sight of the Lord by following Babylonish gods, defiled the house of the Lord in Jerusalem with them, mocked the messengers of God that came to him, scoffed at the prophets of God and despised the Words of God to him, and rebelled against the king of Babylon (II Chr. 36:10-16). Therefore Nebuchadnezzar sent his army against Jerusalem, and the people ended up eating the flesh of their own sons and daughters in the siege that lasted almost two years, as God had prophesied to them He would bring about because they had offered up their own children "**to burn their sons in the fire as burnt offerings to Baal**" (Jer. 19:5, 9). Nebuchadnezzar broke down the walls of Jerusalem, had the gold, silver, and bronze taken to Babylon, burned the house of the Lord and all the houses of Jerusalem with fire, slaughtered Zedekiah's sons before his eyes and then put out Zedekiah's eyes, bound him in fetters, and brought him to Babylon as well as all the people left in Jerusalem (II Ki. 25:1-21; II Chr. 36:17-21). Thus Judah was led away into exile in Babylon in 587 B.C. and the kingdom of Judah was no more.

Now, while the Jews were in the Seventy Years Captivity in the land of Babylon, the Medes and Persians attacked the city of Babylon in 539 B.C. They cut off the water by diverting the Euphrates River that ran through the city into the marsh lands and marched under the walls in the river bed and took the city. This attack and victory was accomplished in one night without a battle as prophesied by Daniel against Belshazzar the king when he interpreted the "handwriting on the wall" (Dan. 5).

Such is the case today. The Lord often destroys a Babylonish kingdom by cutting off the spiritual water, the Spirit of God, and then either the leader or the organization, or both, are taken captive by spirits of Satan (often confusion, lust, alcohol, or greed) and the work comes to naught, sometimes immediately.

And so, Babylon the great will be destroyed soon "**in one hour**" (Rev. 18:10, 17, 19)!

As a final note for God's glory, it is significant that when the Jews were taken captive in Babylon, they lost the language of Hebrew, the original God given language that was part of what united the people of God. So now, when people come out of Babylon, they speak the different spiritual languages of the various Babylonish kingdoms from which they depart. While in Babylon, they do not understand one another's spiritual speech and doctrines, but when they come out to build the true kingdom of God, they unite under the headship of our Lord Jesus Christ and learn the true doctrines of the church under His apostles. When natural Israel was restored to their land from the many different kingdoms of this world in our generation, they were restored to their original language of Hebrew as prophesied (Jer. 31: 23 KJV). What a glorious day it will be soon when the Lord pours out His Spirit in great power and glory to perfect and unite His church in love and peace, restores us to a devotion to the apostle's teaching and understanding of the Word of God, to complete the purifying preparations of His Bride for His Coming! (Dan. 12:9-10; Hag. 2:9; Acts 2:42; Eph. 4:3, 11-13; 5:26-27; Col. 3:14-15; Rev. 19:7-9).

Babylon: God's Word to Us Now!

Now that we have seen what Babylon is — the mother, the daughters, and the spirits that have developed this system even into various types of independent congregations — what should we do?

The very first thing that we must do is to seek the Lord with all of our hearts! We must seek His face to get the direction that we should go, and the timing if we are to move; but we must also be willing to stay where we are if that is the Lord's will. Many have disobeyed the Lord and have been sent into Babylonian Captivity, and it would be just as wrong and devastating to leave against the will of God as it was for the Jews who rebelled against the Lord and were destroyed because they refused to submit to Nebuchadnezzar and the Babylonian Captivity of long ago. We must come to the point of being willing to obey God no matter what the cost, and to serve Him in His way no matter what people think, or say, or do!

Concerning Babylon as a land of spiritual captivity, it would be revealing if we stopped a moment to think about this, considering what we have learned thus far.

Babylon, a system which promotes primarily a controlled single public gathering, can be compared in many ways in various degrees to a prison. To see this, let us consider the definition of a prison and compare it to a meeting place of spiritual captivity.

Prison: A public place, properly arranged and equipped (where one's children are removed for safe keeping) for the reception of persons legally restrained (placed there by God for disobeying His Word), forcibly confined (often by man's spiritual coercion, compelled by pressure or threat), where one lacks freedom of action or expression or movement (where no one is allowed to function except by order of the warden pastor), where one's liberty is restrained (praise and worship), where one does not have the use of one's inheritance and possessions (gifts and ministries), a place of involuntary confinement for debtors (those who do not pay their tithes and offerings, or their debt to love one another) and law breakers (the unrighteous, those who refuse to obey the laws of God, the lawless) committed by process of law (God's judicial decree), a place where ones who have surrendered (given up the fight of faith) or been taken captive by their enemy (the spirits of Babylon) are kept as prisoners of war, where political prisoners are banished to lesser wards (those who are getting wise to the system enough to do something about it), where one is considered a prize (taken as a spoil by worldly reasonings and vain deceit), where often one wears a marked uniform or haircut that is indicative of one's particular prison (not just the dress of certain sects, but also those that follow man more than Christ), where on certain occasions an exchange of prisoners is accomplished, but, praise God, a place from which one can be paroled for good behavior (godly, righteous, sacrificial living), or even released entirely (for dedicated discipleship).

Another aspect of Babylon which we have seen so much of that we need to make a few concluding remarks about is the great fact of its being such a mixture, a mixture of truth and error. As a result, some people are tempted to believe that as long as there is some good, it is alright, and they can still participate in the mixture. But what does God say? If we go to His word, we will find out. We have numerous examples of God's people worshipping the true God and also worshipping in Babylonian idolatry at the same time.

In fact, when Moses was up on Mt. Sinai for forty days and forty nights (receiving the Ten Commandments in stone, the instructions for the tabernacle, and the laws of the Old Covenant), and delayed in coming down, the people immediately wanted Aaron (whom Moses was being given instructions to anoint, fill with the Spirit, and sanctify) to make them Babylonish gods to go before them, which they had learned of from the Egyptians (Ex. 24:12 - 32:4). It was not the absence of leadership, but God anointed, filled, and holy leadership (Ex. 28:41 lit.). Without these spiritual works of God within, men will not be led by the Spirit of God, but by the people, the flesh, and some deceiving spirit. Aaron gave way under pressure from the people and made an altar and the golden calf to worship, and blindly said, "**Tomorrow, a feast to Yahway [Jehovah; The Lord]**" (Ex. 32:5 lit.). What a horrible mixture! They thought they were having a banquet, and singing and dancing in worshipful celebration to the true God whom they had come to know; but God said they were stiffnecked and had corrupted themselves, and He was so angry that He wanted to wipe them all out. Moses interceded and the nation was spared, but was so angry when he saw the calf and the dancing that he broke the stone tablets of the Ten Commandments, threw the golden calf back into the fire, ground it to powder, and made the people consume it in their water (Ex. 32:11-20). Then Moses prophesied God's judgment, and 3000 brothers, friends, and relatives were put to death that day, and the next day the people were smitten with a plague (Ex. 32:25-35). Beloved, God hates a mixture!

The scripture is full of other examples where the people of God mixed their true faith with the worship of Babylonish idolatry (Amos 2:4 - 5:27; Acts 7:42-43; II Ki. 17:6-41; Zep. 1:4-6; Judg. 17, 18; Eze. 8, 9, 14, 16, 23; Jer. 7; I Sam. 7 are a few for your study). In fact, this mixture was the main sin of the Israelites and the reason for God's judgment throughout their history, why the northern kingdom of Israel was led into Assyria forever (II Ki. 17:23), and why the southern kingdom of Judah was led into Babylonian captivity and thus were purged from this terrible wickedness (II Chr. 28:1-5, 16-23; 33:1-11; 36:5-6; II Ki. 23:26-27; 24:8 - 25:21; Jer. 3:6-10; 7; 9:12-16; 11:1-17; 22:8-9; 25:1-11).

It is tragic that we have the same situation today as in those days of old when God told them not to worship both Him and their idols; but as it is written, **"they did not listen, but they did according to their earlier custom. So while these nations feared the Lord, they also served their idols; their children likewise and their grandchildren, as their fathers did, so they do to this day"** (II Ki. 17:40-41 NAS).

But let us pray that all of God's people will heed the admonition and turn away from every form of idolatry as when **"Samuel spoke to all the house of Israel, saying, 'If you return to the Lord with all your heart, remove the foreign gods and the Ashtaroth from among you and direct your hearts to the Lord and <u>serve Him alone</u>; and He will deliver you from the hand of the Philistines.' So the sons of Israel removed the Baals and the Ashtaroth and <u>served the Lord alone</u>"** (I Sam. 7:3-4 NAS). And then we could expect supernatural victory over the enemies of God as they did from the Philistines who had been oppressing them for years for we read that **"the Lord thundered with a great thunder on that day against the Philistines and confused them, so that they were routed before Israel. . . . So the Philistines were subdued and they did not come anymore within the border of Israel. And the hand of the Lord was against the Philistines all the days of Samuel"** (I Sam. 7:10, 13 NAS). And thus the Lord will rout the enemies of Christ out of His church as well!

Remember, God hates a mixture; and do not believe that we can Christianize pagan customs and get by with it. When we do, we receive the wicked spirits that instituted these customs in the first place. Also, please take note that the scripture says, **"No lie is of the truth,"** and to think that one can sanctify a lie is gross deception! (I Jn. 2:21).

Now then, many who have learned by this time what Babylon is will have heard the Word of the Lord, maybe in different ways such as I did long ago on one occasion when being asked to join a congregation where I was instrumental in bringing revival; but the Lord said, **"Be not entangled again with the yoke of bondage"** (Gal. 5:1 KJV). The leader soon did not heed the prophetic words that the Lord was bringing to him personally in a morning prayer meeting; he said, "I am ordained in this denomination!" even though he had just been ordained by the Lord through the laying on of hands and prophecy into apostolic ministry; and he made it plain that his commitment was to the denomination, not to what God was revealing; and so he soon was forced to leave that congregation, and spent many years after that elsewhere in Babylon, only to be forced out again at their normal retirement age into nothing, with nothing. What a shame! God is sovereign. He rules! And when we put an organization or people before the Lord, that is idolatry, and we will be judged, that is for sure!

Many upon learning of what Babylon is, will have heard the very plain Word of the Lord coming to them, **"Come out of her, my people"** and have obeyed, and have gotten out of whatever Babylonish structure in which they were involved (Rev. 18:4 NAS). Still others need more prodding, and must look more closely at God's Word to us. He said, **"Come out of her, my people, that you may not participate in her sins and that you may not receive of her plagues"** (Rev. 18:4). Here God is revealing to us that when we participate in a Babylonish kingdom of some type, we are participating in the sins of that structure, denomination, congregation, or whatever, even though we do not agree with those sins and are actively trying to stop them or to reform the system. We will receive God's judgment upon us the same as those within who are responsible, because the whole system and everyone within is being judged. If we have the fear of the Lord, we will depart! For some, however, their idolatry will keep them in and they will perish with the system.

Let me give an example of this kind of idolatry. Many years ago a brother and I were ministering to a couple whose daughter was in an adulterous situation. I had been teaching for a number of weeks on the church, the structure and the sectarianism of the body of Christ; and one Friday night God spoke prophetically that their daughter was in adultery because they were in adultery. The husband we were ministering to had taught a very successful Sunday school class in the congregation of a major denomination of which he was a member. The pastor had become jealous of this brother's success, and so the brother had to resign from teaching. However, even though this husband and wife were not attending the church services anymore because of this situation, they were still officially on the books as members. So two days later on Sunday afternoon they wrote a letter of resignation from the denomination. That very night their daughter returned home!

I wish the story had a better, more rewarding and fulfilling ending. But not willing to go on in what God was bringing them into, after a time, they went to another denomination and became involved, committing spiritual adultery again; so their daughter went back into adultery with the man, his marriage broke up, and she married him in and into adultery! (Mt. 5:27-32; 19:9). When the sins of the fathers are visited upon the children, they very often demonstrate the sins of the parents (Ex. 20:5-6; Hos. 4:6-14)!

Now, for those who find themselves within a Babylonish structure, what should you do? You must seek the Lord with all of your heart. If the structure is a part of the mother or a daughter of Babylon, so to speak, a denomination that is committed to its own ways, you probably will be led to come out, but you might find the Lord using you for a season so as to bring others with you. You might be able to enlighten a leader who will then be able to lead a whole congregation or at least a significant part, or the faithful portion of it, out into freedom and to denounce any and all Babylonish customs as God reveals them. Here we can learn from the examples of old when it was God's time to lead His people out of Babylonian Captivity. First Zerubbabel, whose name means "begotten in Babylon," led many out to Israel and the temple was built; then Ezra, meaning "help," another prophet, led many out; and finally Nehemiah, meaning "Yahway has consoled," led many out, rebuilt the walls of Jerusalem, and took steps to have the city fully inhabited. Before Ezra left he proclaimed a fast for those leaving, and after the people fasted and sought the Lord, God moved marvelously in protecting them all during the journey. Although some of the people left Babylon for the Land of Promise, others stayed behind; some of them came out later. But some liked it so well in Babylon, that they stayed behind and died there; they never experienced the joy and rewards of building the true temple of God in His land. What a tragedy! I know of no other way to build the living temple of God than to fast and pray, to seek God with all of your heart, and to trust Him to give wisdom and direction in a consecrated holy walk of loving obedience. He always does. Praise His holy and faithful name!

Another type situation we should mention is when we find ourselves in a Babylonish type structure due to the fact that the leader is a Saul type person rather than a David. The sins of Babylon were and are the sins of the Saul type kingdoms, and when we find ourselves involved, and come to understand it, we must seek the Lord! The Lord can then either lead us out, or can change the leadership as He did in Israel of old. Many Sauls have been being removed by the Lord all over the world, and His Davids are being brought forth, men who have renounced all selfish ambitions, pride, rebellion, unbelief, and the fear of man!

So, what we must see here is that it is not enough to come out of Babylon, but we must be willing to follow the Lord and His leaders and enter His land; that is to say, His true church, structured by His true Word, under the freedom and authority of His true apostles, and be willing to be "**built upon the foundation of the apostles and prophets, Christ Jesus Himself being the corner stone**" (Eph. 2:20 NAS). Let me ask you a question. Are you committed to building the true church only, or a synagogue system in Babylon? If you say that there were synagogues in Israel, and that the Lord Jesus taught in them, I will say, Yes, He did, but he taught the people there that He was building the kingdom of God, and that "**No one tears a piece from a new garment and puts it on an old garment; otherwise he will both tear the new, and the piece from the new will not match** [KJV: agree with; Greek: συμφωνει, *sumphonei,* from which we get our word symphony, be in harmony with] **the old. And no one puts new wine into old wineskins; otherwise the new wine will burst the skins, and it will be spilled out, and the skins will be ruined. But new wine must be put into fresh wineskins.** [Then both are preserved for their purposes.] **And no one, after drinking old wine wishes for new; for he says, 'The old is good** *enough.*'" (Lk. 5:36-39 NAS; Mt. 9:16-17; Mk. 2:21-22). And the King James Version ends it thus: "**No man also having drunk old wine straightway desireth new: for he saith, The old is better**" (Lk. 5:39). And so we have people today saying the same things, "The old ways [the Babylonish ways of their traditions] are good enough." They are content, as many of the Jews were content to stay in Babylon, but they lost their eternal rewards, joy, and the blessings of God which come from building the true Jerusalem of God in His way. Some people even go so far as to say, "The old way is better." They too are not up to the exciting adventure of following Jesus outside the religious camp, bearing His reproach, because they do not have the faith necessary to pursue the rewards which are far greater than the riches of this life (Heb. 11:26).

But what of the early apostles? They came out of the synagogue system and built the body of Christ, the true temple of God!

Some would make mention of the temple in Jerusalem, but we would answer, there was only one temple ever allowed, and it was built under the Old Covenant, not the New. It was a special place for prayer, worship, and teaching in Jerusalem, and was a type of the true temple in heaven to which we are to come now, and thus it was destroyed in 70 A.D. as prophesied by the Lord

Jesus Himself. Now we are beckoned to come to the heavenly Jerusalem, for <u>we</u> are the true temple of God (Jn. 4:21-24; Gal. 4:21-31; Heb. 12:22; Rev. 3:12; 21:2, 10; I Cor.3:16-17; II Cor. 6:16; Eph. 2:21-22). Consider the example of the early church, they took advantage of the early temple, prayed and taught there, but soon their leaders were beaten, Stephen and James were killed, and the disciples scattered by a great persecution. All along they had been meeting from house to house daily, eating their bread with gladness and sincerity of heart, and when being scattered, continued as witnesses to the Lord, meeting anywhere and everywhere — but never building special buildings for religious worship (Acts 2:46; 5:42; 20:20; Rom. 16:4-5; I Cor. 16:19; Col. 4:15; Phile. 1:2). They put all their energies and finances into building the true church, the true temple of God, the body of Christ!

They only went into Jewish synagogues to preach the Word of the Lord and make converts before they were either thrown out or had to leave and separate the disciples from those who opposed the truth so they could experience the new wineskin of the free body of Christ (Acts 13:14 - 14:6; 17:1-17; 18:4-28; 19:8-10). They never built a "Christian Synagogue!"

As we close this teaching on Babylon, let us look at several scriptures with which God closes His revelations about Babylon to us. I would encourage you to read The Revelation, chapter 16:17 through 19:6, some of which we have discussed before, but there are several items we did not cover which would be helpful now.

First, as the Roman Empire, dressed in her regal scarlet, was responsible for putting to death thousands of the witnesses of Jesus in the first few centuries of the Christian faith, so too when these spirits of ancient Babylon finally entered into the church and Roman Catholicism came into being, she added the purple of royalty to the scarlet of Rome, and also eventually became responsible for the killing of thousands of the witnesses of Jesus. The one who gives a witness, Greek μαρτυριον, *marturion*, "testimony," is a "witness," Greek μαρτυσ, *martus,* from which we get the English word "martyr"; and the fact that so many of the faithful witnesses of Jesus have given their lives for their testimony of Christ has resulted in the word martyr now being synonymous with one who has given their life for the faith.

Thus the scriptural vision is fulfilled that John saw and wrote to us about, **"And I saw a woman sitting on a scarlet beast. . . . And the woman was clothed in purple and scarlet. . . . And I saw** the woman drunk with the blood of the saints, and with the blood of the witnesses of Jesus. And when I saw her, I wondered greatly" (Rev. 17:3, 4, 6 NAS).

And "wonder" we should, and would, if we knew the history of persecutions for the faith down through the centuries since the beginning of the Christian church.

The greatest book of testimony to these persecutions is the classic we have referred to previously, *Fox's Book of Martyrs,* which records the accounts of thousands of martyrs for Jesus, not only through the period of the early church under the severe persecutions of Pagan Rome, but later under Papal Rome until the year that the book was originally completed in 1574, with later additions until the early 1800's.

History records that when it was first published in England where the Church of England had just come to prominence under Queen Elizabeth after the terrible reign of Bloody Mary who had given "all power into the hands of the papists," that "it was ordered by the bishops to be placed in every cathedral church in England, where it was often found chained, as the Bible was in those days, to a lectern for the access of the people" (Editor's comments, *Fox's Book of Martyrs,* FBM). And "When one recollects that until the appearance of the *Pilgrim's Progress* the common people had almost no other reading matter except the Bible and *Fox's Book of Martyrs,* we can understand the deep impression that this book produced; and how it served to mold the national character" (Douglas Campbell in FBM).

Thousands more could be added to the list of martyrs from the hands of Babylonish Christianity, and few people realize that more witnesses of Jesus have died in this century than ever before. Right now, saints are being killed because of their testimony and stand for the truth of God's Word, and their refusal to participate in Babylonish ways, and many more will be (Rev. 6:9-11; 14:12-13; 20:4).

Another scripture that should be commented on is when Babylon falls, an angel cries out, **"Fallen, fallen is Babylon the great! And she has become a dwelling place of demons and a prison of every unclean spirit, and a prison of every unclean and hateful bird"** (Rev. 18:2 NAS). As we have learned from history, that idolatrous Pagan Rome was an infestation of wicked, evil spirits — sexual debauchery, greed, and murder prevailed, as well as the original spirits of Babylon — so too did Papal Rome become the same. And now Babylon, in whatever stage we find her, is becoming the same. Unclean and hateful spirits imprison people, they bind those who give themselves either to the idols of man, or the idolization of man. Paul makes it very plain that behind every idol is a demon (I Cor. 10:14-21).

Also, it would be good to remind ourselves that the idolatry of Babylonian whoredoms is spiritual fornication in relation to God, therefore it will result in the judgment of degrees of sexual impurity or fornication in its participants. It is to be observed that when idolatry of various kinds grows and proliferates, it becomes more and more self-centered, and its own physical fornication therefore often includes one of the most detestable forms, homosexuality.

We also learn from this passage that Babylon is a home for unclean and hated birds. It behooves us to consider several of these birds to better understand the nature of men who make the Babylonish church systems their home. These are primarily the birds appropriately dressed in black, in various degrees of unclean ugliness. First we have the small black birds and their larger cousins, the crow and the still larger raven. Black birds are noisy creatures, and also disliked because they chase the gentler birds away. But the crow is especially hated by farmers because it pulls up sprouting corn and eats it. This is like religious leaders who uproot from the faith those who just start to come into an intimate experience with Jesus. Crows also eat the young of other birds, and the religious systems produce many who, in the words of the prophet, eat and devour God's people (Mic. 3:1-3; Eze. 34). Also, the crow can be made to talk like a parrot, and this certainly reminds us of religious leaders and people who can speak the right words, but it is not from their heart. The much larger raven feeds a lot on seeds and fruit, as well as eating dead fish and other carrion. In the same manner, there are religious people who Satan uses to devour the good seed of the Word of God when sown in a heart, by contradicting, discouraging, and discounting the reality found in the scriptures. Also, one does not have to be serving long in the kingdom of God before one sees good fruit devoured by Christian leaders who are caught up in their Babylonish ways, and therefore invalidate the Word of God working in the lives of God's people as they insist on holding to their dead traditions (Mt. 15:1-20; Mk. 7:1-23). Since the fish was a sign used by the early Christians to identify themselves, and the raven loves dead fish, this reminds us of how the religious leaders of the dead professing Christians, or even true Christian leaders who are caught up in dead, lifeless, or just carnal religious services, devour the substance of those involved in their systems. Other hated black birds such as the vulture and buzzard also thrive on dead animals and rotten flesh of any kind, and so too do the systems of Babylon thrive on the carnal, rotten fleshly nature of man to sustain themselves. Oh, how true that Babylon has become "**a prison of every unclean and hateful bird.**"

Another scripture that needs to be mentioned is when God considers the sins of Babylon to be ready for final judgment, we hear a voice from heaven say to us, "**Pay her back even as she has paid, and give back to her double according to her deeds; in the cup which she has mixed, mix twice as much for her. To the degree that she glorified herself and lived sensuously, to the same degree give her torment and mourning**" (Rev. 18:4-7 NAS). This payback should begin by obeying God's command to us, "**Come out of her, my people,**" and then actively exposing her and the works of darkness that she has committed (Rev. 18:4; Eph. 5:11).

More scriptures remind us of the extreme wealth and lavish worldly ways that the leaders of Babylon heap to themselves. We read about, "**the wealth of her sensuality**" and "**she who was clothed in fine linen and purple and scarlet, and adorned with gold and precious stones and pearls**" (Rev. 18:3, 16 NAS). Compare the multiplied millions of dollars of wealth that the Pope and his leaders have as compared to Peter, the one they claim as the first Pope, who said, "**I do not possess silver and gold, but what I do have I give to you: In the name of Jesus Christ the Nazarene — walk!**" (Acts 3:6 NAS). And Peter, although not having worldly riches, was rich in faith and raised the lame man up and he was healed (Acts 3:1-10). Babylon produces the exact opposite of what God produces!

Another amazing comparison of the exact similarity of Pagan Rome with Papal Rome is the statement that she was filled with not only all kinds of valuable merchandise and forms of wealth and goods, but also of "**slaves, and souls of men**" (Rev. 18:12-13 KJV). We all know of the slavery of the Roman Empire, and have possibly seen portrayed even on film the men put on Roman slave galleys, but few know of the true Christians, some of which were actually Roman Catholic Christians, but most non-Roman Catholic Christians, thus persecuted during the centuries of the Inquisitions, during the latter times of which Protestant Christians were taken captive by the Roman Catholic Church during the Protestant Reformation, and sent to the galleys as slaves to endure the most horrible treatments until they expired from the tortures and deprivation of proper food and clothing, only for being faithful witnesses of Jesus (FBM). **"Of whom the world was not worthy!"** (Heb. 11:35-40).

Oh, that we would be such slaves of Jesus, and slaves of righteousness, even if it means becoming a slave of men, and not be slaves of a false religious system, slaves of sin, and actually slaves of Satan himself (NAS - Mt. 10:24-28; 20:27; 25:14-30; Lk. 17:10; Jn. 15:20; I Cor. 7:22; 9:19; Eph. 6:6; Jn. 8:34; Rom. 1:1; 6:16-23; 16:17-18; II Tim. 2:24-26; Acts 26:18).

When we consider the sufferings of the Catholic Inquisitions, and the other horrendous injustices perpetrated against innocent men, women, and children, is it any wonder that the heavenly voice cries out against Babylon, **"For this reason in one day her plagues will come, pestilence and mourning and famine, and she will be burned up with fire; for the Lord God who judges her is strong"** (Rev. 18:8 NAS). And again, **"for in one hour such great wealth has been laid waste!** (Rev. 18:17 NAS, 19).

Many years ago, according to an FBI report, the radical left-wing forces of antichrist were declaring how they were going to literally burn down the Roman Catholic Church buildings and those associated with her, and destroy the system. This will be fulfilled as God has spoken in Revelation 17:15-18!

And what should be our response? To those who know the Lord, the scriptures and history, and His will, we will respond to the Word of the Lord, **"Rejoice over her, O heaven, and you saints and apostles and prophets, because God has pronounced judgment for you against her"** (Rev. 18:20 NAS).

"And a strong angel took up a stone like a great millstone and threw it into the sea, saying, 'Thus will Babylon, the great city, be thrown down with violence, and will not be found any longer ... because all the nations were deceived by your sorcery [Greek: φαρμακεια, *pharmakeia*, "pharmacy," medication, or sorcery which consists of deception by such means as drugs, potions, poisons, medicines, magic, and elaborate rituals]'" (Rev. 18:21, 23 NAS).

When we analyze Babylon for what it really is, its secular as well as religious developments, we can then understand the next statement, **"And in her was found the blood of prophets and of saints and of all who have been slain on the earth"** (Rev. 18:24 NAS).

When we then understand this, we can then understand the fourfold Hallelujahs that immediately follow:

"After these things I heard, as it were, a loud voice of a great multitude in heaven, saying, 'Hallelujah! Salvation and glory and power belong to our God; because His judgments are true and righteous; for He has judged the great harlot who was corrupting the earth with her immorality, and He has avenged the blood of His bond-servants on her.'

And a second time they said, 'Hallelujah! Her smoke rises up forever and ever.'

And the twenty-four elders and the four living creatures fell down and worshiped God who sits on the throne saying, 'Amen. Hallelujah!'

And a voice came from the throne, saying, 'Give praise to our God, all you His bond-servants, you who fear Him, the small and the great.'

And I heard, as it were, the voice of a great multitude and as the sound of many waters and as the sound of mighty peals of thunder, saying, 'Hallelujah! For the Lord our God, the Almighty, reigns."

(Rev. 19:1-6 NAS)

This leads us to the next section to learn more clearly what the true church is, how it is structured and led under the headship of our Lord Jesus Christ, **"The Head of the church"**!

CHAPTER 3

The true New Testament church!

In this chapter, we wish to present a picture of the true New Testament church as it is given to us in the scriptures, established by the Lord Jesus Christ and His apostles, after His crucifixion for our sins and His resurrection from the dead. Jesus had said to Peter, "**And I also say to you that you are Peter, and upon this** [Gk., this the] **rock I will build My church; and the gates of Hades shall not overpower it. I will give you** [Gk., singular] **the keys of the kingdom of heaven; and whatever you** [sing.] **shall bind on earth shall be bound in heaven, and whatever you** [sing.] **shall loose on earth shall be loosed in heaven**" (Mt. 16:18-19 NAS). This scripture has been misinterpreted by the vast majority of the church for centuries because of our rebellion and carnality. The Roman Catholics have interpreted the church to mean an organization of man built upon Peter, built with the traditions of men invalidating the Word of God, and have built Babylon in all of its mass confusion. The Protestants, on the other hand, (knowing that the true church is certainly not the Roman Catholic denomination of man with all of its sordid history and persecution of the true saints of God) have rejected the truth that Jesus built His church upon Peter; and they have in large part not only rejected Peter's words, but also the words of the other apostolic writers, especially Paul who was built upon Ananias who was built upon Peter and "**the eleven**," and they have built other carnal organizations.

Very simply, Peter was chosen by the Lord to preach His Word first to establish the church; first to the Jews, on the day of Pentecost (Acts 2), and first to the Gentiles when he preached to Cornelius and his household (Acts 10). The Jews knew that Peter had been used to establish the church with them, when on the day of Pentecost Peter had preached to the crowd gathered from so many parts of the known world and three thousand souls had been added to the church, the "called out" people of God. There is to be only one church, so Peter confirms that this interpretation included all of the non-Jews when he says to the apostles and elders of the Jerusalem church that he had been chosen by God to open the door of God's kingdom with the keys of the gospel message to the Gentiles, also. Peter said, "**Brethren, you know that in the early days God made a choice among you, that by my mouth the Gentiles should hear the word of the gospel and believe. And God, who knows the heart, bore witness to them, giving them the Holy Spirit, just as He also did to us**" (Acts 15:7-8 NAS).

Many Christians are fearful of acknowledging that the church is built upon Peter because they see the church as a man-made organization, structured as a congregation or denomination, instead of the spiritual structure that God reveals to us in the Word. They confess that the church is built upon Christ only — but that is not what Christ said, or what the scriptures teach. Christ is the bedrock foundation, of course, as the scripture says, "**For no man can lay a foundation other than the one which is laid, which is Jesus Christ** (I Cor. 3:11 NAS); but, then upon that foundation is Peter and the other apostles, then the prophets, and then all of the other saints of God, as the scriptures also say, "**So then you are no longer strangers and aliens, but you are fellow citizens with the saints, and are of God's household, having been built upon the foundation of the apostles and prophets, Christ Jesus Himself being the corner stone**" (Eph. 2:19-20 NAS).

One might ask, "What is the real importance of this?" The answer is that it teaches us a matter of relationship — relationship with God and Christ and the Holy Spirit, and the proper relationship with one another and the leadership of His church. Many of those who believe that the church is the Roman Catholic Church built upon Peter have no relationship with the Father,

Christ, or the Holy Spirit; God is only part of a head theology. This was the case of the Jews who had a correct theology about God in many respects, but did not have a relationship with God. In fact, when they professed to be children of God through Abraham, Jesus denied it, and said, **"You are of your father the devil,"** because their works were of the devil (Jn. 8:44 NAS). One has only to look at their fruits, as Jesus said, to know them. These kind of Roman Catholics can not have a spiritual relationship with true Christians either; in fact, in many places in the world they are persecuting and killing them. Those who are within the Roman Catholic structure and are true Christians, and desire a right relationship with other Christians, are taught that this would only be possible by the others becoming Roman Catholic, and this is impossible for spiritual Christians to do. Now, the sad fact is that this situation is true of most others who are part of some Christian denomination or man-made structure of the church; they understand their "Church" to be the only correct one, and others ought to join them to be saved, or at least be really "good Christians." Unless they see the true church is the body of Christ, and <u>then</u> understand how it is to be structured, they also fall victims to the same destructive, carnal theologies. And as a result their relationship with other Christians is adversely affected, and thus their relationship with God. Jesus said, **"'You shall love the Lord your God with all your heart, and with all your soul, and with all your mind.' This is the great and foremost commandment. The second is like it, 'You shall love your neighbor as yourself'"** (Mt. 22:37-39 NAS). Jesus also said if we were going to be known as disciples of His, that we are to **"have love for one another"** (Jn. 13:35 NAS). And if we are going to love one another as He loves us, we must first love God with all of our hearts, and that means we must be willing to know and obey His Word! (Jn. 14:21-24). If we are to have proper relationships with God and other Christians, we must understand proper apostolic church structure. Moreover, if we are to understand it, we must first be willing to practice it (Jn. 7:17). So, if our hearts are set on loving and thus obeying the Lord, let us now look at the proper structure of the true New Testament church.

The structure of the New Testament church is very simple! There is only one church, both in heaven and on earth. For those of us on the earth, since there is only one church, the only thing that is to separate Christians is distance. (We will not be talking about sin and its effect in this discussion.) Therefore, all of the Christians in one locality are to be united, they are one church. All of the people that were "**of God**" were named with His name and identified simply by their location — the New Testament churches were identified individually by the city they lived "in" or "at" — such as the church "**in Jerusalem**" or "**at Jerusalem**" (NAS, Acts 11:22; 8:1), "**the church of God which is at Corinth**" (I Cor. 1:2), "**the seven churches that are in Asia**" (Rev. 1:4), one of which was "**the church in Ephesus**" (Rev. 2:1), and others. Sometimes the church was identified simply by the fact that they were the holy and faithful people in the Lord, such as when Paul wrote to these same people and did not use the word "church", but wrote "**to the saints** [holy ones] **who are at Ephesus, and who are faithful in Christ Jesus**" (Eph. 1:1 NAS). Now, what about the governmental structure?

New Testament rule.

In this section we want to look at several scriptures to begin to see the beauty and simplicity of the governmental structure of the New Testament church.

First, Isaiah prophesied these familiar and wonderful words:

> "**For unto us a child is born, unto us a son is given: and the government shall be upon his shoulder: and his name shall be called Wonderful, Counsellor, The mighty God, The everlasting Father, The Prince of Peace. Of the increase of his government and peace there shall be no end, upon the throne of David, and upon his kingdom, to order it, and to establish it with judgment and with justice from henceforth even for ever. The zeal of the Lord of hosts will perform this.**"
> (Isa. 9:6-7 KJV)

Here we have it so very clearly, that the Lord Jesus Christ has the authority to rule over His church, and that this authority on earth is until the end of the age and for ever. Jesus said:

> "**All authority has been given to Me in heaven and on earth. Go therefore and make disciples of all the nations, baptizing them in the name of the Father**

and [of] the Son and [of] the Holy Spirit, teaching them
to observe all that I commanded you; and lo, I am with
you always, even to the end of the age."

(Mt. 28:18-20 NAS)

Recognizing that the Lord Jesus has the authority in His
church, how then does He delegate this authority, and to whom?

First, we see that He ordained apostles and gave authority
to them, and they went everywhere under His authority —
preaching, teaching, baptizing, and making disciples (Mk. 3:14-15;
Mt. 28:18-20; Jn. 15:16). As the church grew, it was necessary to
establish local rulers because the apostles would be traveling in
order to establish the church properly in other places, and so we
find elders (Acts 11:30; 14:23; 15:2, 4, 6, 22, 23).

Now the questions arise, "How were elders ordained?
Whose authority were they under? What are the qualifications?"
It is first stated that this was the ministry of the apostles. Paul,
who was a teacher, and Barnabas, a prophet (both ministering in
the church in Antioch), were set apart by the Holy Spirit as apostles
(Acts 13:1-4; 14:4, 14; I Tim. 2:7). And this is how, we might add,
that apostles are ordained today, as well as the other ministry gifts;
they are ordained by Jesus, speaking by the Holy Spirit, often
through an anointed servant. Paul wrote that after the resurrection
and Jesus ascended on high "**He gave gifts to men. . . . And He
gave some as apostles, and some as prophets, and some as
evangelists, and some as pastors [shepherds] and teachers**" (Eph.
4:8, 11 NAS).

Again, the apostles were the ones responsible for ordaining
elders. The first occurrence written of this was through Paul and
Barnabas as they prayed and fasted. We read, "**And when they
had ordained them elders in every church, and had prayed with
fasting, they commended them to the Lord, on whom they
believed**," and they then continued on their apostolic journey (Acts
14:23-24 KJV). Also, this responsibility is very plainly given to us
in Paul's letters to two younger apostles, Timothy and Titus. But,
let us first establish their apostolic ministry because tradition often
tells us that Timothy and Titus were pastors, or bishops, but this is
not true. That teaching is from the Babylonish church, sometimes
inserted as superscriptions before the Roman Catholic scriptures,
or subscriptions after the King James Version, in Paul's letters to
them.

Paul's salutation in his first letter to the Thessalonians reads:

"**Paul and Silas and Timothy,**" and then he identifies all three of them as being apostles when he states: "**Nor of men sought we glory, neither of you, nor yet of others, when we might have been burdensome, as the apostles of Christ**" (I Thes. 1:1; 2:6 KJV). Other post-ascension apostles positively identified besides Paul, Barnabas, Silas, and Timothy, are Titus, Epaphroditus, James the Lord's brother, and Apollos (II Cor. 8:23 lit. Gk.; Phil. 2:25 lit. Gk.; Gal. 1:19; I Cor. 4:6-9). And from the way these men traveled and ministered, we can come to understand their apostolic ministry. From the similar instructions to both Timothy and Titus, we can understand more clearly the apostolic ordination of elders and ministry.

Now, we want to see several things from the scriptures just given or referred to. First, the elders were ordained to serve the people of God in a local area, identified as a city or church. They were not ordained to serve a congregation separate from other Christians in their area. We were given the scripture where Paul and Barnabas ordained elders in every church (Acts 14:23), and in Paul's letter to Titus, he instructed the younger apostle who was ministering on the island of Crete to "**set in order what remains, and appoint elders in every city as I directed you**" (Tit. 1:5 NAS). We can realize several things from these verses. One, it confirms the reality that the body of Christ in a church or in a city are synonymous, as God's people are to be one, and not divided. Another thing is that the people were considered a church before they had elders and everything was in order. The church is simply the people of God, not a particular structure. Also, Titus was a junior apostle functioning under the authority of a senior apostle, Paul. And as an apostle, Titus was responsible for ordaining men as elders who met certain qualifications; and Titus was to function with his apostolic authority in exhorting and reproving them and the rest of the church, including older men and women, as needed (Tit. 1:13; 2:15). Paul wrote to Titus, "**These things speak and exhort and reprove with all authority. Let no one disregard you.**" This was similar to the word Paul gave to the young apostle, Timothy, when he wrote, "**These things command and teach. Let no man despise thy youth**" (I Tim. 4:11-12 KJV).

Another important practice that we learn from the scriptures that we have just given, and the teaching on "**one mind, and one accord,**" is that the apostles taught the elders that they were to look to the Lord Jesus in their midst as the Chief Shepherd and get their directions from Him. So when the apostles left, the elders were to know how to function and to be functioning directly under the authority and person of the Lord Jesus, not the apostles from a distance; and of course this means that neither were they to be under the authority of what has been developed since that time — various man-made, independent, or denominational hierarchies.

We also need to see that after an apostle left an area, the local elders were commanded to maintain the proper apostolic doctrines that they had been taught, and that other apostles might come through the area who would also function with them in the one united church in their city. We read that the church in Corinth had been founded by Paul, and yet also received the apostolic ministries of both Apollos and Peter; but the church was admonished not to be divided into groups following just one of these apostles, nor for some to separate themselves and think they were only following Christ (I Cor. 1:9-15; 3:4-7; 4:15; 9:1-2). Paul wrote, **"Now I exhort you, brethren, by the name of our Lord Jesus Christ, that you all agree, and there be no divisions among you, but you be made complete in the same mind and in the same judgment. For I have been informed concerning you, my brethren, by Chloe's people, that there are quarrels among you. Now I mean this, that each one of you is saying, 'I am of Paul,' and 'I of Apollos,' and 'I of Cephas,' and 'I of Christ'"** (I Cor. 1:10-12 NAS).

The traveling ministry of Apollos which becomes apostolic is interesting as it starts with him **"speaking and teaching"** with a limited understanding of the Christian faith at Ephesus where Priscilla and Aquila heard him and **"took him aside and explained to him the way of God more accurately"** (Acts 18:24 - 19:7 NAS). Apollos then goes over to Achaia and we read the first account of his helping the church in Corinth which Paul had established. It was after Apollos left that Paul writes to the Corinthians his first letter in which we find that Apollos has at some point been ordained as an apostle, and Paul uses Apollos and himself as examples in teaching the Corinthians (I Cor. 1:10-17; 3:1 - 4:14). Paul confirms specifically the apostolic ministry of Apollos when he writes, **"Now these things, brethren, I have figuratively applied to myself and Apollos for your sakes, that in us you might learn not to exceed what is written, in order that no one of you might become arrogant in behalf of one against the other. . . . For, I think, God has exhibited us apostles last of all, as men condemned to death"** (I Cor. 4:6, 9 NAS).

Paul also gives us insight that Apollos is travelling directly under the Holy Spirit (as when Paul and Barnabas had been called into their apostolic ministries, Acts 13:1-4; 14:4, 14), while Timothy, a young apostle, is travelling directly under Paul's authority when he writes, "**For this reason I have sent to you Timothy, who is my beloved and faithful child in the Lord**" (4:17), and then in concluding the letter writes, "**Now if Timothy comes, see that he is with you without cause to be afraid; for he is doing the Lord's work, as I also am. Let no one therefore despise him. But send him on his way in peace, so that he may come to me; for I expect him with the brethren. But concerning Apollos our brother, I encouraged him greatly to come to you with the brethren; and it was not at all his desire to come now, but he will come when he has opportunity**" (I Cor. 16:10-12 NAS).

Paul's love and concern for Apollos, however, is evidenced in the one other reference about Apollos in the scripture, when he instructs the young apostle, Titus, "**Diligently help Zenas the lawyer and Apollos on their way so that nothing is lacking for them**" (Tit. 3:13 NAS).

When the apostles were in a city where there was an established church, they were with the elders as co-elders (συμπρεσβυτεροσ, *sumpresbuteros; sum* means "with" and *presbuteros* means "presbyter," an older man; therefore *sumpresbuteros* is translated "fellow elder," I Pet. 5:1 NAS); and when the apostles left the city, "**they commended** [παρεθεντο, *parethento*, committed, intrusted] **them** [the elders] **to the Lord, on whom they believed**" (Acts 14:23 KJV).

Now that we have seen that the apostles ordained and instructed the elders, let us look at several scriptures that prove that the elders were indeed the shepherds (Latin: pastors), and also called bishops; that these were not separate offices in a hierarchy. Peter wrote, "**Therefore, I exhort the <u>elders</u> among you, as your fellow elder and witness of the sufferings of Christ, and a partaker also of the glory that is to be revealed, <u>shepherd</u> the flock of God among you, <u>exercising oversight</u>** [επισκοπουντεσ, *episkopountes* (this Greek word is not found here in many Greek texts, including Panin), it is the participial form of *episkopos; epi* meaning "over," *skopos* meaning "seer," therefore it means "functioning as <u>overseers</u>"; often translated <u>bishops</u> — this word being derived from the Medieval Latin, (e)biscopus; e.g. the Episcopal Church is ruled by bishops; the Presbyterian Church is ruled by πρεσβυτεροι, *presbuteroi*, presbyters, meaning elders; but in the New Testament church these were the same men, the elders were the bishops who shepherded the one flock in each city] **not** under compulsion, but voluntarily, according to the will of God; and not for sordid gain, but with eagerness; nor yet as lording it over those allotted to your charge, but proving to be examples to the flock. And when the <u>Chief Shepherd</u> appears, you will receive the unfading crown of glory. You younger men, likewise, be subject to your elders; and all of you, clothe yourselves with humility toward one another, for God is opposed to the proud, but gives grace to the humble" (I Pet. 5:1-5 NAS).

When Paul called the <u>elders</u> of the church in Ephesus over to the island of Miletus he said to them, "**Be on guard for yourselves and for all the flock, among which the Holy Spirit has made you <u>overseers</u>** [επισκοπουσ, *episkopous,* overseers, <u>bishops</u>] **to <u>shepherd</u> the church of God which He purchased with His own blood. I know that after my departure savage wolves will come in among you, not sparing the flock; and from among your own selves men will arise, speaking perverse things, to draw away the disciples after them** [themselves]. **Therefore be on the alert, remembering that night and day for a period of three years I did not cease to admonish each one with tears. And now I commend** [παρατιθεμαι, *paratithemai,* commit, intrust] **you to God and to the word of His grace, which is able to build you up and to give you the inheritance among all those who are sanctified"** (Acts 20:28-32 NAS).

Notice again that the elders were to be the bishops and shepherds of the one flock, one church, in the city of Ephesus. The people had been taught "**publicly and from house to house,**" so there were many different places where they were meeting, but there was only one church in the city! (Acts 20:20). Paul's public meeting place was the school of Tyrannus, and he also had personally gone around the city from house to house (Acts 19:9).

One might wonder why there are three different words used to describe a leader of the local church, but this can be easily understood when we compare their functions to a man, the leader of the family. A married man is the elder of the family, the older man, and that is precisely what the Greek word for elder (πρεσβυτεροσ, *presbuteros*) means, literally, "older man"; and it is always in the masculine and never in the feminine when referring to an elder of the church. He is also the overseer of the family, and that is what the Greek word for bishop means (επισκοποσ, *episkopos,* *epi* meaning "over," *skopos* meaning "seer"), the one responsible in taking the oversight, the supervisor, of the family. He is also the one responsible for providing, protecting, caring for, and feeding the family; this makes him the shepherd of the family. [The Greek word ποιμην, *poimen,* is always translated shepherd in the New Testament except one time. That exception is when it refers to a ministry brought into our understanding from the Roman system, and therefore is from the Latin translation of the word for shepherd, "pastor," being brought into our English with even the same spelling. It is given in a list of four other ministries, and therefore, if this is not known so as to be able to trace the word in scripture for proper understanding, it cannot be interpreted except by tradition (Eph. 4:11).] Continuing on with the different words describing the different functions of a man, we might add that a man is also the husband, but this is only toward his wife, not the children. Only Christ is spoken of as our husband corporately (II Cor. 11:2-3); and we, the church, are His bride (Isa. 54:5; Jer. 31:32; Rev. 19:7; 21:2, 9). An elder of the church is never the husband of more than one woman, for the scriptures say he must be "**the husband of one wife**" (I Tim. 3:2; Tit. 1:6). Therefore, a man is only the head of his wife, never a church; only Christ is head of "a" or "the" church (Eph. 5:23).

To further confirm the fact that an elder is also a bishop and shepherd, we find the words "elder" and "bishop" used together in referring to the same position and describing the same functions when qualifications are given to Timothy and Titus (I Tim. 3:1-7; Tit. 1:5-9). Paul wrote, "a **bishop**" (I Tim. 3:2 KJV), and "**ordain elders . . . for a bishop**" (Tit. 1:7, 9 KJV).

Elders are worthy of double pay when working hard in studying and teaching the Word of God; for Paul wrote, "**Let the elders that rule well be counted worthy of double honour** [Gk. τιμησ, *times,* value, and referring to money in this context and elsewhere (I Tim. 5:3, 9, 16, 18; Mt. 15:4-9)], **especially they who labour in the word and doctrine**" (I Tim. 5:17 KJV).

And as overseers, elders are given the responsibility to rule, they are prepared for the function of being a bishop by first successfully overseeing their own family before overseeing the family of God. Paul wrote, "**A bishop then must be . . . one that ruleth well his own house, having his children in subjection with all gravity; (for if a man know not how to rule his own house, how shall he take care of the church of God?)**" (I Tim. 3:2-5 KJV).

In conclusion of this point of elders being both overseers and shepherds, we can see this when there are only two major ministries of oversight in a church, a local city church, given in Paul's greeting to the church in Philippi. He wrote, "**Paul, and**

Timotheus [Gk. for Timothy], **the servants of Jesus Christ, to all the saints in Christ Jesus which are at Philippi, with the bishops [overseers] and deacons [servants]**" (Phil. 1:1 KJV). The bishops (overseers), which are the elders and pastors (shepherds), have the oversight of the church as a whole, which includes the spiritual food; the deacons, the word taken from the Greek word for servants (διακονοι, *diakonoi*), have the oversight of serving the physical food. Although the deacons (servants) may be effective preachers and ministers in the spiritual realm (such as Stephen, Acts 6:1 - 7:60), they are not ruling elders of the church. When we see positions in the church as callings and ministry gifts to serve the people of God, instead of offices with titles to be served, we shall better understand what has become traditionally confusing because of our Babylonish backgrounds and unscriptural translations.

New Testament meeting.

In the New Testament scriptures we find that the church, the Christians, met in many different places, but primarily in the homes of believers. Although there were public gatherings, most of the meeting and fellowship was done in the family homes of the family of God. It was here that the believers met regularly, most of them daily, for fellowship, prayer, ministering to one another, and breaking bread with one another. In larger meeting places where more could come together, if not all of the believers from a local community, there would be more of the same, but naturally the Holy Spirit (since He was available to direct all meetings as well as the believers themselves) would have each meeting's agenda appropriate for those present, and would direct according to the various ministry gifts present. There was not any standard ritual or agenda set by man or tradition, but each meeting was under the headship of our Lord Jesus Christ who was present and ministering by His Spirit. The activity of the Holy Spirit was manifested continually as the believers worshipped the Father in spirit and truth, and songs of praise and adoration to God were an important part of the meeting. After people came together, at the time when they started to focus on God and wait upon Him (to look together to Him in a meeting), it was only natural to enter His presence with praise and thanksgiving, and once they had entered in corporately, to continue to look to Him for direction from His throne. It is only tradition and teaching, supported by pulpits and pews, that have most Christians today looking to man for direction and everything else. We have built structures to exalt man, spiritual thrones for our leaders and often actual ones, and wonder why there is so little response from His throne. We must humble ourselves and pray, turn from our wicked ways and seek His face, and He will restore us, and much more.

Let us now look at the scriptures which support these truths. In the same chapter where we find the first tremendous growth of the church (the chapter after we find the church praying and waiting on God to begin with), we find that God did it by pouring out His Spirit upon the disciples, and multitudes came to know the Lord. They were preached to with signs from heaven, in sin-convicting power, baptized in water, and received the Holy Spirit as there were three thousand souls added that day to the church. The very next verse gives us the answer as to what believers should then do. "**And they were continually devoting themselves to the apostles' teaching and to fellowship, to the breaking of bread and to prayer[s]**" (Acts 2:42 NAS). The next verses confirm that the believers met together in their homes daily as the preachers also proclaimed the gospel publicly. And their commitment in Christian community was with such grace, and God moved through them in such power, that it has astounded the church ever since.

> "**And everyone kept feeling a sense of awe; and many wonders and signs were taking place through the apostles. And all those who had believed were together, and had all things in common; and they began selling their property and possessions, and were sharing them with all, as anyone might have need. And day by day continuing with one mind in the temple, and breaking bread from house to house, they were taking their meals together with gladness and sincerity of heart, praising God, and having favor with all the people. And the Lord was adding to their number day by day those who were being saved.**"
> (Acts 2:43-47 NAS)

And this grace was not just momentary, or incidental, for we read as it continued:

"And when they had prayed, the place where they had gathered together was shaken, and they were all filled with the Holy Spirit, and began to speak the word of God with boldness. And the congregation of those who believed were of one heart and soul; and not one of them claimed that anything belonging to him was his own; but all things were common property to them. And with great power the apostles were giving witness to the resurrection of the Lord Jesus, and abundant grace was upon them all. For there was not a needy person among them, for all who were owners of land or houses would sell them and bring the proceeds of the sales, and lay them at the apostles' feet; and they would be distributed to each, as any had need." (Acts 4:31-35 NAS)

This pattern of public proclamation together with home ministry continued in spite of severe persecution. Even though the apostles were beaten for it, we read that "**Every day, in the temple and from house to house, they kept right on teaching and preaching Jesus as the Christ**" (Acts 5:42 NAS). We see this practice of the church meeting in homes (sharing in fellowship, meals, and prayers, as the apostles travelled from house to house teaching) confirmed in the account of Peter's imprisonment after James was killed. We read that although there was only one church in Jerusalem, it met in many different homes. Although "**the church at Jerusalem**" is spoken of in the singular, and "**prayer for him was being made fervently by the** [one] **church to God**," it was being accomplished by the thousands of people in the many private homes of the believers where they gathered together in small groups to avoid the persecution (Acts 11:22; 12:5, 12, 17). We read that after Peter was released by the angel of the Lord in answer to their prayers, "**he went to the house of Mary, the mother of John who was also called Mark, where many were gathered together and were praying**" (Acts 12:12 NAS). And after he told them what had happened, "**he said, 'Report these things to James and the brethren.' And he departed and went to another place**," confirming in this history of the original New Testament church the pattern of home meetings (Acts 12:17 NAS).

Paul followed this same pattern, though he was also persecuted for it. He tells the elders of Ephesus:

159

"You yourselves know, from the first day that I set foot in Asia, how I was with you the whole time, serving the Lord with all humility and with tears and with trials which came upon me through the plots of the Jews; how I did not shrink from declaring to you anything that was profitable, and teaching you publicly and from house to house, solemnly testifying to both Jews and Greeks of repentance toward God and faith in our Lord Jesus Christ."

(Acts 20:18-21 NAS)

And this apostolic pattern was not because they did not have sufficient funds in Ephesus to build a Christian synagogue, because they destroyed occult books alone worth over fifty thousand days' wages (Acts 19:19; Mt. 20:2).

We see that Paul taught this pattern by both word and example, and throughout his letters we read that it was continued by those he discipled.

"The churches of Asia greet you. Aquila and Prisca greet you heartily in the Lord, with the church that is in their house" (I Cor. 16:19 NAS). Written from Ephesus about A.D. 55-57.

"Greet Prisca and Aquila, my fellow workers in Christ Jesus, who for my life risked their own necks, to whom not only do I give thanks, but also all the churches of the Gentiles; also greet the church that is in their house" (Rom. 16:3-5 NAS). Written in A.D. 58 after they had moved to Rome.

"Gaius, host to me and to the whole church, greets you" (Rom. 16:23 NAS). Written from Corinth where Gaius was able to accommodate the entire Christian community at times in his home.

"Greet the brethren who are in Laodicea and also Nympha and the church that is in her house" (Col. 4:15 NAS). Another scripture confirming that women may host the church in their own house (Acts 12:12).

"To Philemon our beloved brother and fellow

worker . . . and to the church in your house: Grace to you" (Phile. 1:1-3 NAS). Here the apostle again confirms the fundamental practice of leaders and those working in the gospel to regularly host the church in their own homes.

Now that we have seen so very clearly in the scriptures that the Christians met primarily in homes for fellowship, prayer, ministering to one another, and breaking bread with one another, let us consider briefly why.

Let us ask ourselves, how much fellowship takes place at most Sunday morning meetings? Not much, as it is hard to fellowship with the back of someone's neck, even if we've hugged it in a brief greeting. Services start and end on a schedule that does not facilitate for much real fellowship. An informal home setting does! And that is where we can really get to know one another — and ourselves, our visions, our hearts in serving the Lord.

Let us ask ourselves, how much prayer takes place on Sunday morning for the real needs of the congregation? Not much, as it takes personal sharing and different people praying to accomplish this, not just the leader. Again, the home is a wonderful place to share and pray about all that anyone might have upon their hearts. And prayer is to be the main practice of the church, not preaching and teaching. Jesus said, **"Is it not written, 'My house shall be called a house of prayer for all the nations'? But you have made it a robbers' den"** (Mk. 11:17 NAS; Isa. 56:7; Jer. 7:11; Mt. 21:13; Lk. 19:46). It was not to be a public building for preaching, as important as this is, but the church is the people, to be meeting as He directs! New Testament preaching took place more outside the meetings, in the public arena, than inside, as recorded in the scriptures. What we really call churches today are not churches, but privately owned corporate buildings, used for the (semi-private) proclamation of the Word of God (hopefully); but the real functions of the believers still take place in homes, though only to a very small degree because they are not only not being taught, but actually discouraged or prevented from meeting as the Lord teaches us in the scriptures and by His Spirit!

Next, let us ask ourselves, how much ministering to one another takes place on Sunday morning? Not much, as it is also done mostly by leaders, if at all. [And we might ask the question, "Who and what kind of leaders are there?" Leaders are usually

161

controlled by who owns the buildings. They are often trained and controlled by denominations as to what they can do and teach, and they come and go as denominational headquarters directs; or leaders are controlled by a small group of local people, sometimes but not always including the pastor himself, who have responsibility for the building; or if owned by the "pastor," he controls the message and the ministry, and the people come and go.] But the home is such a wonderful place to minister to one another, in the privacy of a small gathering where certain needs can and will be made known, but will not be revealed in a large public gathering.

And let us ask ourselves, how much breaking of bread together is there on Sunday morning? Very, very little, if any! An occasional meal is served in a basement, but those are seldom, and usually not much time for fellowship is scheduled when they do occur.

Now, we have briefly reviewed three of the four major practices of the early church: "**And they were continually devoting themselves to the apostles' teaching and to fellowship, to the breaking of bread and to prayer[s]**" (Acts 2:42 NAS), and ministry to one another. Now, let us ask ourselves, "How much of the apostles' teaching is done today?" It might surprise you, but very little of the pertinent truths. This is evident in the neglect of the other three major practices of the early church, and the lack of current church practices lining up with the Word of God or with one another. The very fact that there are so many differences in doctrine proves that most of the church is wrong, or we would not hold to such different views and opinions as to the proper interpretation of scripture and the oneness of truth!

So you see beloved, we must repent, rethink and re-evaluate our meeting practices, and get back to the Word and ways of God if we are to be obedient and successful in the church!

Let us close this section on the practice of meeting in private homes by reminding ourselves of just the incidences of their use given to us in the book of Acts, the authentic history book of the true New Testament church. First, we find the apostles abiding in an upper room, waiting on the Lord there with over one hundred other disciples, praying for the coming of the Holy Spirit; and revelation was given by the Lord for the ordination of a new apostle to replace Judas who fell (Acts 1:13-26). Next, we find the initial great outpouring and manifestations of the Holy Spirit in the house where they were praying on the day of Pentecost, and the first large evangelistic preaching initiated from that house (Acts 2:1-41). The new church met daily for fellowship, prayer, and sharing their lives, financial resources, and food with one another in their homes (Acts 2:42-47). Paul received his sight, was filled with the Holy Spirit, and was ordained to preach the gospel in the house where he had been praying and fasting for three days (Acts 9:8-20). The healing of paralyzed Aeneas which caused the whole cities of Lydda and Sharon to turn to the Lord happened in the house where he had been bedridden for eight years (Acts 9:32-35). The raising from the dead of Dorcas at Joppa took place in the upper room where she had been laid (Acts 9:36-42). Then the hospitality of Simon the tanner given to Peter who had been used of the Lord to perform this mighty miracle was in Simon's house by the sea there in Joppa (Acts 9:43; 10:6). Next, Cornelius the centurion was praying and fasting in his house in Caesarea at the 3 pm hour of prayer when the angel of the Lord appeared to him, and directed him to send to Joppa for Peter (Acts 10:3, 30-32). It was on the housetop of the tanner's house the next day while Peter was praying that he had the wonderful vision from God to initiate salvation to the Gentiles; and then the three men arrived from Cornelius and he gave them lodging in the house (Acts 10:9, 19-23). Soon it was in Cornelius' house that the first Gentiles were saved and received the gift of the Holy Spirit (Acts 10:22, 24-28, 44-47). Then Peter stayed and ate in Cornelius' house with those who had gathered there (Acts 10:48; 11:3).

Next, it was in the private homes of the church in Jerusalem, such as the house of Mary the mother of John, who was also called Mark, that they gathered in smaller groups to pray for Peter when he was imprisoned because of the persecution (Acts 12:12). Then it was in the house of Lydia at Philippi that Paul and his companions stayed after receiving the Macedonian call in a night vision to first go to Europe (Acts 16:15). It was there in Philippi after the earthquake at midnight that Paul led the jailer and his entire household to the Lord in the jailer's house (Acts 16:32-34). And it was in Lydia's house again that they met with the brethren and comforted them before leaving the city (Acts 16:40).

At Corinth Paul stayed in the home of Aquila and his wife Priscilla (Acts 18:1-3). It was there in Corinth that Paul went to the house of Titius Justus, whose house was next to the synagogue which Paul left after the Jews refused the gospel, and led many to the Lord (Acts 18:7-8). It was later in an upper room in Troas on a Sunday night that Paul ministered so long that a boy fell asleep on a window sill after midnight and fell three stories to his death; but Paul brought him back to life, ate food with them, and continued talking with them until daybreak before departing (Acts 20:6-12). When Paul and his company arrived in Caesarea, they stayed with Philip the evangelist in his house for many days; and it was in this house that Agabus the prophet warned Paul by the Holy Spirit what would befall him in Jerusalem (Acts 21:8-11). When Paul and his companions arrived in Jerusalem, they lodged with Mnason of Cyprus (Acts 21:16). Then after the Jews rose up against Paul and he was taken into protective custody by the Romans, they were shipwrecked on the island of Malta on the way to Rome where Paul entered into the home where the father of the leading man of the island lie sick and Paul healed him there (Acts 28:8). Then many who had diseases came to where Paul had been lodged in such a friendly manner and were healed (Acts 28:9). The last reference of Paul using a home to minister in and from is found in the last two verses of this great book of New Testament history. It is a fitting summary statement of the use of homes where open discussion and dialogue can take place so effectively. It is thus written that after Paul was taken to Rome for trial, **"he stayed two full years in his own rented quarters, and was welcoming all who came to him, preaching the kingdom of God, and teaching concerning the Lord Jesus Christ with all openness, unhindered"** (Acts 28:23, 30-31).

Dearly beloved, let us return to meeting in our homes!

New Testament membership.

In this section we wish to consider church membership. Is it important? Is it helpful or harmful? Does it help build the body of Christ, or does it help destroy it? Where is our church membership scripturally? Is it in a house fellowship, a local congregation, a denomination, or is it in the body of Christ only? These questions and others, we will consider.

First, let us pray from the scripture, and then quote all of the scriptures in the New Testament that pertain to this subject, and see what God has to say on the subject.

Paul prays in the Ephesian letter a prayer that we would do well to pray now for ourselves as we consider church membership. He prayed [and now we pray] that:

> "The God of our Lord Jesus Christ, the Father of glory, may give to you [us] a spirit of wisdom and of revelation in the knowledge of Him . . . the eyes of your [our] heart may be [being] enlightened, so that you [we] may know what is the hope of His calling." "And He put all things in subjection under His [Christ's] feet, and gave Him as head over all things to the church, which is His body, the fulness of Him who fills all in all." (Eph. 1:17-18, 22-23 NAS)

Paul then states that:

> "There is [only] one body." (Eph. 4:4)

To the saints at Colossae, he writes of Christ:

> "In the heavens and on earth . . . He is also head of the body, the church; and He is the beginning, the first-born from the dead; so that He Himself might come to have first place in everything." "Now I rejoice in my sufferings for your sake, and in my flesh I do my share on behalf of His body (which is the church) in filling up that which is lacking in Christ's afflictions." (Col. 1:16, 18, 24 NAS)

And since Paul likens the body of Christ to a human body so that we, as members, can better understand it, he writes to the Romans:

> "For just as we have many members in one body and all the members do not have the same function, so we, who are many, are <u>one body in Christ</u>, and <u>individually members one of another.</u>" (Rom. 12:4-5 NAS)

Thus we see in Paul's letters that he identifies the church as the body of Christ, and that there is only one body in the universe. He writes further to the Ephesians:

165

"By revelation there was made known to me the mystery, as I wrote before in brief. And by referring to this, when you read you can understand my insight into the mystery of Christ, which in other generations was not made known to the sons of men, as it has now been revealed to His holy apostles and prophets in the Spirit; to be specific, that the Gentiles are fellow heirs and fellow members of the body, and fellow partakers of the promise in Christ Jesus through the gospel, of which I was made a minister, according to the gift of God's grace which was given to me according to the working of His power."

(Eph. 3:3-7 NAS)

"I, therefore, the prisoner of the Lord, entreat you to walk in a manner worthy of the calling with which you have been called, with all humility and gentleness, with patience, showing forbearance to one another in love, being diligent to preserve the unity of the Spirit in the bond of peace. There is one body and one Spirit, just as also you were called in one hope of your calling; one Lord, one faith, one baptism, one God and Father of all who is over all and through all and in all. But to each one of us grace was given according to the measure of Christ's gift. Therefore it says, 'When He ascended on high, He led captive a host of captives, and He gave gifts to men.' (Now this expression, 'He ascended,' what does it mean except that He also had descended into the lower parts of the earth? He who descended is Himself also He who ascended far above all the heavens, that He might fill all things.) And He gave some as apostles, and some as prophets, and some as evangelists, and some as pastors [shepherds] and teachers, for the equipping of the saints for the work of service, to the building up of the body of Christ; until we all attain to the unity of the faith, and of the knowledge of the Son of God, to a mature man, to the measure of the stature which belongs to the fulness of Christ. As a result, we are no longer to be children, tossed here and there by waves, and carried about by every wind of doctrine, by the trickery of men, by craftiness in deceitful scheming; but speaking the truth in love, we are to grow up in all aspects into Him, who is the head, even Christ, <u>from whom the whole body, being fitted and held together</u> by <u>that which every joint supplies</u>, according to the <u>proper working of each individual part</u> [member], causes the <u>growth of the body</u> for the <u>building up of itself in love.</u>"

(Eph. 4:1-16 NAS)

"Therefore, laying aside falsehood, speak truth, each one of you, with his neighbor, for <u>we are members of one another.</u>" (Eph. 4:25 NAS)

Christ nourishes and cherishes the church "because <u>we are members of His body.</u>"

(Eph. 5:30 NAS)

From the above scriptures we can see that there is only one body, one true church, and that we must see ourselves as members of that one true church, which must not be divided by carnal means and methods, by false and selfish teachings which are from beneath, not from above. These truths are special revelation that is first given to holy apostles and prophets of God by the ministry of the Holy Spirit. We can see that all of the body of Christ is to be connected in very practical ways, by which each joining supplies food and spiritual necessities to other members of this one universal body; and that this fitting together is only accomplished by first, the ministry of present day apostles and prophets given until we all come to the spiritual, functional, and practical unity of the faith, as well as spiritually minded evangelists, shepherds, and teachers, and then other maturing members of the body (see also I Cor. 12: 27-29).

The believing Jews are fellow members with the Gentile believers; the church is not to be divided.

"For all of you who were baptized into Christ have clothed yourselves with Christ. There is neither Jew nor Greek, there is neither slave nor free man, there is neither male nor female; for you are all one in Christ Jesus." (Gal. 3:27-28 NAS)

Concerning communion, Paul writes:

"Is not the cup of blessing which we bless a sharing in the blood of Christ? Is not the bread which we break a sharing in the body of Christ? Since there is one bread, we who are many are one body; for we all partake of the one bread." "For he who eats and drinks, eats and drinks judgment to himself, if he does not judge the body rightly."

(I Cor. 10:16-17; 11:29 NAS)

Consequently, we see that division between members in the universal body of Christ is sin, and brings judgment upon those responsible and practicing division! Many communion services are divisive in themselves when they exclude "outside" members of the body from participating, and thus the righteous weakness, sickness, and death from the hand of the Lord is evident (I Cor. 11:30).

To follow this serious note, Paul gives us a very detailed portion of scripture from which we can see that our membership is in the one body of Christ, and not in a small house fellowship, a larger "local congregation," or even an entire city; and these scriptures give us reasons why we must practice this truth.

Let us understand that Paul is including all Christians everywhere when he writes:

"To the church of God which is at Corinth, to those who have been sanctified in Christ Jesus, saints by calling, with all who in every place call upon the name of our Lord Jesus Christ, their Lord and ours."

(I Cor. 1:2 NAS)

Now then, let us understand that the following scripture refers to the entire body of Christ, not a city, not a congregation, or anything less.

"Now concerning spiritual gifts [Gk. πνευματικων, pneumatikon, spirituals], brethren, I do not want you to be unaware. You know that when you were pagans, you were led astray to the dumb idols, however you were led. Therefore I make known to you, that no one speaking by the Spirit of God says, 'Jesus is accursed'; and no one can say, 'Jesus is Lord,' except by the Holy Spirit.

Now there are varieties of gifts, but the same Spirit. And there are varieties of ministries, and the same Lord. And there are varieties of effects, but the same God who works all things in all persons. But to each one is given the manifestation of the Spirit for the common good. For to one is given the word of wisdom through the Spirit, and to another the word of knowledge according to the same Spirit; to another faith by the same Spirit, and to another gifts of healing by the one Spirit, and to another the effecting of miracles, and to another prophecy, and to another the distinguishing of spirits, to another various kinds of tongues, and to another the interpretation of tongues. But one and the same Spirit works all these things, distributing to each one individually just as He wills.

For even as the body is one and yet has many members, and all the members of the body, though they are many, are one body, so also is Christ. For by one Spirit we were all baptized into one body, whether Jews or Greeks, whether slaves or free, and we were all made to drink of one Spirit. For the body is not one member, but many. If the foot should say, 'Because I am not a hand, I am not a part of the body,' it is not for this reason any the less a part of the body. And if the ear should say, 'Because I am not an eye, I am not a part of the body,' it is not for this reason any the less a part of the body. If the whole body were an eye, where would the hearing be? If the whole were hearing, where would the sense of smell be? But now God has placed the members, each one of them, in the body, just as He desired. And if they were all one member, where would the body be? But now there are many members, but one body. And the eye cannot say to the hand, 'I have no need of you'; or again the head to the feet, 'I have no need of you.' On the contrary, it is much truer that the members of the body which seem to be weaker are necessary; and those members of the body, which we deem less honorable, on these we bestow more abundant honor, and our unseemly members come to have more abundant seemliness, whereas our seemly members have no need of it. But God has so composed the body, giving more abundant honor to that member which lacked, that there should be no division in the body, but that the members should have the same care for one another. And if one member suffers, all the members suffer with it; if one member is honored, all the members rejoice with it. Now you are Christ's body, and individually members of it. And God has appointed in the church, first apostles, second prophets, third teachers, then miracles, then gifts of healings, helps, administrations, various kinds of tongues. All are not apostles, are they? All are not prophets, are they? All are not teachers, are they? All are not workers of miracles, are they? All do not have gifts of healings, do they? All do not speak with tongues, do they? All do not interpret, do they? But earnestly desire the greater gifts."

(I Cor. 12:1-31 NAS)

If we are to benefit from various ministries and gifts which the Lord has given to His body, we must recognize that they are given to the body as a whole, not to any one portion of it! They are given to build up the one true universal church, and must be seen in this light. Membership is in the body, not a congregation, whether it is five people, five hundred, five thousand, or five million. And not even a city, for we, as individual members of the body of Christ, travel here and there, and must be accepted and responsible where ever we are. On the street or in the office, at play or at work, in assembly or out, we are always in church because we are the church, and we are to be ready and willing to function wherever we are, and we must recognize that all Christians are members of the one body of Christ, and must be accepted everywhere as such! Sectarianism is a deadly sin! It grieves the Holy Spirit who is given to make us one! It grieves the Lord Jesus Christ who died to make us one, and who agonized in prayer before He did so that we might be one. It grieves our heavenly Father who provides all that we are, all that we have, and all the benefits of salvation, that all of his children do not love and accept one another. We must stop lording it over one another when He has made Jesus our Lord! Our God is the one who paid the price to make us one, and we must repent of our divisions and learn how to function together in love if we are going to succeed in the remaining days of this age, and be rewarded in eternity. Jesus is Lord!

When we split the body of Christ up into congregations or denominations with our own membership, it divides the body of Christ. It is not scriptural, but traditional! It is not spiritual, but carnal.

We just read how all true Christian are all baptized into one body by one Spirit! And that the various ministries that Christ gives, and various manifestations of the Holy Spirit, are given to the body for the edification of all of the body in love. When one member is affected, all are affected, and we must see this whether we thoroughly understand it or not. God deals with us according to our hearts and attitudes, and they must be filled with love for Him and for all of His children. "**Whoever believes that Jesus is the Christ is born of God; and whoever loves the Father loves the child born of Him**" (I Jn. 5:1 NAS).

There is never an incidence in scripture where Christians are members of anything less than the entire body of Christ. All modern membership is sectarian, divisive, carnal, and under the judgment of almighty God, our Lord Jesus Christ, and His Holy Spirit! It is of Babylon, and fostered by spirits of pride, selfish ambition, rebellion, unbelief, and fear!

We must congregate as the Spirit leads us, recognizing that He is in our midst as Head, and any of His children present are our legal, full brothers and sisters in Christ. We are not stepbrothers or half brothers, unrecognized or unwanted, but full brothers of our heavenly Father. The problems from our spiritual sickness of carnal division are exacerbated, however, due to the fact that our mother, the church which is above, is misunderstood and therefore practiced so incorrectly as a carnal church congregation or denomination from the earth (Gal. 4:26). Therefore we are in spiritual slavery instead of freedom, to the degree that we do not understand and practice the truth (Gal.4:22 - 5:1).

Various carnal reasons are given to justify local church membership, but they are just that — carnal justification for our building according to the carnal ways of men, and not according to the spiritual will of God! It is building carnal temples according to tradition, the way others have done it, the way men are taught in carnal schools, and not according to the way in heaven. When Moses was told to build the tabernacle, he was commanded to build

171

it according to how he had seen it while up on the mountain of God. Today, true apostles will build and help others to build in the true way; but rebellion, pride, selfish ambition, unbelief, and the fear of man and the fear of losing members, respectability among our peers, cause men to build incorrectly and with so much "**wood, hay,** [and] **stubble**."

Therefore, I believe it would be helpful to bring to our attention and emphasize that within three chapters, Moses was told four times to build "**the tabernacle**" and "**all its furniture**" according to the "**pattern**" and "**plan**" for each which he had been "**shown in the mountain**" (Ex. 25:9, 40; 26:30; 27:8 NAS). The purpose, God said, was for His people to "**construct a sanctuary for Me, that I may dwell among them**" (Ex. 25:8 NAS). This same truth is for us in building a sanctuary for God today, the church, that He might dwell and manifest Himself among us now (Eph. 2: 21-22). And the Lord Jesus Christ, our high priest of the New Covenant, is the chief "**minister in the** [heavenly] **sanctuary**" where we are now able and beckoned to come boldly before the throne of grace; and as such He repeats the warning Moses received from God "**when he was about to erect the tabernacle; for, 'See,' He says, 'that you make all things according to the pattern which was shown you on the mountain'**" (Heb. 8:2, 5 NAS). Thus if we are to please God, and thereby experience all the benefits which are given to us in this "**better covenant, which has been enacted on better promises**," we must go up on the mountain of God also, seeking His face by prayer and fasting, in total consecration and humble service to Him, to have revealed to us His pattern for His tabernacle, the church, and then build accordingly (Heb. 8:6 NAS). Building as most do, in a sectarian and man centered, led, and controlled way, according to the carnal traditions of men, does not accomplish the will of God, does not bring to His church all of the glorious and wonderful benefits and manifestations of His presence, and will not result in joyful eternal rewards but sorrowful eternal loss (I Cor. 3:8-18).

There are those who justify church membership for various reasons, but it would be well to acknowledge that whole groups and movements have been built upon a proper understanding of the truth, and do not have memberships. However, although a group does not have church membership, it may deteriorate into carnality and become just as sectarian in spirit, or even more so, than those who do! But, we must not make that an excuse for not following the Lord fully; we must determine to worship Him not

172

only in Spirit, but in truth as well (**for the Father seeketh such to worship Him**), not according to the vain traditions and carnality of men (Jn. 4:23-24 KJV; Mt. 15:3-9; Mk. 7:6-13).

The carnal mind wants local church membership so as to hold a particular group together, not realizing that it is causing the very opposite in the Lord's church. When we come to realize this, we will be confronted with the reality of who we are really working for — the Lord or ourselves, and thus for the spiritual benefit of God's people, or for the carnal benefit of ourselves and other carnal groups. We are to be held together by love and peace, which come through spiritual commitments; not carnal means which come from erroneous and carnal commitments (Col. 3:14; Eph. 4:3).

Some leaders might think that local membership is needed to determine who they are responsible for and to, but that leads to failure to be responsible for many outside our membership for whom we are responsible. We are responsible when gathered together for all who are in our midst as the Lord leads us, whether true Christians, or unbelievers, or those who are not Christians but profess to be. The Lord looks and judges us "as one" (Josh.7; I Cor. 5:6). All are considered by God and should be by us according to their profession of faith, not according to whether they have signed some earthly membership roll or not (I Cor. 5:11). All who profess to be brothers and sisters in Christ must live according to certain standards (I Cor. 5:9-13). When dealing with all those who profess to be Christians, it's according to His membership roll, not ours!

We must come to see and practice universal membership if we are to grow and mature into all that the Father and our Lord Jesus Christ have planned for us. We can tell our progress by discerning the presence and anointing of the Holy Spirit as He works throughout our assemblies and beyond, and how we relate to all other members of His body! If we limit church membership, we limit relationship with those outside that membership. How tragic!

In closing this section on church membership, let us summarize briefly. Church membership is not in a congregation, group, denomination, movement, or even a city, but it is in the one universal body of Christ which is in heaven and earth. Any practice contrary to this truth is carnal and divisive. It brings judgment from God, depending upon the nature, intention, and destructiveness to the body of Christ.

Let us now quote a few scriptures that reveal our carnality in the church, and our eternal loss because of it.

> **"God is faithful, through whom you were called into fellowship with His Son, Jesus Christ our Lord. Now I exhort you, brethren, by the name of our Lord Jesus Christ, that you all agree, and there be no divisions** [Gk. σχισματα, *schismata,* schisms, dissensions, rendings] **among you, but you be made complete in the same mind and in the same judgment. For I have been informed concerning you, my brethren, by Chloe's people, that there are quarrels among you. Now I mean this, that each one of you is saying, 'I am of Paul** [a man of power and demonstration of the Spirit; maybe "I'm a Pentecostal" or "I'm a Charismatic"],**' and 'I of Apollos** [a man of eloquence; gifted orators; maybe "I'm a Methodist," or "I'm a Baptist"],**' and 'I of Cephas** [a man of boldness; maybe "I'm a Lutheran" or "I'm a fundamentalist"],**' and 'I of Christ** ["I belong to the Church of Christ," or even "the church of Christ", or "I'm a Catholic"].**' Has Christ been divided? Paul was not crucified for you, was he? Or were you baptized in the name of Paul?"**
> (I Cor. 1:9-13 NAS)

Please note that our fellowship is in Jesus, not doctrine about Jesus. Therefore, we can have fellowship with all Christians, unless they are in gross sin! Also, the church in Corinth was not divided as we are today; they were still meeting together, but were carnal and factious (I Cor. 11:18-19). The church had not at this time received such false teaching as to completely divide the church as we have today. And if I missed including your group in the list above, please forgive me.

Thus when we remember that Paul was writing to all of the Christians in Corinth as well as to all other Christians everywhere (that means all of us), we can have a better understanding of what he meant when he went further and wrote:

> **"And I, brethren, could not speak to you as to spiritual men, but as to men of flesh** [carnal]**, as to babes in Christ. I gave you milk to drink, not solid food; for you were not yet able to receive it. Indeed,**

even now you are not yet able, for you are still fleshly [carnal]. For since there is jealousy and strife among you, are you not fleshly, and are you not walking like mere men? For when one says, 'I am of Paul,' and another, 'I am of Apollos,' are you not mere men? What then is Apollos? And what is Paul? Servants through whom you believed, even as the Lord gave opportunity to each one. I planted, Apollos watered, but God was causing the growth. So then neither the one who plants nor the one who waters is anything, but God who causes the growth. Now he who plants and he who waters are one; but each will receive his own reward according to his own labor. For we are God's fellow workers; you are God's field, God's building.

According to the grace of God which was given to me, as a wise master builder I laid a foundation, and another is building upon it. But let each man be careful how he builds upon it. For no man can lay a foundation other than the one which is laid, which is Jesus Christ. Now if any man builds upon the foundation with gold, silver, precious stones, wood, hay, straw, each man's work will become evident; for the day will show it, because it is to be revealed with fire; and the fire itself will test the quality of each man's work. If any man's work which he has built upon it remains, he shall receive a reward. If any man's work is burned up, he shall suffer loss; but he himself shall be saved, yet so as through fire.

Do you not know that you are a temple of God, and that the Spirit of God dwells in you? If any man destroys the temple of God [the one true body of Christ, its unity or any of its members], God will destroy him, for the temple of God is holy, and that is what you are.

Let no man deceive himself. If any man among you thinks that he is wise in this age, let him become foolish that he may become wise. For the wisdom of this world is foolishness before God. For it is written, 'He is the one who catches the wise in their craftiness'; and again, 'The Lord knows the reasonings of the wise, that they are useless.' So then let no one boast in men. For all things belong to you, whether Paul or Apollos

**or Cephas or the world or life or death or things
present or things to come; all things belong to you,
and you belong to Christ; and Christ belongs to God."**
(I Cor. 3:1-23 NAS)

So we see how the Lord is going to judge us with rewards or
loss depending upon the quality of our work, not quantity of
activity, in building the body of Christ. And we are to benefit from
all of the great Christian men of the past who have brought to the
universal church, the body of Christ, the truths we have been given
down through the centuries; they all belong to us.

Unfortunately, in our carnality, we have not understood
properly the one true body of Christ — church structure, function,
discipline, and membership, and our responsibilities to them —
although we have held tightly to the head. Consequently, the Lord
has had to move separately in different parts of His body, but He
has not had a united body through which He can demonstrate to
the world all that He desires. But, it is coming!

In some respects, the body of Christ has been like a disjointed
or spastic body, but as God moves and pours out more of His Spirit,
and we experience more of His innervating and uniting work, we
are going to see the body of Christ arise as never before in the
history of man; and God will demonstrate to the world His creation
in Christ, and therefore reveal as never before His Son to a lost
world and soon ending age.

Let us press on therefore to know the Lord and His body
more fully, and therefore understand God's warning to us all of:

**"not holding fast to the head, from whom the
<u>entire body</u>, being supplied and held together by the
joints and ligaments, grows with a growth which is
from God."** (Col. 2:19 NAS)

Remembering always the admonition and truth that we have:

**"laid aside the old self with its evil practices, and
have put on the new self who is being renewed to a
true knowledge according to the image of the One who
created him — a renewal in which there is no
distinction between Greek and Jew, circumcised and
uncircumcised, barbarian, Scythian, slave and freeman**
[Methodist, Presbyterian, Episcopalian, Roman

176

Catholic, Baptist, Fundamentalist, Holiness or Pentecostal, Charismatic or Evangelical, independent or dependent], **but Christ is all, and in all.**

And so, as those who have been chosen of God, holy and beloved, put on a heart of compassion, kindness, humility, gentleness and patience; bearing with one another, and forgiving each other, whoever has a complaint against anyone; just as the Lord forgave you, so also should you. And beyond all these things put on love, which is the perfect bond of unity. And let the peace of Christ rule in your [our] hearts, to which indeed you [we] were called in one body; and be thankful." (Col. 3:9-15 NAS)

Finally, since the weapons of our warfare are not carnal but spiritual, in battling to bring unity and harmony to the body of Christ and to defeat Satan's work of destroying the body, when asked what we are a member of, let us answer with love and thankfulness, with understanding and appreciation, as Jesus did: **"It is written"**; and then with Paul and the saints in Rome to whom he wrote, and with all of the Christians down through the ages:

"Just as we have many members in one body and all the members do not have the same function, so <u>we</u>, who are many, <u>are one body in Christ</u>, and <u>individually</u> <u>members one of another</u>."
(Rom. 12:4-5 NAS)

Amen, and Amen!

New Testament picture.

When we began this chapter on "**the church**," our stated goal was "to present a picture of the true New Testament church as it is given to us in the scriptures, established by the Lord Jesus Christ and His apostles, after His crucifixion for our sins and His resurrection from the dead."

We have endeavored to picture the church in words, and now we wish to picture the church in graphic illustration, both the true spiritual New Testament church and the carnal Babylonian church. By these terms we mean: The spiritual church is the true New Testament church which is indwelt, empowered, structured, and led (mostly) by the Spirit of God (as she matures). The Babylonian church is composed of organizations of man, a mixture of true believers and those that are only professing to be believers, structured according to the traditions and interpretations of man, and led by a mixture of God's Spirit and **"the spirit that is now working in the sons of disobedience"** (Eph. 2:2 NAS). Energized by Satan using the spirits of Babylon and every other conceivable unclean spirit of lust and greed (Rev. 18:2; II Tim. 3:1-9; II Pet. 2:1-22; Jude vv. 4-19), the Babylonian church follows men and **"the tradition of the elders"** (Mt. 15:2; Mk. 7:5; see also Isa. 29:13; Col. 2:8) according to the varying degrees of Babylonish doctrines which they hold to.

There are a number of differences which we can note from the graphics, and there is more that is not shown.

First, the Babylonian Church is composed of many separate "Churches," each with its own independent government and structure of different kinds depending upon the tradition from which they come. Of course, many are supremely governed by a hierarchy outside the congregation, but all of them are governed and structured independently of other "Christians" in their city. This sectarianism is illustrated by the solid lines around each individual congregation. They all have different names put upon the people so that they recognize themselves as belonging to one particular congregation, not the whole, the true church of the Lord in the entire city and beyond. In the spiritual church, believers carry His precious name only.

As we look at the members, we see some that are saved, that are truly children of God, and some that are not saved; this is illustrated by true believers having an open, white circle; and the unbelievers are filled with black, indicating that their hearts have not been regenerated by the Spirit of God. The spiritual church is united, because the leadership sees itself as united under the headship of Jesus Christ, and the "elders of the city" are shepherding and overseeing the one true flock in the city together. These leaders are the "elders," " shepherds," and "bishops," and regularly meet together for prayer and fasting, fellowship, teaching and ministering to one another and to the Lord as the Holy Spirit leads, recognizing themselves in their individual giftings and together governing the one church in their locality under Christ

178

the Head in their midst. They have renounced the Babylonian doctrines and practices from their backgrounds in order to support the truth of God and the headship of Jesus Christ in every respect, both individually and corporately.

Notice from the graphics that what was once a "Pastor" and recognized as the "Head" of an independent congregation in the Babylonian system, is in the spiritual system a fellow elder of the city with other men of God, looking to Jesus as the "Head" and "Chief Shepherd" in their midst, getting direction, inspiration, and life from Him as He moves by His Spirit both directly and through his fellow elders, as well as other members of His body. The elders together rule the one church in their city in plurality, not independently but dependently, dependent upon the Lord and one another.

Men who were elders of congregations in the Babylonian Church under a Pastor may or may not be elders in the spiritual church. And of course, some were not even saved and true believers, and this is true of other "Church members" as well!

Membership in the Babylonian Church is congregational, with all the attendant requirements and commitments demanded, but in the spiritual church, membership is recognized and taught as in the body of Christ only, and all requirements and commitments are first to the Lord as given by His Word and Spirit. No unbeliever is recognized as a member, and no believer is recognized as a non-member! The solid lines around the congregations also emphasizes the sectarian carnality of the independent and divisive Babylonish Church memberships; whereas, in the spiritual church there is only membership in the total, one body of Christ, so there are no lines around the congregations in the city. In the Babylonian structure meetings such as one of the home groups or the media ministry have broken lines around them to signify that they have no sectarian membership but teach and practice body-wide church membership. However, this is not always the case with many home groups or media ministries. The city has no solid line either as we are not even members of a locality alone, but "**fellow members of the body**," "**one body**," and "**members of one another**" throughout the city and beyond.

In the Babylonian Church, meetings are set according to tradition and the degree of life within and allowed by hierarchical leadership; but in the spiritual church, meetings are where ever, when ever, and however the Lord, the Head of the church, directs; and His life flows accordingly (Mt. 18:19-20).

The modern Babylonian Churches in any large Christianized city.

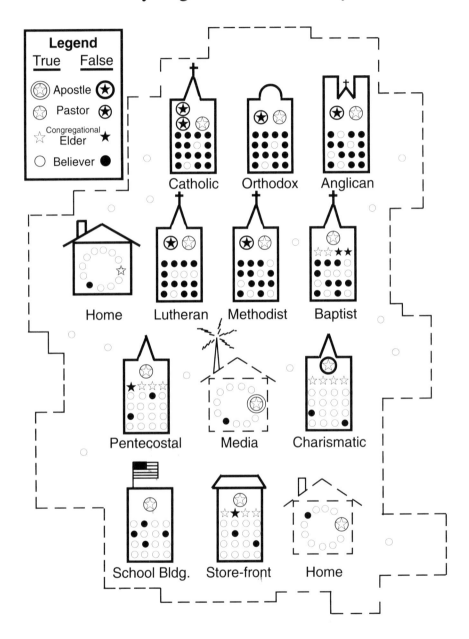

The one true church in the same city.
And "the elders of the church [city]." Acts 20:17

Example: "The church which was in Jerusalem." Acts 11:22
"The seven churches [cities] which are in Asia." Rev. 1:11 KJV

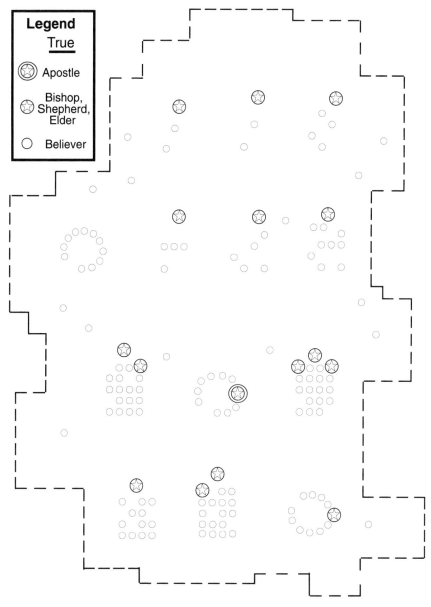

Legend

__True__

⊚ Apostle

⊛ Bishop, Shepherd, Elder

○ Believer

During this time of such Babylonian sectarianism, notice there are believers outside the "Churches" who are members of His body. They often flow freely within the body, and consequently are called "church tramps," "church hoppers," "uncommitted," or worse; and although some may have spiritual needs and deficiencies, many are just more spiritual than the castigating carnal leadership which needs to be ashamed of themselves and repent of their carnal Babylonish ways and words!

Notice also that although a man may be a true shepherd, he may think, or have been told or prophesied to, that he is an apostle because of his "success" as a Babylonish "pastor" — but he is not! He does not teach "**the apostles' doctrine**," does not have the apostles' "**revelations**," and the understanding of the "**mystery of Christ**" (Eph. 3:1-12), and is not backed up by the Lord in that authority because he is not called by the Lord into that ministry. (For example, consider the Charismatic Church graphic.) Men must repent for assuming any position, ministry, or authority which Christ has not given or be severely chastened, either in this life, the next, or both!

The true apostles with 20/20 vision will be teaching "**publicly and from house to house**" (Acts 20:20), and using writings as Paul and the first apostles in Jerusalem did, and also using the additional media of the present such as radio, television, tape recordings, and the internet. In any particular city, there may be no apostles, or there may be one or more depending upon the leading of the Lord at any given time.

The most significant differences in graphical summation that we must see and understand between the Babylonian Churches and the true church are the structures and government, and the sectarian membership and function versus the all inclusive non-sectarian membership and function within the total body of Christ. The placement of the members is the same in both graphics, in order to account for their participation in the Babylonian system versus a spiritual system, not to demonstrate seating arrangements or even participation throughout the city. This has been addressed in words elsewhere in this book. Obviously, when Christians are properly shepherded and have a spiritual view of the entire body of Christ, they will also be encouraged to flow freely and widely throughout the city and beyond in experiencing and building the entire body of Christ, and then we can also expect to experience powerful revival and evangelism!

There are many other truths that may not be observed from the graphic pictures, but can be understood from the previous word pictures, so let us take note of some.

The spiritual New Testament church
vs
The carnal Babylonian Church

In the spiritual church, all the people are Christians and members of the same church, the body of Christ; and they are under spiritual leadership. In the Babylonian church, the people are divided into separate congregations, each with its own sectarian membership, composed of mixtures of all non-Christians, varying degrees of both carnal Christians and non-Christians, or all carnal Christians. The leadership is the same mixture, and instead of recognizing the Lord Jesus as the head, it looks to a hierarchy or itself as the head. Only when local leaders meet together and recognize the truth of the headship of Christ over each and every meeting of Christians, as well as the total church, and learn to wait upon Him for the direction and anointing of the Holy Spirit for all the Christians in any given area, can they grow and understand what true spirituality is and what Christ's plans and purposes for the church are.

Consequently, Babylonish leaders also look to denominational doctrine or their own interpretation of scripture, rather than meeting together and waiting on the Lord for His truth to come forth, and particularly, the "**teaching of the apostles**" (Acts 2:42 lit.).

In the spiritual church, Christians meet whenever and wherever the Lord leads; this results in daily fellowship, edifying, helping, and loving one another, and reaching out to those to whom they are being led. In the carnal church, they follow carnal man and the patterns of the Babylonian heritage from which they descended — either of a denomination, or of men which they follow from books, experience, or fellowship; this results in only weekly [and weakly] "worship" services, but depending upon the spirituality of the leaders there may be one or two more "meetings."

In the spiritual church, Christians are taught to be concerned with building up the body of Christ; but in the Babylonian church, the concern is with a particular congregation or movement, even at the expense of harming or destroying the proper functioning of the body of Christ, or its members. Or worse yet, the concern is building up a physical building at the expense of the spiritual and financial well being of the members themselves.

In the spiritual church, home meetings are foundational and essential; but in the Babylonian church they are either forbidden, or else erroneously controlled by man, customs, or doctrine, rather than by the Holy Spirit of God. Consequently, Christian homes are deteriorating, both spiritually and financially, while special buildings are built with idolatrous zeal and greed.

In the spiritual church, every member is important and able to function freely under the anointing of the Holy Spirit; whereas in the Babylonian church only selected people are permitted to function, and only as freely as heritage or headquarters permit. Because of this, small intimate meetings are forbidden or looked to as unimportant, and the size of the meetings is the standard of success. Large impersonal meetings are more comfortable for those not seeking wholeheartedly the kingdom of God (whether they be the leaders or those being led).

In the spiritual church, Christians seek for and receive all of the ministries, gifts, and manifestations of the Holy Spirit, and people function freely in their particular individual anointings; but in the Babylonian church the practice of these different anointings is in various mixtures, many being denied expression and only a very few being practiced, and certainly only those that will not challenge the beliefs or positions of the hierarchy of the Church.

In the spiritual church, members are equipped to carry on ministry outside the assembly (a place of spiritual training), and a worldwide vision of the body of Christ is held forth; but in the Babylonian church what is held in highest esteem is attendance in meetings, financial contributions to the local work, and volunteering for programs and activities.

In the spiritual church, members help one another; but in the Babylonian church, everyone in need is referred to the "pastor" or a specialist outside the Church (often someone not even saved), whether it's the people themselves (the house of God) or the furnishings of their physical house that need repair.

In the spiritual church, a good meeting is where the Lord has His way, and moves through whomever He chooses; but in the Babylonian church, it is a good sermon or teaching from the leader. The emphasis is more on the head than the heart, forgetting the scripture, **"knowledge puffs up, but love builds up"** (I Cor. 8:1 lit.).

In the spiritual church, prayer is extremely important, both private and corporate; but in the Babylonian church, a simple "Pastoral" prayer is the most often heard publicly, and private prayer is also unbelievably small, both in quantity and quality.

In the spiritual church where God chooses, the qualifications for leadership are character and spirituality; but in the Babylonian church where man chooses, the qualifications are formal education and degrees in worldly ways. We must realize that to serve is more important than to know (Lu. 22:25-27; Gal. 5:13-14; I Cor. 13:1-3).

In the spiritual church the emphasis is to "go" — go and make disciples of all nations — quality first and then quantity; but in the Babylonian church the emphasis is to "come" — come and help us build the size of this congregation — quantity first, and quality is low priority, if at all.

In the spiritual church the goal of leaders is to serve others (the Lord's vision; Mt. 20:25-28); but in the Babylonian church the goal is to gather others to serve the leader (his own vision; Rom. 16:17-18).

Consequently, in the spiritual church, members are discipled, trained and qualified to serve from within the local work. But in the Babylonian church, members who wish to be trained, are stifled or exported to be trained to serve elsewhere; and professional clergy are imported to lead and control. In the spiritual church emerging ministry is encouraged and trained to come up along side, versus being suppressed and rejected, or at least held in lower esteem.

In the spiritual church, leaders are in plurality, responsible for shepherding one another, working cooperatively with one another. In the Babylonian church they are isolated, structured to working competitively with one another. Fired up, versus burned out! Edified, versus edifices!

In the spiritual church, leaders are recognized as being sheep as well as shepherds, and are therefore cared for along with the rest of the flock. In the Babylonian church the "clergy" are so singular and elevated above and separated from the "laity," they are without proper care and more easily fall prey to many wiles of the "evil one."

In summation, in the spiritual church the commitments are to the Lord primarily, and then to the work; but in the Babylonian church the commitments are primarily to carnal ambitions and idolatrous practices before any commitment to the Lord. Humility, faith, truth, love, obedience, the kingdom of God, and the fear of the Lord are liberating virtues and goals prayed for in the spiritual church; as opposed to pride, unbelief, misbelief, rebellion, selfish ambition, and the fear of man that are bonds of slavery in every Babylonish carnal structure.

"Dear Father, please help us to be Your servants, filled with Your Spirit to do Your will and not our own — to pursue love and spiritual gifting that we might be better used to build your kingdom, and not our own. Help us to be like Jesus, that others might see Him and be drawn to Him, and not to ourselves. Dear God, please help us in Jesus' name we pray. Amen, and Amen. Amen!"

CHAPTER 4

"One Mind, and One Accord"

What we are about to consider now is a principle that I call "One Mind, and One Accord"; but it has been called by others "Unanimity," and "The Headship of Christ," which are all very good and descriptive terms of what we shall explain.

Basically, the doctrine is this:

> When two or more believers gather to find and do the Lord's will, it is not decided by a majority vote, but waiting upon the Lord for His mind to be revealed to each believer in whom dwells the Holy Spirit, until they all come into the same undivided judgment concerning the situation.

The scripture repeatedly reports to us this principle when it is written that they were all of "**one mind, and one accord.**" That is "unanimity," it is looking to the Lord Jesus who is head of His church to manifest His mind to us so that we can be assured of His will and then do it!

I first learned of this teaching through an excellent book on early church history and doctrine entitled *The Churches of God* by G. H. Lang. His eleventh chapter, which I recommend you read, is: "Unanimity: A Divine Rule of Church Order and Christian Co-operation." It is a beautiful treatise, and in its original form was his first published work, under the title, *Unanimity: The Divine Method Of Church Government*. Both are very thorough explanations of this most important doctrine and apostolic practice.

Let us look now at various other revelations from the Old Testament scriptures that reveal to us that God has always operated by this principle and expects us to do the same. Later we shall look at the New Testament scriptures.

In the very first verses of the holy scriptures we discover that God is one and yet is a plurality. For example, we find: "**In the beginning God created**" and "**the Spirit of God was moving,**" and "**Then God said, 'Let Us make man in Our image, according to Our likeness; and let them rule. . . .' And God created man in His own image, in the image of God He created him; male and female He created them. . . . Then God said, 'Behold, I have given'**" (Gen. 1: 1, 2, 26, 27, 29 NAS). Here we have found God to be the creating Father, the Spirit, and the speaker of the spoken Word; acknowledging that He is a plurality, "**Us . . . Our**"; but acting as one, "**His . . . He . . . I.**" He speaks and creates in a unity and harmony of His own nature as one; yet He is three persons in one. This is of course confirmed in the New Testament.

God the Father, God the Son, and God the Holy Spirit, all speak and act as one. It is unthinkable that They move from a majority position, of two against one. They move in "**one mind, and one accord**" always! Notice too that They acted in unity when They made man; They made him according to Their image and likeness, in other words, to operate like Themselves! They made "**man,**" singular, and then said, "**let them rule,**" plurality. This shows us that our rulership is to be from the same position of unanimity as Theirs. It shows us that a man and his wife are to aspire to this principle also, although the man is the head and is responsible for and must make final decisions. God is the head of Christ, Christ is the head of man, and man is the head of woman, but we are all to aspire for unanimity (1 Cor. 11:3). Notice also that after it is written that God said, "**Let Us**", that we find Him creating man, then the woman, and "**Then God said, 'Behold I,'**" indicating to us again that God speaks from unity and to unity as one, and that all things are "**from Him and through Him and to Him. . . . To Him be the glory forever. Amen**" (Rom. 11:36).

As we have seen God's creative power manifested in the unity of the Godhead at creation, we see also the power for evil in unity soon thereafter at the building of the tower of Babel, or Babylon. "**And the Lord said, 'Behold, they are one people, and they all have the same language. And this is what they began to do, and now nothing which they purpose to do will be impossible for them'**" (Gen. 11:6 NAS). So we see that unity is a most powerful condition. Therefore, if we are going to do successful battle against the enemy, we must be in unity with the Lord — and unanimity is the way to get there!

When God gave instructions to the Israelites to build a tabernacle (which is a type of the church, the tabernacle in which God dwells), they were to make a number of different and separate curtains (representing different parts of His church); but they were to "**join the curtains to one another with the [gold] clasps, that the tabernacle may be a unit [one]**" (Ex. 26:6 NAS). We are to be joined together in the gold of His faith, tried in the fires of His workings, "**one body in Christ**," united together for His purposes! (Rom. 12:5). We are to be "clasped" together by the bonds of His love and peace, the only uniting bonds that will ever hold us together (Col. 3:14; Eph. 4:3).

Moses declared, "**Hear, O Israel! The Lord is our God, the Lord is one! And you shall love the Lord your God with all your heart and with all your soul and with all your might**" (Deut. 6:4-5 NAS). If we hear this word and do it, we shall be one also! And, in fact, if we do not love God with everything within us, we shall not be one and shall not accomplish His purposes in our lives or in the church!

To continue further in revelation from the Old Testament concerning this principle, let us consider what happened under Solomon, the son of David, realizing that we are under Jesus Christ, the greater son of David today. We find that when a number of things had been completed in unity, then God moved mightily. First, when Solomon had finished all of the work for the house of the Lord, he brought all of the dedicated silver and gold and utensils into the treasuries of the house of God. Then he assembled all of the elders of God's people. There was much sacrifice by the people, and all of the priests present (today that is all of us) restored the ark of the Lord (containing the law of God) to its proper place (our hearts and lives). The priests who had come forth from the holy of holies (a time of communion with God), together in unity without regard for their different groupings (no sectarianism here), completely sanctified themselves (spirit, soul, and body). Then when the priests (remember that this is all of us) with the anointed musicians and singers lifted up their voices in thanksgiving to praise and to glorify the Lord, and to be heard "**as one . . . with one voice . . . saying, 'He indeed is good for His lovingkindness is everlasting,'** then **the house, the house of the Lord, was filled with a cloud, so that the priests could not stand to minister because of the cloud, for the glory of the Lord filled the house of God**" (II Chr. 5 KJV, NAS). Oh, let us understand and continue to pray for this today!

This unity is accomplished among God's people by God Himself when He cleanses them from all sin, and they remove all the detestable things and abominations from their midst; for God says, "**I shall give them one heart, and shall put a new spirit within them. And I shall take the heart of stone out of their flesh and give them a heart of flesh, that they may walk in My statutes and keep My ordinances, and do them. Then they will be My people, and I shall be their God**" (Eze. 11:17-20 NAS). Ezekiel also prophesies that God's people will no longer be divided, but be one nation having one king and one shepherd over them; and that God shall dwell in their midst forever, manifesting Himself in the sanctuary by His sanctifying presence! (Eze. 37:15-28).

In the New Testament, the most striking and familiar passage for unity is the high priestly prayer of our Lord Jesus Christ. It was given to us the night He was betrayed, His last night upon the earth before He was crucified for our sins and the sins of the whole world. He had concluded supper for the Passover, and these were His last words before He went out to the garden of Gethsemane to pray. This is a prayer to the Father for us, for all who shall believe in Him: "**that they may be one, just as We are one; I in them, and Thou in Me, that they may be perfected in unity [into one], that the world may know that Thou didst send Me**" (Jn. 17:22-23 NAS). Here again, we see that God's desire for us is to be so united in harmony of purpose and will that we are all totally committed to the Father's will and that of the Lord Jesus, that we are one and the same in our judgments and decisions with one another and with God Himself. This means that we are of "**one mind, and one accord.**"

We shall now see how the New Testament church operated.

In the book of Acts, our authentic record of the history of the church, we find a key for this important experience in the first reference. It is written of the eleven apostles that remained after Judas fell: **"These all continued <u>with one accord</u> in prayer and supplication"** (Acts 1:14 KJV). The NAS translates it, **"These all <u>with one mind</u> were continually devoting themselves to prayer, along with the women, and Mary the mother of Jesus, and with His brothers. And at this time Peter stood up in the midst of the brethren (a gathering of about one hundred and twenty persons was there together), and said, Brethren, the scripture . . ."** (Acts 1:14-16 NAS).

The phrase **"with one accord"** or **"with one mind"** is a translation of the Greek word *ομοθυμαδον, homothumadon.* The prefix *ομο, homo,* from *ομοσ, homos,* means "same"; and *θυμαδον, thumadon,* from *θυμοσ, thumos,* means "glow, ardor, passion"; thus *ομοθυμαδον, homothumadon,* means a state in which people are brought into **"one mind, and one accord."** The Latin Vulgate translates the word as "unanimiter" which is brought into our English as "unanimity." The Bauer, Arndt & Gingrich lexicon defines the word as: "with one mind or purpose or impulse; unanimously." Also, we can see from the words from which it is derived that it can not be a passive state, but one created through intense desires and effort. That is precisely what we find as we continue to look at this word in the scriptures. Let us notice that this experience was first mentioned as the result of <u>continual meeting for prayer</u>. There were ten times as many people praying together than the eleven apostles, and many of the people were women. We need to remember that out of their **"one mind, and one accord"** came their direction from the scripture (to let the office Judas held, be given to another: Matthias).

The next time *homothumadon* is used they were <u>continuing in prayer</u>: **"And when the day of Pentecost was fully come, they were all with <u>one accord</u> in one place"**; and then the Holy Spirit was poured out so powerfully and dramatically (Acts 2:1-4 KJV). Although this word *homothumadon* does not appear here in the most accurate manuscripts (but it is *ομου, homou,* which means "together"), it is clear that they were still in this state of one mind and in one accord together praying for the Holy Spirit which the Lord Jesus had promised and told them to wait for. Today if we will do the same, we can have a wonderful visitation of the Holy Spirit also.

After the Holy Spirit was poured out, **"they were continually devoting themselves to . . . prayer,"** and thus they were **"day by** day continuing with <u>one mind</u> [*homothumadon*] in the temple," our next reference (Acts 2:42, 46 NAS). The results were astonishing: "**they were continually devoting themselves to the apostles' teaching and to fellowship, to the breaking of bread and to prayer** [lit. the prayers]. **And everyone kept feeling a sense of awe; and many wonders and signs were taking place through the apostles. And all those who had believed were together, and had all things in common; and they began selling their property and possessions, and were sharing them with all, as anyone might have need. And day by day continuing with one mind in the temple, and breaking bread from house to house, they were taking their meals together with gladness and sincerity of heart, praising God, and having favor with all the people. And the Lord was adding to their number** [lit. to the church] **day by day those who were being saved**" (Acts 2:42-47 NAS).

The next reference has them praying again. Immediately after the apostles had been threatened and released by the chief priests and the elders, and returned to their own, we read: "**And when they heard this, they lifted their voices to God with <u>one accord</u>** [*homothumadon*]" (Acts 4:21-24 NAS). We can see from these first three references that the apostles and other disciples were continually praying. This last reference gives us their prayer which was so powerful that God shook the place where they were all gathered together praying. The result was that they were not only filled with the Holy Spirit again, and began to speak the Word of God with boldness, but also "[lit. **the multitude] of those who believed were of one heart and soul.**" Such great grace was upon them that they were sharing whatever they owned and selling their properties and laying it at the apostles' feet. And the apostles were distributing the proceeds and witnessing with such great power it amazes us even today! (Acts 4:25-37 NAS).

It is in this context of such an outpouring of God's grace that greed was revealed in their midst, and the judgment of God brought such fear that it produced the next reference of "**one mind, and one accord**" (Acts 5:1-16). This is very interesting, as it shows us the power of the fear of God in maintaining a true unity in purity. Ananias and Sapphira were judged for their sins of greed, lying, and putting the Spirit of the Lord to the test: by death! I might add, you will see this judgment increasingly as the end of this age comes to a close. Consequently "**great fear came upon the whole church, and upon all who heard of these things. And at the hands of the apostles many signs and wonders were taking place among** the people; and they were all with <u>one accord</u> [*homothumadon*] in Solomon's portico. But none of the rest dared to associate with them; however, the people held them in high esteem" (Acts 5:11-13 NAS).

The next occasion for this word which tells us of how the Holy Spirit of God unifies people for His purposes is when Philip preached Christ to the Samaritans. Because of the great release of the true power of God, it brought them into unity, for we read, "**the multitudes with <u>one accord</u>** [*homothumadon*] **were giving attention to what was said by Philip, as they heard and saw the signs which he was performing. For in the case of many who had unclean spirits, they were coming out of them shouting with a loud voice; and many who had been paralyzed and lame were healed. And there was much rejoicing in that city**" (Acts 8:6-8 NAS).

Now, the last occurrence in the book of Acts for "good" is when the apostles and elders met in Jerusalem with Paul and Barnabas "**to see about this word**" (lit. from 15:6) concerning whether the Gentile brethren needed to be "**circumcised according to the custom of Moses**" to "**be saved**" (Acts 15:1-6 NAS). We need to look at this portion of scripture very carefully, as many erroneous interpretations have been made concerning it; for it contains very valuable insight as to how these men functioned together under the Holy Spirit's direction and anointing. First the apostles and elders gathered together and debated among themselves the issue at hand (vv. 6-7). Then God chose Peter (an apostle and the one to whom God had first given the "**keys of the kingdom**" to open the door of salvation to the Jews and the Gentiles) to stand up and speak forth his judgment; and all the men were silent under the Holy Spirit's presence (Mt. 16:19; Acts 2; 10; 15:7-12). As the entire church continued in the apostles teaching, they remembered Peter's explanation of how God had first started saving the Gentiles, and had done so under the direction of the Holy Spirit, accompanied with His manifestations of the supernatural (Acts 2:42; 10; 11). They were reminded again through Peter that they are being saved by grace and not by keeping the Law (which no matter how right it was and how hard they tried, no one was ever able to keep, except of course the Lord Jesus), and that God is saving both themselves, as Jews, and the Gentiles by faith through the grace of the Lord Jesus (Acts 15:7-11). During the silence of the presence of the Lord, Barnabas and Paul began relating what signs and wonders God had done through them among the Gentiles, which confirmed what Peter had said (v. 12). After Barnabas and Paul stopped speaking, James arose under the Holy Spirit's anointing and confirmed with scripture what Peter had said, and then spoke forth his concluding judgment as to what they consequently should do (vv. 12-21). All of the apostles and elders agreed with James' judgment that this was what the Holy Spirit wanted done; and as they shared this with the whole church, the church also agreed that this should be done (v. 22). A letter was written from the apostles and the men who were elders, to the Gentile brethren; in it they explained that they had "**become of one mind** [*homothumadon*]," and that "**it seemed good to the Holy Spirit and to us**" what should be done (Acts 15:23, 25, 28 NAS).

What we must see from this, dear brethren, is that a serious matter of doctrine was decided only after the leaders had come to "**one mind, and one accord.**" The men who were involved were: first the apostles; and secondly the other elders of the church, the shepherds of the flock (some of whom were prophets and teachers as well) (I Cor. 12:28; Acts 15:2, 4, 6, 22-23, 32; I Pet. 5:1-4; Jam. 3:1). Peter was not the head of this meeting, the Lord Jesus was; and the Lord's presence was known and sensed through the Holy Spirit. James was not the head of this Jerusalem church, nor the president of this council of leaders, Jesus was! Peter and the other ten (James the brother of John had been put to death with the sword), and Barnabas, Paul, and James (the Lord's brother) were all apostles, recognized and respected as such; and they spoke under the anointing of the Holy Spirit. The elders understood this (the headship of the Lord Jesus Christ), how He is present in every meeting to direct and manifest Himself by His Spirit, if we will but wait upon Him and give Him and His chosen vessels their proper place.

We must do away with our church traditions that are contrary to God's word, and return to the realization that we are a kingdom with the King present. We are not a democracy or hierarchical structure of Babylonish darkness, but the very kingdom of God and light on this earth! We can have the "**light of life**," if we will open our eyes and see! But alas, our hardened hearts and selfish ambitions, our rebellious ways and demonic pride — these have blinded our eyes so that we can not see the obvious. We are like God's people of old. "**Give us a king**" that we can see with our natural eyes and hear with our natural ears, a mere man; not the One who is ever present with us, who is discerned by our spiritual eyes and spiritual ears, the very "**Lord of glory, King of kings and

Lord of lords." He is the all powerful God who is not only mighty to save, but so desirous of us having His never failing direction, instead of our fumbling failures! Let us repent! Repent now!! What is your decision, brother? Let me remind you, it has eternal consequences, both now and forever!

Now, let us continue on in the epistles to see that God is consistently exhorting us to be of "**one mind, and one accord**," and that this is not only a most important but a well established principle in His Word.

We read, "**For whatever was written in earlier times <u>was written for our instruction</u>, that through perseverance and encouragement of the Scriptures we might have hope. Now may the God who gives perseverance and encouragement grant you to be of the <u>same mind</u>** [αυτοσ φρονειν, *autos phronein*] **with one another according to Christ Jesus; that with <u>one accord</u> you may with <u>one voice</u>** [ινα ομοθυμαδον εν ενι στοματι, *hina homothumadon en eni stomati;* lit. **in order that with one accord in one mouth you may**] **glorify the God and Father of our Lord Jesus Christ**" (Rom. 15:4-6 NAS). Notice that God must grant us by His grace to be of the same mind in order that we then will be in one accord and consequently speak with one voice! We will only be of one mind when we relinquish our own and wait upon Him for His!

Paul exhorts the Corinthians also. "**Now I exhort you, brethren, by the name of our Lord Jesus Christ, that you all agree** [lit. <u>speak the same thing</u>]**, and there be no divisions** [lit. **schisms**] **among you, but you be made complete in the <u>same mind</u> and in the <u>same judgment</u>**" (I Cor. 1:10 NAS). In the second letter he again exhorts them to "**be of one mind**" (II Cor. 13:11 KJV).

To the Philippians he writes, "**Conduct yourselves in a manner worthy of the gospel of Christ; so that whether I come and see you or remain absent, I may hear of you that you are standing firm in <u>one spirit</u>, with <u>one mind</u>** [lit. **soul**] **striving together for the faith of the gospel**" (1:27 NAS). Then when he repeats this a few verses later, Paul reveals to us really how we can attain this condition. "**Fulfil ye my joy, that ye be <u>likeminded</u>** [lit. of the <u>same mind</u>]**, having the same love, being of <u>one accord</u>** [lit. **joined in soul**]**, of <u>one mind</u>** [lit. **minding one thing**]**. Let nothing be done through strife** [εριθειαν, *eritheian;* lit. **selfish ambition**] **or vainglory** [lit. **self-glory**]**; but in lowliness of mind let each esteem other** [lit. **one another as**] **better than** [υπερεχοντασ, *huperechontas;* lit. **to hold above**] **themselves. Look not every man on his own things, but every man also on the things of others.**

Let this mind be in you, which was also in Christ Jesus, who, although He existed in the form of God, did not regard equality with God a thing to be grasped [seized], but emptied Himself, taking the form of a bond-servant, and being made in the likeness of men. And being found in appearance as a man, He humbled Himself by becoming obedient to the point of death, even death on a cross. Therefore also God highly exalted Him, and bestowed on Him the name which is above every name"** (Phil. 2:2-9 KJV & NAS).

The above scripture verses give us not only the goal, the exhortation to be of **"one mind, and one accord,"** but how to attain this in the Lord. To the degree that we humble ourselves, surrendering all of self and becoming a bond-slave with no rights of our own, will we be able to walk regularly in **"one mind, and one accord."**

Now, we need to consider more carefully this business of majority rule, since it is by far the most common method of church government today. It is of the world, because the world seldom can attain to "one mind, and one accord," except when the situation is obvious. The world operates in the spirit of this world, which is the spirit of the evil one. We have four more occurrences in the book of Acts where the word *homothumadon* is used, and they are all examples of this evil.

The first occurrence is when Stephen was testifying to the unbelieving Jews and telling them they were always resisting the Holy Spirit, for they had now betrayed and murdered the Lord Jesus (Acts 7:51-60). God then gave him a vision of the heavens opening up and the Lord standing at the Father's right hand. When he told them this, Stephen was filled with the Holy Spirit, but they were filled with the spirit of the evil one; for "**Then they cried out with a loud voice, and stopped their ears, and ran upon him <u>with one accord</u>** [*homothumadon*]," and stoned him to death (Acts 7:57 KJV).

The second occurrence in Acts of the spirit of this world uniting unbelievers is when Herod "**was very angry with the people of Tyre and Sidon; and <u>with one accord</u>** [*homothumadon*] **they came to him**" seeking peace. Shortly afterward at his oratory, they tried to puff him up and gain his favor by declaring he was a god and not a man. An angel of the Lord struck him because he did not give God the glory, and so he was eaten alive with worms and died (Acts 12:20-23; Josephus has an interesting description of this: Antiquities of the Jews XIX.viii.2). Isn't it remarkable how the people of this world unite in the same spirit when their souls or their lives are at stake, as in these two incidents. But we have two more.

The third occurrence is after Paul had been teaching in Corinth for eighteen months unafraid because the Lord had revealed to him that He had many people in the city. The Jews of the synagogue had resisted the truth of the gospel and the Holy Spirit, so Paul turned away from them to the Gentiles. Then the Jews got so angry about this that they "**with one accord** [*homothumadon*] **rose up against Paul and brought him before the judgment seat**" accusing him of teaching the people to worship God contrary to the law (Acts 18:12 NAS). Gallio, the proconsul of that area, refused to hear the Jews, and drove them away from the judgment seat. Then the people took hold of Sosthenes, the new leader of the Holy Spirit rejecting congregation (the "new" leader, because the one when Paul had come had been won to Christ), and beat him right there before the judgment seat where he and the other Jews had sought punishment for Paul (Acts 18:8-17).

Can you see how the unbelieving can unite in a spirit of antichrist, particularly when envy and selfish ambition reigns in their hearts, so that they turn in a united persecution on the one who is in the true Spirit of Christ? But praise be to our God, judgment is sure, both now and forever. However, let us consider this truth and not let it happen to us, and be unbelieving believers, in persecuting those who are moving in the Holy Spirit in ways we do not understand or believe.

The fourth and last occurrence of this most interesting word in the book of Acts is of a most interesting and significant situation. Paul had been preaching in Ephesus; and a silversmith of idols gathered other craftsmen and workers of his trade, and warned them that their prosperity was in danger because Paul was "**saying that they be [are] no gods which are made with hands**" (Acts 19:26 KJV). They used a religious ploy by charging that Paul was not only turning away many from their (idolatrous) craft, but he would cause the temple of their great Babylonish goddess, Diana, to be regarded as worthless, and be dethroned from her world-wide worship and majesty. This caused Satan to move and fill them with great wrath. "**And the city** [in which, many had come to know the truth] **was filled with the <u>confusion</u>**" (Acts 19:29 NAS). This word means literally "a pouring together, a commingling," hence its translation as "confusion" or "confounding." Truth and error, the Spirit of God and the spirit of greed, had collided head on. The uproar was so great that the majority did not even know why they had all come together. It was in this state of shouting and incitement against Paul, full of rage and confusion, that "**they rushed <u>with one accord</u>** [*homothumadon*] **into the theater, dragging along Gaius and Aristarchus, Paul's traveling companions from Macedonia**" (Acts 19:29 NAS).

God marvelously preserved His servants in this exciting story. What we want to understand here is that two of the greatest bondages that men have, <u>religious traditions</u> and <u>the love of money,</u> can enable Satan to so excite a mob that they will be totally united "**in one mind, and one accord**" against the truth of God's Word. We have seen this in the four scriptural incidents given, two with antichrist Jews and two with Gentiles (one was a morally corrupt people and the other a totally Babylonish religious mob). And unfortunately this can happen in a church today that is not a true church. However, even in Babylonish Christianity, God is faithful to raise up voices of protest against error, provided this mixture of truth and error still has some who are indwelt with the Holy Spirit. But unless people humble themselves and look to their Lord and King (being sensitive to the indwelling Holy Spirit who alone can quicken us in the Spirit of truth to know His will in any matter that comes before us) the majority of Christians can and often will be in the wrong. That is why we need to wait upon the Lord until we all come into "**one mind, and one accord**."

To confirm this, let us look at the two very well known examples in scripture where the people of God acted on a majority vote instead of waiting for unanimity — and the consequences were so disastrous!

First was when Moses was told by God to send out a leader from each of the tribes of Israel to spy out the land of Canaan which He was going to give the sons of Israel (Num. 13 & 14). We remember the story, how they listened to the ten who gave an evil report rather than to the two who gave a good report. Not only was the majority wrong, it brought disastrous results. It immediately cost the ten their lives as God killed them with a plague; and then the whole congregation of God who listened to their wicked words and rebelled against the Lord were doomed to wander in the wilderness forty years (a year for every day the leaders they had listened to had spied out the land) until their carcasses would be wasted in the wilderness. What a shame!

This is a major incident in the history of God's people, so let us look at aspects of it more closely. The leaders were fearful because they judged an immediate challenge with their eyes rather than remember the greatness of God and what He had done for them in bringing them out of Egypt. The years of servitude under the Egyptians had more influence than the more recent grand and marvelous victory God had given over Pharaoh and his army. They were terrified of the giants in the land, and disregarded the fact that it would be God who could and would give them victory, not themselves.

We must have no confidence in the flesh, only in our great God! We must not listen to Satan and yield to his spirits of fear, unbelief, and rebellion. The majority of the leaders gave out an "**evil report**" by saying that they were not able to go up against the people of the land for they were too strong for them; the people were of such great size, giants! And consequently, because of a wrong spirit, they saw themselves as grasshoppers compared to their enemies; and they believed their enemies saw themselves that way also, which later would be found as a lie of the devil (Num. 13:31-33). It was afterward when Israel was to enter the land, God would put a spirit of fear upon their enemies so that their hearts would melt and be fearful of the Israelites and fearful of God for what He had done to Israel's enemies (Josh. 2:9-11). The issue is not our abilities but God's! The result of Israel's bad leadership ministering fear and unbelief to the people was that the people cried, gathered together against God, and turned upon their God appointed leadership. They murmured, complained, and wished they were either back in Egypt or dead. They rebelled and planned to appoint new leadership which would lead them according to their unbelief. When Joshua and Caleb, the minority leaders, tried to encourage the people and exhort them not to rebel nor fear, the people all agreed to stone them to death. But God intervened with His glorious presence and now "reports" on them! The people were spurning (rejecting with contempt) and not believing in Him; they had put Him to the test and not listened to His voice, in spite of seeing His signs and His glory which He had performed in Egypt. Because Moses interceded for them, God forgave them according to His mercy, but judged them according to His righteousness. They had rejected the land of promise, so they would never enter into it. They accused God of hating them, because they said their wives and children would become a prey, so their own corpses would fall in the wilderness. Because of their spiritual fornication, their children would have to suffer during God's long judgment; but their children would be the ones to eventually enter and possess the promised land. What a tragedy! The whole nation had to wander for forty years! And, except for the two faithful leaders and the innocent children, they had to die in a wilderness without ever seeing or receiving their God promised inheritance.

We can see from this story the importance of godly leadership, so let us look more carefully at theirs. First was Joshua, who from his youth was a close attendant to Moses, and faithfully followed his words and ways (Num. 11:28). Important! The other was Caleb, whom God called "**My servant**," and said that he had a "**different spirit**" and "**has followed Me fully.**" This expression, "**followed me fully**," is used seven times concerning this incident. Once it is stated that the people did not follow the Lord fully, once that Joshua and Caleb had, and five times that Caleb had (therefore, he would see and enter the promised land and gain his inheritance). Forty-five years later after entering the promised land, he won the mountain of the giants and the city of Hebron (then called Kiriath-arba, meaning "the city of Arba"; Arba being the greatest giant of all (Num. 14:24; 32:11-12; Deut. 1:36; Josh. 14:8-15).

And this is the critical issue, will we "**follow the Lord fully**" or only part way? It is obvious from the fact that God has repeated this seven perfect times that He considers this factor of utmost importance! Do we? I believe that only eternity will tell how this effects our ministries now and our eternal destiny and rewards later. "Babylon" nurtures half-hearted responses and deceives the vast majority into choosing lukewarm commitments! In fact, the theology of "Babylon" is one of comforting the lukewarm and tickling their ears; it is a "Theology of the Lukewarm!"

Now, let us learn some more lessons from the meaning of the names of the twelve spies.

First, Joshua, the son of Nun, of the tribe of Ephraim, means "Jehovah is salvation"; thus first and foremost we must follow our Savior if we are ever to enter our promised land. Moses changed his name from Hoshea meaning "Salvation" to Joshua meaning "Jehovah is salvation"; thus we must forever realize our Savior is God and God is our Savior and not any man. He was the son of Nun, which means fish; and this gives us a double witness as the word fish in Greek, *ΙΧΘΥΣ, ICHTHUS,* has an acrostic which the early Christians used which meant:

Ιησουσ Χριστοσ Θεοσ Υιοσ Σωτηρ,
Iesous Christos Theos Huios Soter,
Jesus Christ God's Son our Savior.

The leaders we follow must also be men who follow the Savior wherever He leads, and not the traditions of men. His Word, as given to us by His holy apostles and prophets, both from the scriptures and from others past and present, must be our guide as we and our leaders follow under Christ's headship. He is our military Commander-in-chief and we must make a commitment to **"follow the Lord fully."** We can not stress this enough. Ephraim means "fruitful"; and when we are truly led by our Savior, we will always be fruitful in whatever we do.

Second is Caleb, the son of Jephunneh, of the tribe of Judah. The meaning of Caleb is uncertain, but it is believed to mean either "dog" or "bold." Either way, we must have that faithful characteristic of a dog's loving service and commitment to his master until death, which Caleb certainly had; as well as faith in God, and boldness to take on the biggest giants of them all, praise the Lord! He was the son of Jephunneh meaning "it will be prepared," and his father had undoubtedly prepared him well. He was of the tribe of Judah, which means "praise"; and we must always go forth with praise to our God. We saw this shortly after they entered the promised land and shouted the victory as the walls of Jericho, which means "fragrant," came tumbling down miraculously. What a sweet smelling <u>fragrance</u> to our God when we are <u>prepared</u> and go forth <u>faithfully</u> and <u>boldly</u> in <u>praise</u>, <u>following</u> our <u>Savior</u> <u>fully</u> to reap a <u>fruitful harvest</u>.

Now for the ten rebellious spies and what we must not be if we are to enter into our promised land now.

The first is Shammua the son of Zaccur from the tribe of Reuben. Shammua means "one that is heard," "heard-about," or "renowned" or "fame." And certainly this spy was being heard, busy talking, instead of listening. He was talking unbelief, fear, and rebellion rather than listening to what God had said, was saying, or was about to do. He missed it forever! And how many leaders miss God for the same reason. Just look and observe how many are busy talking, preaching and teaching, and doing so little listening to God — doing so little hiding away in their prayer closet to listen for the only One who can lead into victory and fruitfulness. And then it can mean one who loves to be heard and be famous. What shame is being brought upon the body of Christ by those with such selfish ambition and pride. But God will shake everything and everyone, and only those who are building upon the unshakable rock of Christ's words and His kingdom will see it through these last days (Mt. 7:15-27; Heb. 12:25-29). This talker was the son of Zaccur meaning "thoughtful," and "mindful," which makes me laugh. How he wishes he had been more thoughtful of what he said and of God's instruction and power, than of his observations and the conclusions of his own mind in the promised land. He was from the tribe of Reuben, which means "behold a son." Here again we need to hear what God is saying; and that is to "behold The Son," our Lord, Savior, Head, and our Commander-in-chief who always causes us to triumph in Himself. Too many are beholding "their son" and what they have produced and not what God has produced.

The second wicked spy is Shaphat the son of Hori from the tribe of Simeon. Shaphat means "he hath judged," and God certainly did. Because of his leading the people of God in rebellion, he was judged unworthy to even live. He was the son of Hori, which means "cave-dweller"; and how many men have been brought into ministry, birthed by men who when they see trouble, go find a hole to hide in. And some are so fearful they even learn to live there. We must be bold and believe God; we must be as Caleb who said, **"Let us go up at once, and possess it; for we are well able to overcome it"** (Num. 13:30 KJV). Simeon means "heard"; and we repeat, we must listen to what we have heard God say to us, and do what he has told us to do, and not listen to our own fears and circumstances. They had mightily been delivered from Egypt by following what God had said through their leader Moses, in spite of what looked like an impossible situation at the Red Sea with Pharaoh's army storming down upon them; but God had spoken, and so delivered them according to His word. They now rebelled against His word spoken through Moses, took a majority vote, because they would not be persuaded to follow God's way, and perished! Shaphat! "He hath judged!"

Next is Igal the son of Joseph from the tribe of Issachar. Igal means "He Redeems"; and we are reminded of what happens when we get our eyes off our Redeemer and upon the enemy, we fail. His father's name, Joseph means "may he add, or increase"; and how we need to be reminded that our heavenly father wants to add to us so that we increase, but He will not when we are disobedient and unbelieving. Issachar means "he will bring a reward" or "there is recompense"; and here we need to be reminded again from "our fathers" that there is recompense with God — success and blessing for obedient faith, and judgment and death for unbelief and disobedience.

Next is Palti the son of Raphu from the tribe of Benjamin.

Palti means "deliverance," and is an abbreviation of Paltiel meaning "deliverance of God." How God is trying to drive home the point that there is no deliverance without Him, that we must not leave Him out of the picture, that there is no abbreviated way for victory, that we must keep our eyes on Him and follow Him completely!

We could continue making application from the meaning of names but since this is not the emphasis of this teaching, we will give you the meanings and leave the rest to you. Raphu means "healed" and Benjamin means "son of the right hand."

Next is Gaddiel the son of Sodi from the tribe of Zebulun. Gaddiel means "God is my fortune," Sodi means "intimate," and Zebulun means "habitation."

Next is Gaddi the son of Susi from the tribes of Joseph and Manasseh. Gaddi means "my fortune," Susi means "a horseman," Joseph means "may he add, or increase," and Manasseh means "forgetting."

Next is Ammiel the son of Gemalli from the tribe of Dan. Ammiel means "my kinsman is God," Gemalli means "abundance," and Dan means "judge."

Next is Sethur the son of Michael from the tribe of Asher. Sethur means "hidden," Michael means "who is like God?" and Asher means "happy."

Next is Nahbi the son of Vophsi from the tribe of Naphtali. Nahbi means "concealed," Vophsi means "additional," and Naphtali means "my wrestling."

Next is Geuel the son of Machi from the tribe of Gad. Geuel means "majesty of El (God)," and Machi possibly means "pining" or "bought," and Gad means "fortune."

Now that we have seen the meaning of the names of the spies and some application, let us look briefly at the meaning of the names of the men God chose Himself to represent the tribes of Israel as they entered to possess the promised land. The first twelve the people had asked for, and Moses appointed them from the leaders the people had chosen (Deut. 1:13-15; 22-24; Num. 13:1-16); but now after forty years the Lord chose them. When the tribes of Reuben, Gad, and part of the half tribe of Manasseh decided to stay on the east side of the Jordan for their inheritance, God chose a priest, plus a leader over all, and a leader for each of the remaining nine and a half tribes Himself (Num. 34:13-29). Moses, which means "drawn out" because he was drawn out of the water, represents one of us as we are drawn out and born of the waters of baptism. As one of us, Moses' choices were the best that a human being could make because he was the meekest man upon the face of the whole earth, referring to his humble, submissive obedience. But his choices could not be compared with the choices that God made. This is now to be done by Jesus, who is not subject to the limitations of human frailty, but is omniscient, omnipresent, and omnipotent; who will always cause us to triumph! What a lesson to learn!

The first man God chose is Eleazar the priest. Eleazar means "God has helped"; and in those days the priests were the ones who inquired of the Lord for His Word and direction. When we function properly with the priests of God, the special prayer warriors interceding before and during the battles of the Lord, God will help us on to victory every time in battling for our promised land.

God's next choice is Joshua the son of Nun, "Jehovah our Savior," whom Moses chose as representative leader of the tribe of Ephraim, but God chose as the commander-in-chief of the whole nation of Israel (Num. 27:15-23). Eleazar as high priest, Joshua as the leader of the nation, and Moses as lawgiver stand in representation of Jesus who is now our High Priest, Commander-in-chief, and King. The Lord spoke to Moses saying that Eleazar and Joshua shall apportion the promised land to each tribe for inheritance; now, Jesus Christ is our High Priest and Commander-in-chief giving gifts as promised unto men. The Lord also said to Moses to "take **one leader** of every tribe to apportion the [promised] land for inheritance" to that tribe (Num. 34:17-18 NAS). From this we may be able to see a picture of the grace of God flowing from Christ, to leaders chosen of God, and then to the people.

Then the first leader chosen by God of the twelve tribes was again Caleb, of the tribe of Judah, the son of Jephunneh. After forty years, he was doubly "prepared," and his "faithfulness" and "boldness" in following the Lord fully was fully rewarded.

Then God chose a leader for the tribe of Simeon, Samuel the son of Ammihud. Samuel means "name of God"; and this is the only name we can go forward in, to obtain victory. So many try to go in their own name or one they have made up, and end up defeated. Ammihud is from "Ammi" meaning "my people" or "kinsman," plus "glory" or "majesty" or "praiseworthiness." Compounded it tells us that we must be a people that are praiseworthy if we want to enter our "promised land." Individually we must be born of a people that are praiseworthy. That is, we must be a part of a church fellowship of trusted, faithful saints that are upholding us in prayer, if we are to go forward in victory. And we are to do all, from and to the glory of God.

For the tribe of Benjamin, God chose Elidad the son of Chislon as leader. Elidad means "God has loved," and Chislon means "hope." Jesus tells us that those who have God's commandments and keep them are the ones He loves and will manifest Himself to in victory — and these certainly are the only ones born of hope. Hallelujah!

And for the tribe of Dan, God chose a leader, Bukki the son of Jogli. Bukki means possibly "tested," and Jogli means "led captive" or "exiled." We must be reminded that only those who have been tested and proven faithful will enter the promised land, others will be led captive to Babylon.

God chose a leader for the tribe of Manasseh, Hanniel the son of Ephod. Hanniel means "favor or grace of God"; and Ephod means "a covering," and it was the name of the holy garment that the priests wore. Without question we need the grace of God, the unmerited favor of our God. There is no victory except by the grace of God! And as we grow in grace we will come to realize that we must be covered. As priests of God, we must worship before Him **"in holy attire"**; we must be dressed in a holy manner according to His word (I Chr. 16:29; Psa. 96:9; 110:3). God has clothed Himself in **"splendor and majesty,"** and He covers Himself **"with light as with a cloak"** (Psa. 104:1-2). He has promised that **"His glory shall be seen upon thee [us]"** as we take Him seriously and clothe ourselves in both positional and practical righteousness and holiness (Isa. 60:1-2 KJV).

God chose a leader for the tribe of Ephraim, Kemuel the son of Shiphtan. Kemuel means "assembly of God," and Shiphtan means "judging." Here we have a very significant revelation, because if we are to go forward in victory, we must go forward as a true assembly of God which is born of judgment. This is a big lack in the church today. Leadership for the most part does not teach the necessity of judging ourselves so as to be pure, holy vessels; and it does not judge sin in the congregation so as to keep it pure and holy. We must judge sin, and (when not repented of) purge out the old leaven, and have no fellowship with the works of darkness. We must remove those from the assembly of God who are living in gross sins, or we will be defeated as a people! (Josh. 7, I Cor. 5 & 6).

God chose a leader for the tribe of Zebulun, Elizaphan the son of Parnach. Elizaphan means "God has concealed," and the meaning of Parnach is uncertain to many scholars, but one I discovered believes it means "very nimble." God has concealed many things from us, and that is why we must not only seek His face earnestly and persistently, but we must continue until we come to **"one mind, and one accord."** Often our timing for some action is not yet right, and by withholding unanimity He stops us from proceeding before He is ready. How many wrong decisions have been hastily made by majority vote, only to be found out later that if they had only waited a little longer — God had wonderful results for them. God has concealed even the meaning of Elizaphan's father's name to some to underscore the importance of this most valuable principle of God's methods for success under His headship! However, to those who are nimble, quick in apprehension, His will and wisdom will be revealed.

God chose a leader for the tribe of Issachar, Paltiel the son of Azzan. Paltiel means "deliverance of God," and Azzan means "strong." Here we have the revelation that we will have our deliverance of God, and that it will be born out of His strength. Formerly, the unbelieving spy's name was "Palti" meaning simply "deliverance," as his eyes were not on the Lord; and his father's name was Raphu, meaning "healed," which tells us we need to be healed from this untrusting attitude which always leads to disaster.

God chose a leader for the tribe of Asher, Ahihud the son of Shelomi. Ahihud means "brother of renown or majesty," and Shelomi means "peaceful." It is absolutely necessary that we see first, Jesus, our brother of glorious majesty and renown; and then that we see also all of our brothers and sisters in Christ as children of the Most High God, fellow heirs of the grace of life and the majestic future Our Majesty has for us all. This will be born out of our striving, not with one another, but to be "peaceful" with one another. This is a result of finding our contentment, our happiness, in Him and Him alone; which is why God chose this faithful one from the tribe of Asher, meaning "happy."

God chose a leader for the tribe of Naphtali, Pedahel the son of Ammihud. Pedahel means "God saves," and Ammihud as before means "my people of glory" or "majesty" or "praiseworthiness." As these faithful leaders will be led by Joshua, meaning "Jehovah our Savior," so also the last man is emphasizing to us this essential truth, that "God saves." We do not need to fear our enemies no matter how big and strong they appear to be. Jesus saves! God saves! This truth is birthed in our hearts and becomes a steadfast practical truth when we are part of a "praiseworthy, glorious, majestic people." This is the second father to be named Ammihud, and thus we close this explanation of names by re-emphasizing the absolute necessity of being knit together in love with a people worthy of God's praises; for He instructs us not to forsake assembling ourselves together as the habit of those who will be defeated, but to assemble in order to stimulate one another to love and good deeds, and to encourage one another all the more as we see the end of this age drawing near (Heb. 10:24-25).

Having examined the meaning of the names of the ten rebellious leaders (who **"restrained the hearts"** of an **"entire generation"** of God's people so that they all did **"evil in the sight of the Lord,"** and thus were **"destroyed"**), and the meaning of the names of the faithful leaders who forty years later successfully led their children into the promised land, we see the extreme importance of listening to God and following Him fully, and not operating by a majority vote to determine the mind and will of God! (Num. 32:7-13).

Now, let us look at the second major time that the children of Israel rebelled against God and demanded the will of the majority. Instead of listening to His voice through His chosen vessel and following Him fully, they followed the vast majority and the entire nation suffered for centuries.

Israel at the time had been ruled for approximately four hundred years by God through judges. It was the time when Samuel, the prophet of God, was coming to the end of his life, and he appointed his sons to help in judging Israel. However, they did not walk in his ways. They perverted justice by taking bribes, and the elders of Israel came to Samuel to solve the problem. However, instead of coming to him to inquire of God as to what to do, they came with their minds made up: they had their own solution. They asked that Samuel would give them a king to rule over them like all the other nations. Now these were heathen, ungodly nations that they wanted to imitate; and it displeased Samuel very much, so he sought God. God told him what I believe is one of the most tragic testimonies in all of the Word of God. God said that the people had not rejected Samuel, but they had actually rejected Him! They had rejected God as their king, and were asking instead that a mere man be appointed king to rule over them like all of the other nations (which of course did not have God as their king). Can you imagine anything so foolhardy? So stupid?

Yet we are doing it today in the church by the millions. We are refusing to allow our wonderful Lord Jesus Christ to rule us and act as our head; instead we are appointing fallible, feeble men to act as our head in His place. We do this by rejecting the principle of unanimity, "**one mind, and one accord**"; and we have chosen to follow the world's system of democratic vote to determine the will of God! How tragic! How stupid! How ignorant we are of God's ways and desires to bless us with Christ Jesus as our head and King. Most congregations miss God in this because they have never been taught the way of God; and having not sought Him in this, they just follow the multitudes that are following each other instead of following the Lord. We are not to follow the multitude in doing evil (Ex. 23:2) — and that is what God calls this. He called it evil when the ten spies refused to follow His word and encouraged the nation to follow the majority report. He called it evil for the nation to do so. He calls it evil today!

What is significant here is several things. The people were rejecting God as their King. For us this means Christ as Lord and Head, King of kings and Lord of lords. He is head of His body, which is the church, and no man must ever take or presume this place. But it is being done constantly. Secondly, they rejected God's rulership over them because they wanted to be like the world. Thirdly, all the people of God were wrong except one man of God! All of the leaders had persuaded all of the people, and this amounted to millions of people; but one man had the mind and heart of God, Samuel! This was not just a simple majority, this was all against one; the one just so happened to be standing with God Almighty. God told Samuel to warn them of what the king they would get would do, and it came to pass.

And what happens to us today? We are oppressed as a people! in church and out. We are as salt without saltiness, as far as our society is concerned. We see God's laws being removed from the books, schools, and government because it has been removed from "The Church." Leadership will not come together to pray and seek the mind of God for their nation, cities, congregations, individuals, or even themselves, for the most part. We are too busy building our own little kingdoms, or else, just too self-indulgent to pray and fast for God's help. "The spirit is willing, but the flesh is weak," Jesus told His chosen apostles; and the same is true with us all today! Therefore we must gather and pray as He said. If we continue to refuse and rebel, only God knows what He will do. Let us cry out for mercy and grace to help us in this desperate time of need!

Another significant thing that the Lord told Samuel was that the people had forsaken Him and were serving other gods. We are serving the gods of materialism, mammon, ease and luxury, sex, and every conceivable idol there is; and we are in Babylonish bondage. We are serving the gods of Babylon, and following the Babylonish ways of life! Instead of the Almighty God, it is the almighty dollar! We hoard it, pull down our "barns" to build bigger, and use the money from the purse as if it was our own, like Judas. Oh, we need God! The kings we have set up, use us, just like those prophesied by Samuel, by taking the tithe that is both Holy and the Lord's, for their own kingdoms! We either set up a king over us, or rule by majority; but we do not allow Christ, who is our head, to rule over us. But He does; and so we reap the sad consequences, both for the present and at the judgment seat of Christ someday — if we make it there! "**Many that are first shall be last**," and that is for changing only the least of His commandments and so teaching others; thus many shall be left out completely!

The whole history of Israel after this event, the history of human kings ruling God's people, is a reminder of the consequences of rejecting the Lordship and headship of Jesus Christ. The church fathers not only persecuted the prophets, but they killed those who preached about the coming of Jesus (Acts 7:52). One king tried to kill the baby Jesus Himself, and the leaders finally did succeed in killing Him! But our God reigns, and turned it into a blessing for the world; but what of those who were guilty?

Today, I have been witness to many groups, congregations, and men who have rejected the headship of Jesus Christ by rejecting unanimity, "**one mind, and one accord**"; and I have seen the tragic results. Also, because God calls us to unity in His word, we must realize that there is a unity which we can accomplish our way, but then there is a unity which God accomplishes His way, and they are quite different.

When I first came to Columbus, I was invited to speak in the largest church moving in the flow of the Holy Spirit. The Lord told me to give the message on "Unanimity," which I did. No one said anything to me, but the leadership failed to heed the Word. Within just a few years, the congregation was torn apart by strife and selfish ambition, and the people scattered; it is now a showcase for the glory that once was. If they had listened to God's Word, man could not have had his way and destroyed the beautiful work that God was doing. Sin became rampant and the House of God became a house of wickedness. King "Saul" ruled, and the Lord moved on.

Another experience was when a congregation I was very familiar with ceased to operate by unanimity when serious differences arose. Instead of calling on an apostle to settle differences, they called on carnal leadership for advice; and the congregation was totally destroyed.

I have seen God raise men up in ministry and instruct them in plurality of leadership; only to see them go, when difficulty arose, for advice from a leader in "one-man-ministry" (such as "the pastor is head" type) rather than to their God appointed oversight. Consequently, when they chose to practice a "one-man-ministry," God judged; and after removing most of the people and they still did not repent, He removed them from that ministry. God will tolerate a "one-man-ministry" for a time when that is all the people know and have been taught, but when a congregation begins with enlightenment and true apostolic teaching and leadership, He will not allow rebellion to go on forever. He will come and remove the candlestick out of its place!

I have seen many small home groups raised up and flourishing, until some man or men rise up against the leadership that God has ordained, and then the ministry dissolves. It literally dries up and is quietly disbanded.

I was asked to be a part of an organization which operated (among the trustees) on the principle of this teaching from the very beginning, and it was very successful. But when the chosen leader rebelled and afterward rejected the "Headship of Christ," everyone resigned but him. He then chose new leaders that had money and worldly position, like organizations that he had been in before, and began operating by the world's democratic method like them. But of course God judged him and he failed, and a very important ministry failed with him. What is tragic is that it had been originally operating with apostles and prophets and elders who fasted and prayed weekly; and this was exchanged for "the way other church organizations do it," with "monied" and "distinguished" people voting on the will of God by majority vote. It went from continual success, until rebellion came in, to the inevitable win and loss record like Israel of old, and then destruction. When Israel followed their prophets they never failed! When they sinned and rebelled, they were in and out of bondages continually; and when they did not repent, the nation was destroyed. What a shame that the church is not mature enough to practice and teach the truth, and prevent such sad circumstances.

It needs to be added that when sin enters in and repentance

is refused, a ministry of faith will find the chastening hand of the Lord quickly, usually on its finances. Then if leadership repents, God restores; but if not, the ministry will either be dissolved, destroyed, or changed drastically until it learns the ways of the Lord. Often when money dries up, men go to carnal methods of fund raising rather than to repent of the sin causing the financial drought and trust God again for His sufficiency. And thus we have so many carnal organizations, ministries, congregations, and so forth, that never will amount to much in the kingdom of God because they do not operate by kingdom principles! The sad thing is that most of the church is so carnal they do not know the difference between the ways of the flesh and the ways of the Spirit. Like Corinth of old, we reject humble apostles (like Paul, who gave everything, and never received from them any financial support whatsoever) and readily accept false ones; and the scripture is fulfilled again which was given to them, "**For you bear with anyone if he enslaves you, if he devours you, if he takes advantage of you, if he exalts himself, if he hits you in the face**" (II Cor. 11:20 NAS). How tragic, but our God reigns!

I have seen other kinds of ministries built by God; and then when important decisions have to be made, agreement is thrown out the window, as the self-willed push their agenda. God has to bring the whole thing then or eventually to a halt. As this was being written, a Christian school was dissolved because of this very thing. We often do not see the hand of God because of the way or the time frame that He works in. When unanimity is rejected and some man or men insist on having their own way, God sometimes (in fact often) lets us have our way; but we will not like the result in the long run.

I remember one beautiful house fellowship God raised up, and when the carnal stepped in and spoke up, the leader was pushed to give them a building according to their traditions and desires. As the revelation of the Lord and His Word were being rejected, the leader was given the word, "**And He gave them their request; but sent leanness into their soul**" (Psa. 106:15 KJV). God did just that, but it took several years of struggle and leanness in their building before that ministry was dissolved and brought to naught. Oh, what lessons we have to learn the hard way!

In fact, one long-time ministry, because of rejecting unanimity, was brought to an end the very week I received another copy of brother G. H. Lang's book, *The Churches of God* , containing chapter XI on "Unanimity." [Since I had lost track of my first copy many years before, and it had gone out of print, I had been praying for years for another copy. I also continued to pray for a re-printing. While writing this teaching I not only found that the Lord had answered by raising up another to re-print the book, but also to reprint brother Lang's original booklet, *Unanimity: The Divine Method Of Church Government*, which I urge you strongly to read and consider.]

We could continue with many testimonies, as I am sure you possibly could, of how people have rejected this apostolic practice and reaped the sad consequences. Therefore, let us consider a little more of the practical consequences of doing so.

When we operate by the principle of "**one mind, and one accord**" or "**unanimity**," we are practicing the headship of Jesus Christ as head of His church. We will all be naturally looking to Him for guidance, and His will in everything. However, when we use the principle of the world and fallen man of majority rule (because they do not have the Spirit of God within to bring them into godly unity) we will be constantly tempted to walk in the flesh in order to have a majority that will agree with us, as we will be aware that it is a majority of us who will decide what is the Lord's will rather than being sensitive to the necessity of everyone coming into the knowledge of His will together. There will be temptations to persuade each other by carnal means; pressures will be brought by some in order to get their way because that will work on the majority of people. But it will not work on the spiritual, and those are the ones who most often naturally have the mind of the Lord in the first place. It should not be too difficult to see that the majority of God's people are carnal, and not spiritual! Paul called all of the Corinthians carnal, and yet they had every gift and every calling available from God! Carnal methods stimulate carnality; spiritual methods stimulate spirituality!

When we look at the works of the flesh as given to us in Galatians Five, we find that right after the soul damning sins of immorality and spiritual wickedness, and right before murders, drunkenness, and such like, we have a list of sins that are not as often thought of or taken as seriously as these others. But right here in the very midst of these damning works of the flesh we find a list that is most significant to our study as they are encouraged by the carnal methods of majority voting which so much of the church has followed the world in practicing.

Let us quote the passage and then study these various

activities that destroy men's souls and carnally organized ministries of the church.

> "**Now the works of the flesh are manifest, which are these; adultery, fornication, uncleanness, lasciviousness, idolatry, witchcraft, hatred, variance, emulations, wrath, strife, seditions, heresies, envyings, murders, drunkenness, revellings, and such like: of the which I tell you before, as I have also told you in time past, that they which do such things shall not inherit the kingdom of God.**" (Gal. 5:19-21 KJV)

First we have the sin of "**hatred**" (KJV), "**enmities**" (NAS), which is from the plural form of the Greek word εχθρα, *echthra,* which is defined as "discord, feud, a principle or state of enmity" (The Analytical Greek Lexicon, AGL); and the state of one who is "hostile, hating and opposing another" (Thayer's *Greek English Lexicon*). The dictionary defines "hate" as: "to dislike greatly, to have a great aversion to" (Webster's 1828 *American Dictionary of the English Language*) and "to regard with a strong or passionate dislike" (*American College Dictionary*, ACD). (As we go through these sins and come to understand them more clearly, we might need to stop and do some repenting ourselves!)

The next sin is "**variance**" (KJV), "**strife**" (NAS), from the plural of the Greek word ερισ, *eris,* which means "contention, strife, wrangling" (Thayer's) and "discord" (Bauer, Arndt, and Gingrich Lexicon, BAG), and the verb form means "to quarrel, to wrangle, to use the harsh tone of a wrangler or brawler" (AGL). The dictionary defines "variance" as "difference that produces dispute or controversy; disagreement; dissension; discord" (Webster's 1828).

Next we have "**emulations**" (KJV), "**jealousy**" (NAS), from the plural of ζηλοσ, *zelos,* which means "jealousy, envy, malice" (AGL) and "an envious and contentious rivalry, jealousy" (Thayer's). Webster gives us a very interesting and significant definition of the word "emulation" in regards to majority voting, and it can be especially noticed in voting for the leadership of a board of trustees, elders, or deacons, as it is defined as: "The act of attempting to equal or excel in qualities or actions; rivalry; desire of superiority, attended with effort to attain to it" and "a striving to equal or do more than others to obtain carnal favors or honors. Gal. v"; also, "contest; contention; strife; competition; rivalry accompanied with a desire of depressing another" (Webster's 1828). Boy, does this ever picture politics, and in the church it is so grievous and tragic!

The next work of the flesh is "**wrath**" (KJV), "**outbursts of anger**" (NAS), from the Greek word θυμοι, *thumoi*, which means "impulses and outbursts of anger"; the singular form is *thumos* which means "passion, angry heat, anger forthwith boiling up and soon subsiding again" (Thayer's).

Next we have a sin that is very important to recognize and reject as it is so common and destructive, and was evident at the tower of Babel. It is εριθεια, *eritheia*, translated "**strife**" (KJV), and "**disputes**" (NAS), but is more properly translated "**selfish ambition**" elsewhere in the NAS (Rom. 2:8; Phil. 1:17, 2:3; Jam. 3:14, 16). One of the Thayer's lexicon definitions of this word is: "used of those who electioneer for office, courting popular applause by trickery and low arts; the verb is derived from εριθοσ, *erithos*: working for hire, a hireling." Thayer also defines it as, "a courting distinction, a desire to put one's self forward, a partisan and factious spirit which does not disdain low arts; partisanship, factiousness." The BAG lexicon adds "disputes or outbreaks of selfishness." Bullinger says in his lexicon, "labour for wages, canvassing, intriguing, party-spirit, faction," and "work for gain, any work for ambitious purposes." Now if this does not picture for us politics today and forever! And that is what we have introduced into the church when we have decided to operate by majority vote, a political process. Consequently we will not only arouse the carnal nature, but provide for Satan an opportunity to use all kinds of unrighteous methods and manifest all types of evil spirits.

The next work of the flesh is διχοστασιαι, *dichostasiai*, "**seditions**" (KJV), "**dissensions**" (NAS), and the singular form is defined as "dissension, division," from the word διχοστατεω, *dichostateo*, "to stand apart" (Thayer's); and we have introduced this also by majority vote. We have not only produced a division by voting, the enemy moves to stir up the carnal nature and all of his hellish activity comes forth. Anyone with any experience can tell of situations they have been involved in or know about where deep divisions occurred between men who otherwise would have been, and previously were, standing together. The root words from which we get this word is διχαζω, *dichazo*, meaning "to cleave, to cut asunder"; and στασια, *stasia*, meaning "standing, station, state"; and so we create the state where men have been cleaved into two or even more factions, where men "stand apart," and unfortunately may never come back together.

Next we have the plural of the word αιρεσισ, *hairesis*, which is translated "**heresies**" (KJV), and "**factions**" (NAS), and literally means "choosing, a choice, that which is chosen, a chosen course of thought and action; hence one's chosen opinion, tenet; according to the context, an opinion varying from the true exposition of the Christian faith (heresy) [II Pet. 2:1]"; and it can also mean "a body of men separating themselves from others and following their own tenets — a sect or party [Acts 5:17; 15:5; 24:5, 14; 26:5; 28:22; I Cor. 11:19; Gal. 5:20; a heretic, Tit. 3:10]" (Thayer's). In actual practice, any one or group that teaches something unacceptable to others is sometimes called a heretic by those others, even though the teaching is not false (Acts 24:5, 14; 28:22). It is not difficult to see that heresies, factions, are just what is promoted by majority voting because instead of men seeing themselves as one group seeking the mind of the Lord together, they will divide into factions seeking to get the most votes for their positions. And when this sinful attitude gets a real hold on men, it is amazing how they will create little parties, and deceive, and very cleverly manipulate people and such things as "Robert's Rules of Order" to get <u>their own chosen</u> positions passed. It is simply deplorable and disgusting, very grievous indeed! And since we live in a democracy where politics is such a way of life, men do the most dishonorable things thinking it is honorable, because after all, they have "the mind of the Lord" on matters, not the other "parties." But Jesus said, "**that which is highly esteemed among men is abomination in the sight of God**" (Lu. 16:15 KJV); and Paul wrote in this regard, "**they which do such things shall not inherit the kingdom of God**" (Gal. 5:21 KJV). Truly this is one of those "**evil works**" that James wrote about where their is "**envy**" and "**selfish ambition**" (Jam. 3:16 KJV/NAS).

And this brings us to the last work of the flesh in this series, "**envyings**" (KJV) from the Greek word φθονοι, *phthonoi*, which the NAS translates "**envying**" in the singular, and means "envy, jealousy, spite" (AGL), "ill-will"; and is "probably akin to the base of" the word φθιω, *phthio*, which means "to pine, waste, shrivel, wither, spoil, ruin" and morally "to deprave, corrupt, defile, [and] destroy" (Strong's *Greek Dictionary of the New Testament*). Webster defines the verb "envy" as: "to feel uneasiness, mortification or discontent, at the sight of superior excellence, reputation or happiness enjoyed by another; to repine at another's prosperity; to fret or grieve one's self at the real or supposed superiority of another and to hate [greatly dislike] him on that account." The noun "envy" reveals in addition that it is "accompanied with some degree of hatred or malignity, and often or usually with a desire or an effort to depreciate the person, and with pleasure in seeing him depressed [also: made powerless, having no authority in a matter, voted down or out]. Envy springs from pride, ambition or love, mortified that another has obtained what one has a strong desire to possess. Emulation differs from envy, in not being accompanied with hatred and a desire to depress a more fortunate person" (Webster's 1828). He gives an older definition of envy as: "rivalry, competition." This was one of the sins of the religious leaders who opposed Jesus (Mt. 27:18; Mk. 15:10), and also a sin that even preachers of the gospel had who opposed Paul the apostle (Phil. 1:15). Times have not changed, as people have not changed, and we can see these works of the flesh not only prevalent but promoted by changing God's kingdom from a theocracy (recognizing Christ as the head in our midst and uniting in "**one mind, and one accord**") into a democracy (voting-in our opinions as the will of God)! We must repent, as God is holding us accountable for how we conduct the affairs of His kingdom, and His judgment is both now and later! Let us seek Him in the "fear of the Lord" else He come and remove our candlestick out of its place (Rev. 2:5)! Let us fall upon the rock and be broken, least He come and grind us to powder (Mt. 21:44; Lu. 20:18)!

So we have seen why the works of the flesh as given to us in Galatians Five, "**hatred, variance, emulations, wrath, strife, seditions, heresies, envyings**," become present when we operate by majority vote and produce factions, and how Satan can then come in and really do his destructive work! When men do not repent of these works of the flesh, nor start doing what God has told them to do and how He has told them to do it, then they will often and eventually have the Spirit of God taken from them like Saul; and then the other works of the flesh like immorality or fornication, impurity, sensuality, drunkenness, carousing, and even sorcery can enter into a man's life and he will be destroyed!

Have you ever noticed how Boards or leaders are often selected? Those chosen are usually not those who will seek God for His will and stand strong for what they believe; maybe they were selected because they will vote the way the choosing man or men vote, or they can be manipulated or easily persuaded of anything, or maybe they have money or standing in the community, or maybe they have some other material or even spiritual contribution that they can make to profit the ministry. But, were

216

they men of God's own choosing?!!

It would be helpful to add here three other types of sin brought to our attention in the scripture that are encouraged by majority voting to determine the will of God. They are very serious sins as they will damn one's soul if not repented of and keep anyone out of the kingdom of God. These sins are found in I Corinthians Chapters Five and Six where we find a list of people with those habitual and unrepented of sins that when found in anyone professing to be a believer they are to be put out of the church and chastened, as they are unfit for the fellowship of God and His people (I Cor. 5:2, 7, 9, 11-13; 6:9-10). [The practice of putting away from among God's people those who commit serious sin is quoted here from many references in the scriptures such as Deut. 13:5; 17:7, 12; 19:19; 21:21; 22:21, 22, 24; 24:7].

The first sin revealed to us in I Corinthians Five that is inspired in the Babylonian and worldly way of majority voting is covetous**ness**, or greed. A covetous person, the word in Greek is πλεονεκτησ, *pleonektes,* meaning "*covetous,*" is "one eager to have more, especially what belongs to others; one greedy of gain" (Thayer's); and "one who has or claims to have more than his share; one who defrauds for the sake of gain" (AGL). The Lord Jesus warned us to: "**Beware, and be on your guard against every form of greed; for not even when one has an abundance does his life consist of his possessions**" (Lu. 12:15 NAS). And this eager desire for more is not just for money or material possessions, it can be for position and power, as Korah, Dathan, and Abiram envied Moses and Aaron and coveted their positions (Num. 16).

The second sin revealed to us here is "railing" or "reviling." The Greek verb λοιδορεω, *loidoreo,* means "to reproach, rail at, revile, heap abuse upon" (Thayer's). The dictionaries define "rail" as: "to utter reproaches, to scoff, to use insolent and reproachful language, to reproach or censure in opprobrious terms" (Webster's 1828); and "to utter bitter complaint or vehement denunciation" (ACD). These dictionaries define "revile" as: "to reproach, to treat with opprobrious and contemptuous language" (Webster's 1828); and "to speak abusively, to regard as vile" (ACD).

The third sin revealed to us here that is encouraged by majority voting is a form of the sin of "**e**xtortion." The verb in Greek, αρπαζω, *harpazo,* meaning "to *extort,*" is defined: "to seize on, to claim for one's self eagerly, to carry off by force; to snatch away" (Thayer's). It is very interesting that the *The American College Dictionary* (ACD) defines extortion as: "*Law.* The crime of obtaining money or other things of value [such as position, authority, etc.] under cover of office [abuse of an office], when none is due or not so much is due, or before it is due." It defines the verb "extort": "*Law.* To wrest or wring (something) from a person by violence, intimidation, or abuse of authority; obtain (money, information, etc.) by force, torture, threat, or the like. To take illegally under cover of office." This word is translated in the New American Standard as "swindle," which is defined by this dictionary: "To cheat; to put forward plausible [having an appearance of truth or reason; seemingly worthy of approval or acceptance] schemes or use unscrupulous artifice [a crafty device, a clever stratagem (a stratagem is a plan, scheme, or trick for deceiving the enemy; a strategy is the skillful management in getting the better of an adversary or attaining an end)] to defraud others; anything deceptive" (ACD). I have experienced this form of extortion as deceit, clever manipulation of the "rules," and distortion of an organization's constitution have resulted in the self-willed and rebellious getting their way. The Church is grieved as the Supreme Court of this land and Federal judges distort the plain and true meaning of our Constitution and laws, and yet it does the same thing! This is a fulfillment of the "law of sowing and reaping"! (Gal. 6:7).

So we can see by the meaning of these words, "covetousness," "greed," "rail," "revile," "extortion," and "swindle," that majority voting to determine the will of God among "elders" or "Boards" can and often results in damnable sins that do not accomplish the will of God, but rather the will of our adversary, "**Satan . . . the accuser of our brethren . . . who accuses them before our God** [and through one another] **day and night**" (Rev. 12:9-10 NAS).

I have personally experienced the working of these sins in majority voting and the "demonic conspiracy" that arises when "**bitter jealousy and selfish ambition**" grip the hearts and minds of people, and together with "**arrogance**" they "**lie against the truth**" (Jam. 3:14-15 NAS). James writes that this wisdom does not come from God, but is of the earth, the way of the world, it is ψυχικη, *psuchike, soulish,* as a person is in his unregenerate state, ruled by his natural senses, and is devilish and demonic! It causes confusion, disorder, and every kind of evil work. Politics is indeed dirty when spiritual matters are at stake and people want their own way, and the carnal nature rules through immature and unspiritual people.

If we have been or are guilty of any of the sins which we

have mentioned, let us quickly call out to God as David did in all of Psalm 51, having seen what happened to Saul: **"Create in me a clean heart, O God; and renew a right spirit within me. Cast me not away from Thy presence; and take not Thy Holy Spirit from me"** (Psa. 51:10-11 KJV). And then after praying the entire Psalm, let us totally repent and change what we can and ask God to change what we can not.

One thing is for sure, we must repent of majority voting to determine the will of God, a carnal method which produces carnality and worse, instead of **"that good, and acceptable, and perfect will of God"** (Rom. 12:2 KJV).

Occasionally we find that we have a "Diotrephes" among us. He was a man **"who loveth to have the preeminence among them [us]"** (III Jn. 9 KJV). He will not receive the good and spiritual brethren God has sent; but he **"boils over against them with empty accusations"** and **"malicious words"**; and **"he forbids others to receive them"** from being a part of the fellowship, board, ministry, or meeting; and he even puts the best of God's chosen vessels **"out"** if he can (lit. from III Jn. 9-11).

In contrast to Diotrephes, we need to be like Demetrius, a man who had a good report; not only from all men, but **"from the truth itself"** (III Jn. 12 NAS). Many men give report that the Word of God is true, but does the Word of God testify that they are true? Does the record of requirements given to us in the Word of God, which is the truth concerning what a man of God is truly to be, give testimony verifying that we are in fact an embodiment of that truth? Is our character and behavior a reflection of the true character and behavior of a man of God as required in God's Word, God's truth? When truth is examined, when circumstances are revealed in situations concerning us, do they bear witness that we are men of truth and integrity? Does the truth give us a good report? It should! John had said at the beginning of the letter that brethren gave testimony of the truth of Gaius, and that Gaius was walking in the truth. John concludes this letter by saying that Gaius knew that John and his associates gave true testimony, and that they and the truth gave Demetrius a good testimony. Do we have a good report among the brethren? We must!

And so we come to a close of this most important apostolic teaching and practice. We must repent of our selfishness and being self-willed (freedom from which is a qualification for being a ruling elder in the body of Christ, Titus 1:7), and we must commit ourselves to Christ as head, and determine that we are going to operate God's way. If we do, we will have God's success. If we do not, after being enlightened, we will enter into darkness, and reap the fruit of our doing (as the rebellious spies of old), and never enter into our "promised land." Let us repent and surrender to God all of our faithless service, and be renewed in the spirit of our mind (Eph. 4:17-27). Let us go on to serve Him in holiness and godly fear each day until the soon coming of our Lord and Savior, Jesus Christ, our head. And as the head of His church, He makes His mind and will known to His church through the principle of "unanimity"; which the scripture reveals to us is waiting on God in serious prayer, fasting when necessary, until we all come into **"one mind, and one accord."**

Besides the eleventh chapter of brother G. H. Lang's book, *The Churches of God*, or his booklet, *Unanimity: The Divine Method Of Church Government,* which I have recommended, I also recommend that you listen to the tape of a leading pastor and teacher, who when appointed to a very formal and traditional congregation was brought together with them into an understanding of this principle. He and the congregation functioned very well for many years under this principle, which he calls the "Headship of Christ." It is a thrilling testimony of God's grace that has been manifested, and is still working in our day. The tape is entitled "Headship and Unity," 13-118 #1, by Everett L. "Terry" Fullam. Let us in these last days grasp this truth and practice it so that we can be found faithful in Him at His soon coming! Amen, and Amen!!

Now, at a date much later than the original writing of this chapter, I am adding some summary statements that are burning in my heart after years of witnessing and experiencing this word.

Consistently attempting to determine the will of God by majority vote:

Creates division, and no longer perfects unity in love; in fact
It destroys brotherly love by inviting thoughts and manners that put one in conflict with another, and creates groups opposed to each other;
It is not perfected in the love of God and the love of one's neighbor, when
It neglects to gently correct, reconcile, and restore those who err;
It indulges the carnal mind in its hostility toward God, for it is not able to submit to God to discern His perfect will;
It is insensitive to the continual need of all growing up together in Christ, for it fosters neglect, animosity, and ill-will;
It ignores the instructions of scripture and is not persuaded to abide graciously in the kingdom of God, but rather it allows some to become hard and disobedient, speaking evil of the way, and they stir up others to get rid of those who oppose their own position, opinion, or desires;
Its wisdom is not from above, but is earthly, soulish, and demonic;
It promotes all the wicked spirits of Babylon, namely pride rebellion, unbelief, selfish ambition, and the fear of man, rather than humility, mutual submission to God and each other, faith, commitment to God's will, and the fear of God;
It quenches, grieves, and hinders the Holy Spirit, but holds to demonic spirits;
It follows Robert's rules rather than Christ's rules, as it copies the world's ways instead of the Lord's;
It is blatantly unscriptural, and actually antichrist;
It presumes on His grace, while denying the purposes of God;
Instead of bringing in the sweet fragrance of The Rose of Sharon,
It spreads and overcomes us in the foul odors of Hell itself;
Therefore,
It does not accomplish the will of God, and thus it demands His sovereign judgment!
It necessitates prayerful contemplation, and complete r e p e n t a n c e !

CHAPTER 5

Discipline
in the church

To know and understand discipline in the church and the necessity of its application is of utmost importance if we are to be manifesting the love of God and striving on toward our perfection in the Lord Jesus Christ! "**Whom the Lord loves He disciplines**" and therefore whom we love we discipline even as a father his beloved children (Heb. 12:5-11 NAS).

The word "**discipline**" and its various forms appear in the New American Standard version of the bible forty-seven times. The most prevalent Hebrew word is *musar,* and the most prevalent Greek word is παιδεια, *paideia,* and both are translated in the King James Version variously as "discipline, chastening, or correction." The word παιδεια, *paideia,* which comes from the root word παισ, *pais,* meaning "a child," means literally "child training."

Discipline starts with oneself, then in a family, and then in the family of God. An elder must first have self-discipline over his own life, then over his wife, and later over his children, before he can exercise good and loving discipline over the church. The scripture says that an elder must be: "**One that ruleth well his own house, having his children in subjection with all gravity; (For if a man know not how to rule his own house, how shall he** take care of the church of God?)" (I Tim. 3:4-5 KJV). The Greek word for "**rule**" is προιστημι, *proistemi;* the root *istemi* means literally "to stand, place, or set" plus the prefix *pro* means "before." Therefore, the word means "to place over, to preside over, superintend" (Thayer's lexicon).

The words for "**in subjection**" are εν υποταγη, *en hupotage.* The meaning of εν, *en,* is "in"; υπο, *hupo,* means "under"; and ταγη, *tage,* means "to place, appoint, assign, order." Consequently, the words are defined to mean "to have in subjection, in submission, in subordination, in obedience" (Bauer, Arndt & Gingrich lexicon).

The word for "**gravity**," σεμνοτησ, *semnotes,* means "gravity, dignity, seriousness, honor, probity, purity," and is spoken in reference of those entitled to "reverence and respect" (Thayer's and B.A.G. lexicons).

Now, in the scriptures to Timothy and Titus, Paul has given us the qualifications for an elder, which are part of the job description for that position of service in the church of one's locality. As we just explained from Paul's letter to Timothy, part of those qualifications involve having proper discipline in the home, so that one can know how to have proper discipline in the church. Again, Paul writes similarly to Titus of the necessity of good discipline in the home when he says that an elder must be one "**having children who believe, not accused of dissipation or rebellion. For the overseer must be above reproach as God's steward**" (Tit. 1:5-7 NAS). Then Paul goes on to mention self-discipline and some of the aspects of discipline in the church when he says that an elder must also be "**self-controlled, holding fast the faithful word which is in accordance with the teaching, that he may be able both to exhort in sound doctrine** [teaching] **and to refute those who contradict. For there are many rebellious men, empty talkers and deceivers, especially those of the circumcision, who must be silenced because they are upsetting whole families, teaching things they should not teach, for the sake of sordid gain. One of themselves, a prophet of their own, said, 'Cretans are always liars, evil beasts, lazy gluttons.' This testimony is true. For this cause reprove them severely that they may be sound in the faith**" (Tit. 1:8-13 NAS).

These last verses emphasize that for "**the elders who rule**" (I Tim. 5:17), discipline in the church is imperative because of the battle that we are in and that the enemy of both our souls and the church of Jesus Christ will stir men up to try and destroy the faith and truth implanted in God's people. Therefore, let us look more carefully at the exact meaning of several of the words used. "**To refute**" comes from the Greek word ελεγχειν, *elegchein,* and means "to convict, refute, confute, generally with a suggestion of the shame of the person convicted"; also,"to find fault with, correct, to reprehend severely, admonish, reprove, to call to account, show one his fault" (Thayer's lexicon).

Now this is to be done to those who "**contradict**" the truths of God's Word. Here the Greek word is αντιλεγοντασ, *antilegontas,* and means literally "to speak against"; and it is translated in the KJV as "**gainsay.**" What an important ministry of the rulers of God's people!

Unfortunately, in the present man-divided church structures making up most of the one true God-made church in each city, the meetings are not freely led of the Holy Spirit of God, and therefore we seldom see the free exchange of teachings and ministry that regularly occurred in the New Testament church. (These structures are the typical type of congregational church structure — man-controlled, man-centered, man-led, principally a one-man ministry or a hierarchy with one man at the top.) Consequently, we seldom see the correction of false teachings that is so needed and necessary among God's people. In fact, men spurn and deny the church the freedom for this purpose that is given to us by God, often with the excuse that it will result in disorder and confusion. However, the result of this denial is the massive confusion of false teaching and division that we see in the body of Christ; because God has ordained freedom to result in the correction of erroneous doctrine and behavior that is so often present. Paul wrote to the Corinthians about this when he said, "**when ye come together in the church . . . there must be also heresies among you, that they which are approved may be made manifest among you**" (I Cor. 11:18-19 KJV). However, because of men's selfishness, they are not adequately interested in the body of Christ as a whole, nor even the quality of their particular little portion of it, but mainly its quantity or their own ways.

Protected pulpits are Babylonish creations which have become the honored thrones of proud dictatorial authority, maintained and guarded for the preservation of the many kingdoms of men, not the one true kingdom of God ruled by humble servant authority.

To continue on with an exposition of Paul's instructions to Titus, we should not be surprised then to find him stating that there are many "**rebellious**" men. Here the Greek word is ανυποτακτοι, *anupotaktoi;* the prefix αν, *an,* means "not"; υπο, *hupo,* means "under"; and τακτοι, *taktoi,* means "orders, control, or authority"; and thus the word means "insubordinate," and is translated "**unruly**" (KJV) and "**rebellious**" (NAS).

Also, there are many "**vain talkers**" (KJV), or "**empty talkers**" (NAS). The Greek word is ματαιολογοι, *mataiologoi.* It is interesting in that ματαιοσ, *mataios,* means "devoid of force, truth, success, result; useless, to no purpose." And λογοι, *logoi,* is the plural form of a very familiar word λογοσ, *logos,* meaning "speech" or "a word which, uttered by a living voice, embodies a conception or idea." What a word for much of the empty preaching and teaching of today!

Also, Paul says there are many "**deceivers**," and here the Greek word is φρεναπαται, *phrenapatai;* φρεν, *phren,* from the root φρην, *phren,* meaning "mind," plus απαται, *apatai,* meaning "deceivers"; and is, therefore, more accurately translated "mind-deceivers," suggestive somewhat of the popular word today, "mind-benders." These are especially from the "**circumcision**," Paul says, which we might think of as from the religious crowd who distort the word of God so cleverly with the aid of "**seducing spirits**." After a little meditation on these words and their implications, please reread the preceding scripture in Titus. Then the tremendous need can certainly be seen for faithful elders who will be able and willing to deal with these kinds of people and maintain proper discipline in the church.

Now that we have seen a little about who is responsible for discipline in the church and why, we should consider how it is to be done. But remember what we said at the beginning?

"Discipline starts with oneself, then in a family, and then in the family of God. An elder must first have self-discipline over his own life, then over his wife, and later over his children, before he can exercise good and loving discipline over the church."

So then, let us consider some aspects of all of these areas of discipline.

First, how do we attain more self-discipline?

I believe our only hope is in the Lord, and if we go to His Word, we'll find the answers. In the Sermon on the Mount, we find three whole chapters of very important teachings that we must understand (Mt. 5, 6, & 7). These are about attitudes and actions, about righteousness in many significant areas. The Lord sums up His teaching with the authoritative declaration that we must hear His words and act upon them if we are to enter His kingdom. We will not expound on the entire Sermon, but let us look at those self-disciplines that He calls righteousness which are very personal and of a private nature, and which He expects us to do.

First, He instructs us about giving alms, which is assistance to the poor (Mt. 6:1-4). When we do this, and do it correctly, we will be rewarded. Our rewards are not only material blessings in return, but many spiritual blessings of growth and development.

Secondly, He instructs us about prayer, and forgiveness (Mt. 6:5-15). We must have a good and adequate prayer life in secret. No one has ever been successful spiritually without communion with God in all of its aspects. And learning to forgive quickly and completely is fundamental.

Thirdly, Jesus expects His disciples to fast (Mt. 6:16-18). Regular weekly fasting is a discipline that is essential for real growth and development, the building of the kingdom of God within ourselves and within others.

Next, Jesus talks about material things (Mt. 6:19-34), that we must **"seek first His kingdom and His righteousness; and all these things shall be added to you [us]"** (Mt. 6:33 NAS).

Paul writes about self-discipline when he likens the Christian life to participating in the olympics. He writes, **"Do you not know that those who run in a race all run, but only one receives the prize? Run in such a way that you may win. And everyone who competes in the games exercises self-control in all things. They then do it to receive a perishable wreath, but we an imperishable. Therefore I run in such a way, as not without aim; I box in such a way, as not beating the air; but I buffet my body and make it my slave, lest possibly, after I have preached to others, I myself should be disqualified"** (I Cor. 9:24-27 NAS). Self-control is a fruit of the Spirit, and whether we wage spiritual warfare, or "the battle against the bulge [our flesh]," it is only available from Him (Gal. 5:23).

Next, if a leader is married, he must know how to function as the head of his household. His wife must be under subjection according to the Word of God, and he must be lovingly leading her into holiness (Eph.5:22-33; I Cor. 11:2-16; 14:34-37; Col. 3:18-19; I Pet. 3:1-7).

"Whom the Lord loves He disciplines," and as Christ (the head of the man) disciplines the husband, the husband (as head of his wife) must discipline her in love the same way (Pro. 3:12; Heb. 12:6; Eph. 5:25, 28-29). Many men are not willing to do this properly, and I have seen many lose their ministries in the Lord because of it. We must not be partial in our dealings, we must love as He loves, impartially, but at the same time holding to the wife in love. This becomes very practical. Let no one abuse his wife, physically or verbally, but often words of admonishment and correction are needed as well as encouragement, and the denying as well as the giving of things. Sometimes a wife needs to stay home when her attitudes and actions are not what they should be. The Lord certainly disciplines men in this way. He withdraws His sweet presence, and refrains from taking them places with Him in ministry.

Any man who is going to be really successful as God counts success in the ministry, must have the Lord first in his life in every aspect. He must rid himself of all idolatry; that is putting anything or anybody before the Lord. He must understand the words of the Lord when He said, "**If anyone comes to Me, and does not hate his own father and mother and wife and children and brothers and sisters, yes, and even his own life, he cannot be My disciple. Whoever does not carry his own cross and come after Me cannot be My disciple**" (Lk. 14:26-27 NAS). The love we have for God must be greater than the love we have for anything or any one, including ourselves. The Lord's requirement for discipleship was given in the midst of parables about land, business, marriage, building, and rulership, as well as His declaration about any family member or oneself; and He closes His teaching about possessions, and the fearful consequence of putting anything before Him. He said, "**So therefore, no one of you can be My disciple who does not give up all his own possessions. Therefore, salt is good; but if even salt has become tasteless, with what will it be seasoned? It is useless either for the soil or for the manure pile; it is thrown out. He who has ears to hear, let him hear**" (Lk. 14:33-35 NAS).

Now, about children. Many scriptures can be given about training and disciplining our children, and I will list some of them. Let us begin by quoting some very famous words of Moses about our responsibility to love God by teaching His Word to our children.

> "**Hear, O Israel! The Lord is our God, the Lord is one! And you shall love the Lord your God with all your heart and with all your soul and with all your might. And these words, which I am commanding you today, shall be on your heart; and you shall teach**

them diligently to your sons and shall talk of them when you sit in your house and when you walk by the way and when you lie down and when you rise up." Deut. 6:4-7 NAS

Next, let us consider a word that God spoke to David through Nathan the prophet about Solomon. It is a word that can be applied to all of us individually, and to small groups, and on up to national leaders that know the Lord.

"I will be a father to him and he will be a son to Me; when he commits iniquity, I will correct him with the rod of men and the strokes of the sons of men, but My lovingkindness shall not depart from him." II Sam. 7:14-15 NAS

Now let us consider some of the words of God through Solomon himself concerning discipline (whom the Lord Jesus commended for his wisdom), which the church has cherished for centuries and therefore used so very successfully in rearing children; but I might add are under such distorted and severe attack today in this lawless and rebellious generation (Mt. 12:42; Lu. 11:31).

"My son, do not reject the discipline of the Lord, or loathe His reproof, for whom the Lord loves He reproves, even as a father, the son in whom he delights." Pro. 3:11-12 NAS

"On the lips of the discerning, wisdom is found, but a rod is for the back of him who lacks understanding [lit., heart]." Pro. 10:13 NAS

"He who spares his rod hates his son, but he who loves him disciplines him diligently [lit., seeks him diligently with discipline]." Pro. 13:24 NAS

"Stern discipline is for him who forsakes the way; he who hates reproof will die." Pro. 15:10 NAS

"Discipline your son while there is hope, and do not desire his death [KJV, and let not thy soul spare for his crying]." Pro. 19:18 NAS

"Stripes that wound scour away evil [KJV, The blueness of a wound cleanseth away evil], and strokes reach the innermost parts."   Pro. 20:30 NAS

"Train up a child in the way he should go, even when he is old he will not depart from it."
Pro. 22:6 NAS

"Foolishness is bound up in the heart of a child; the rod of discipline will remove it far from him."
Pro. 22:15 NAS

"Do not hold back discipline from the child, although you beat him with the rod, he will not die. You shall beat him with the rod, and deliver his soul from Sheol."   Pro. 23:13-14 NAS

"The rod and reproof give wisdom, but a child who gets his own way [KJV, left to himself] brings shame to his mother."   Pro. 29:15 NAS

"Correct your son, and he will give you comfort [KJV, rest]; he will also delight your soul."
Pro. 29:17 NAS

Now two scriptures from the New Testament.

"Children, obey your parents in the Lord, for this is right. Honor your father and mother (which is the first commandment with a promise), that it may be well with you, and that you may live long on the earth. And, fathers, do not provoke your children to anger; but bring them up in the discipline and instruction of the Lord."   Eph. 6:1-4 NAS

"Children, be obedient to your parents in all things, for this is well-pleasing to the Lord. Fathers, do not exasperate your children, that they may not lose heart."   Col. 3:20-21 NAS

It is obvious from the foregoing scriptures alone, when words of correction or other disciplinary measures or restrictions do not bring the necessary correction desired, that physical pain must be used. But then the question arises as to what form of physical discipline should be used. The scriptures we quoted tell us that we can either choose wisdom on our lips, or a rod on our backs; and that the discipline of the rod will effect a change in the inner man, the heart. I believe a rod is just that; it's a thin switch or a thicker rod, depending upon the seriousness of the offense and the size of the child. The purpose is to inflict pain, not damage. When the physical pain of swift and just discipline is done in love and compassion, and is greater than the physical pleasure of the sin committed, a child will change his thoughts and ways.

The physical discipline of a child is the responsibility of the father, and if a mother will use wisdom and the proper admonishments, and warn the child about turning them over to their father for physical correction, both they and the child will be better off. The mother will be more at rest, and the child will be more obedient.

Now concerning discipline in the church, we have already covered scriptures teaching us that it is the responsibility of the elders. These scriptures confirm that an elder must be able and willing to reprove those who error in teaching, but we also need to look at scriptures that pertain to the errors of life (that means sinful behavior) and how we all are to deal with even unrepentant Christians.

When there is sin in an individual's life, we are to pray for them, and God promises to forgive them and give them life (I Jn. 5:16). Sometimes we must go to the individual, admonishing them in humble love in order to restore them (Gal. 6:1). We must always go in the right attitude, humbly and gently, having dealt with ourselves first before going to our brother (Mt. 7:3-5; II Tim. 2:24-26; Jam. 2:12-13).

At other times, when Christians have sinned against us and are not repentant about their sin, we must follow the Lord's instructions that He gave us in Matthew 18:15-35. Here we find that if after we have gone to our brother alone and he doesn't hear us, that means that if he does not listen to us and respond correctly by repentance from his sin, we are then to take with us one or two more because sin is serious. We must do this because if more than one person shows him his sin he may be more apt to accept it, and also because every word must be established by the mouth of two or three witnesses. Finally, if he does not hear the two or three of

231

us, then comes the matter of dealing with sin before the church. Not only is an elder of God's people responsible for teaching and helping people deal with sin on the personal level, but he especially must be willing to deal with sin openly before the church when necessary, recognizing that the discipline of sin on the church level is very important for several reasons. First, an individual must not be allowed to perish without our love and concern; and that involves not only admonishing him about his sin, and praying for him, but loving discipline must be administered to whatever degree necessary so as to do all within our power and that of God to bring the person to repentance and his ultimate salvation.

A second reason that we must continue to deal with sin to the point of bringing it before the entire church is that "**a little leaven leavens the whole lump**" (I Cor. 5:6 NAS). This truth that Paul writes concerning sin in the church should be seen in two aspects. One, sin is pernicious, and infectious. It will influence the behavior of other saints, and therefore must be purged out before it can infect other members of the body and cause them to enter into sin. However, a second aspect must be seen that is not as often considered. This is the fact that the Lord looks at His church as a whole, and judges us accordingly. If we look at the story of Achan, we see that the Lord judged all of Israel when this one man sinned. The account is given to us in Joshua chapter seven where we find Israel going up to battle against the small town of Ai immediately after the very famous and glorious victory over the much larger city of Jericho. Achan took of the spoils for himself (a Babylonian garment and some silver and gold), and buried them in his tent. Consequently the Lord was angry with all of "**the children of Israel**," and when they went to battle, thirty-six innocent men were killed as their invading forces were routed in fear and shamefully defeated. When Joshua fell on his face in supplication before the Lord, the Lord told him to get up off his face because "**Israel has sinned, and they have also transgressed My covenant**" (Josh. 7:11 NAS). God looked at them as a whole the same as He looks at us today. Therefore, we must purge the body of Christ of sin and wickedness if we are ever to see victory over our enemies and the healing of our land. When Israel dealt properly with Achan, God gave a wonderful victory, the same as He will for us when we deal with our "Achans." The spoils of war were to be brought into the treasury of the Lord, not greedily gathered for personal profit; and Babylonish garments are to be abhorred and destroyed, not worn like some proud peacock (Josh.

6:18-24). One man's sin brought a curse on the whole nation, and national disgrace; innocent men died, and their families lost their husbands and fathers; therefore God's righteous judgment in turn was not only the death and dishonor of the man, but the destruction of his whole family.

Therefore, if after a professing member of the body of Christ begins to practice serious sinful behavior, and the matter is brought before the whole church, judged properly, and they are proven guilty but refuse to repent, the church must discipline them. The church must love them enough to pray for them, and depending upon the sin, take whatever action is appropriate to attempt to bring them to repentance and restoration.

We have an incidence mentioned in God's Word where certain Christians were leading an "**unruly**" and "**undisciplined life**," and not according to the example and teaching that their leaders had given them (II Thes. 3:6-16 NAS). Paul and his companions had set the example by working hard, night and day (although as apostles they did not have to, they could have lived off the tithes of God's people), but there were certain Christians who refused to work at all, and were expecting the rest of the church to provide for them. Paul writes to the church that they were to admonish such people as unruly brethren, and then to stay away from them in order that they might be ashamed. Paul gives the church an order and a principle that has been so helpful down through the centuries. "**If anyone will not work, neither let him eat**" (II Thes. 3:10 NAS). This is true Christian love, caring enough about our brothers and sisters to discipline them in love so as to bring them to repentance from their sinful ways.

Because of the seriousness of such sin as rebellion, and teaching things which should not be taught for the purpose of making money, often God's Word to us is to "**reprove them severely that they may be sound in the faith**" (Tit. 1:10-13 NAS). Paul also writes that we are to take note of those who are making division in the church, and causing others to stumble, and turn away from them because they are not serving the Lord but their own selfish appetites (Rom. 16:17-18). For these reasons we are given the Word of God, and it is to be preached "**in season and out of season**" (II Tim. 4:2 NAS). Paul tells Timothy to use it to reprove and rebuke, because in time people will yield to their own selfish desires, and therefore choose to sit under ministers who will teach them what they want to hear in accordance with their own carnal appetites (II Tim. 3:16 - 4:4).

When a person becomes **"factious"** (NAS), **"a heretick"** (KJV), they are to be admonished at least twice, and if they do not repent, they are to be rejected (Tit. 3:10-11). The Greek word is αιρετικον, *hairetikon,* and comes from a root word αιρεω, *haireo,* that means "to choose, to take for one's self, prefer." Paul writes that they are **"perverted"** (NAS), **"turned out of the way** [the true faith]" (literal Greek), and are sinning and have condemned themselves (Tit. 3:11 NAS). One can observe from the context then that a heretic is someone who has chosen to believe a false revelation or teaching and has chosen to cause division in the body of Christ over it because of selfish motivation. The church must reject this kind of person. This is further confirmed by the use of the Greek word αιρεσισ, *hairesis,* which occurs nine times in the New Testament, in either the singular or plural form. It is translated **"sect"** five times the same in both the KJV and NAS (Acts 5:17; 15:5; 24:5; 26:5; 28:22); **"heresy(ies)"** the other four times in the KJV (Acts 24:14; I Cor. 11:19; Gal. 5:20; II Pet. 2:1); and in the NAS, variously, **"sect"** one more time (Acts 24:14), **"factions"** twice (I Cor. 11:19; Gal. 5:20), and **"heresies"** once (II Pet. 2:1). It means "that which is chosen, hence, one's chosen opinion, tenet; a body of men separating themselves from others and following their own tenets; dissensions arising from diversity of opinions and aims" (Thayer's lexicon); and is listed as one of the works of the flesh for which people are condemned (Gal. 5:20-21).

John goes even further and states that a person who has left the true teachings of Christ is not only not to be allowed into your house, but is not even to be greeted with a friendly greeting such as "Hello" (II Jn. vv. 9-10). To do so is to affirm that what he is doing is acceptable, and therefore it encourages him in his evil teachings, and thereby one becomes a partaker of his evil deeds.

The Lord Jesus said that when one sins and refuses to repent, and it is necessary to bring them before the church, **"if he refuses to listen even to the church, let him be to you as a Gentile and a tax-gatherer"** (Mt. 18:17 NAS). This means that they are not to be considered as a Christian (but a Gentile, a heathen), and as one of the publicans (the hated Jewish tax-gatherers for profit employed by the Romans), as a traitor and apostate.

Jesus then immediately goes on to say, **"Truly I say to you, whatever you shall bind on earth shall be bound in heaven; and whatever you loose on earth shall be loosed in heaven. Again I say to you, that if two of you agree on earth about anything that they may ask, it shall be done for them by My Father who is in**

heaven. For where two or three have gathered together in My name, there I am in their midst" (Mt. 18:18-20 NAS).

These verses have been applied to other circumstances, but here in the context Jesus is revealing that when an unrepentant Christian is put out of the church on earth, he is out of the Lord's eternal heavenly kingdom; he is lost! This church discipline may in some circumstances be done among just a few. Who I must add are in right standing with God and under the direction of the true Holy Spirit of God.

This brings us then to the last and most severe form of church discipline, and that is when the Lord uses Satan.

Such was the case when Paul, as an apostle, turned over to Satan two men who had been guilty of evil speaking (Greek: βλασφημειν, *blasphemein,* blaspheme, meaning "to speak evil or reproachfully of God or man, rail at, revile, slander, to injure the good name of another"; in this case most likely against Paul and his companions, but possibly about the Lord Himself), and had sinned against their own conscience and ruined their faith (I Tim. 1:18-20). This action was taken **"so that they may be taught** [παιδευθωσιν, *paideuthosin,* disciplined] **not to"** do so. These are most probably the same men mentioned in Paul's second letter to Timothy. There we find that one had seriously missed the truth concerning the resurrection, teaching that it had already taken place, and thereby was causing some to turn back from their faith (II Tim. 2:17-18). The other had stood vigorously against the teachings of Paul and done many evil things against him personally, for which the Lord would repay him accordingly (II Tim. 4:14-15).

Jesus talked of God using Satan at the end of the chapter in which he spoke of putting people out of the church who refused to repent (Mt. 18:21-35). He teaches that when we do not forgive our brethren of their sins against us, our heavenly Father will deliver us over to the tormentors, which may be either human jailors or demon spirits, or both, to torment us until we repent (Mt. 18:34-35). The word given here is βασανισταισ, *basanistais,* the plural of *basanistes,* which means literally "one who elicits the truth by the use of the rack, an inquisitor, torturer" (Thayer's lexicon). These tormentors have been referred to in the ancient writing of the Apocalypse of Peter as "avenging angels," and by modern experience as meaning either human or spiritual beings. Some people who have been taught **"another Jesus"** (II Cor. 11:4), or who have been taught falsely about our true Lord Jesus, do not understand the seriousness of sin and its eternal consequences, and therefore disbelieve about such discipline, but yet strangely still may believe in an eternal hell, which is far worse because there is no escape. If torment for a brief period will bring someone to repentance, it is a small price to pay in order to escape the eternal torments of an everlasting, fiery, tormenting hell! The scriptures are full of examples of the wrath of God against unrepentant sinners, His own rebellious nation of Israel, and unrepentant Christians (Ro. 1:18; 2:5-11; 11:22; I Cor. 10:1-11; Heb. 10:26-31; 12:28-29). Jesus tells us of some severe judgments upon us if we turn to sin and refuse to repent (Jn. 15:6; Rev. 2:20-23).

With this in mind, let us consider in more detail some scripture that reveals to us the church's responsibility in this type of discipline.

Paul was writing to the Corinthians, and he tells them how to deal with severe sin in their midst, which they had not been dealing with because of their arrogance and lack of concern about the sin or the person committing it. He writes:

> "I do not write these things to shame you, but to admonish you as my beloved children. For if you were to have countless tutors in Christ, yet you would not have many fathers; for in Christ Jesus I became your father through the gospel. I exhort you therefore, be imitators of me. For this reason I have sent to you Timothy, who is my beloved and faithful child in the Lord, and he will remind you of my ways which are in Christ, just as I teach everywhere in every church. Now some have become <u>arrogant</u>, as though I were not coming to you. But I will come to you soon, if the Lord wills, and I shall find out, not the words of those who are arrogant, but their power. For the kingdom of God does not consist in words, but in power. What do you desire? Shall I come to you with a <u>rod or with love and a spirit of gentleness</u>?
>
> It is actually reported that there is immorality among you, and immorality of such a kind as *does* not *exist* even among the Gentiles, that someone has his father's wife. And you have become <u>arrogant</u>, and <u>have not mourned instead</u>, in order that the one who had done this deed might be removed from your midst. For I, on my part, though absent in body but present in spirit, have already judged him who has so

committed this, as though I were present. In the name of our Lord Jesus, when you are assembled, and I with you in spirit, with the power of our Lord Jesus, I have decided to <u>deliver such a one to Satan for the destruction of his flesh, that his spirit may be saved in the day of the Lord Jesus.</u> Your boasting is not good. Do you not know that a little leaven leavens the whole lump of dough? <u>Clean out the old leaven,</u> that you may be a new lump, just as you are in fact unleavened. For Christ our Passover also has been sacrificed. <u>Let us therefore celebrate the feast, not with old leaven,</u> nor with the leaven of malice and wickedness, but with the unleavened bread of sincerity and truth.

I wrote you in my letter not to associate with immoral people; I did not at all mean with the immoral people of this world, or with the covetous and swindlers, or with idolaters; for then you would have to go out of the world. But actually, I wrote to you <u>not to associate with any so-called brother</u> if he should be an <u>immoral person, or covetous, or an idolater, or a reviler, or a drunkard, or a swindler — not even to eat with such a one.</u> For what have I to do with judging outsiders? Do you not judge those who are within the church? But those who are outside, God judges. <u>Remove the wicked man from among yourselves.</u>"

I Cor. 4:14 - 5:13 NAS

Please notice now that some of the Christians were arrogant and puffed up against the apostle who actually founded the church in the faith. They should have been praying and mourning over the sin and the person committing it that was in their midst, but they were not.

Paul gives them a choice, whether he will come with a rod of discipline, or with what he prefers, a loving and gentle spirit, and he has the power of God with him to back up his words.

Then, to deal with the man who was living in sin, he tells them to meet together and to pray in the name of our Lord Jesus and to turn the man over to the disciplining work of Satan (the destruction of one's health or property, or demonic torment against one's person, similar to what Job experienced) in order that even though it might result in the man's death if necessary, it will bring him hopefully to repentance so that he can ultimately be saved. To help this man by disciplining him so as to help him repent and escape the eternal torments of hell is real love, my dear brethren. It is hatred of others not to want them to suffer a little time now, only to suffer much more and eternally later. We learned that clearly from the wisdom of Proverbs, and we must apply it now as the situations demand!

We are told why we must purge sin out of the church; that it is our responsibility to judge those within the church; and that we must not even associate with those who call themselves brothers and yet persist in practicing gross sins! Therefore, excommunication is biblical, and necessary. Because some may not understand, or others practice it falsely, does not absolve us of our responsibilities in these matters.

Dearly beloved, now that we have looked carefully at various forms of discipline, let us check our own hearts and lives, and determine that we will walk before the Lord in holiness and righteousness, and do all that is within our power to see that others who name the name of the Lord do likewise. Amen!

"Dear Father, help us to love you with all of our hearts, our souls, our minds, and our strength, and to love others enough to do whatever is necessary according to your Word and according to your Spirit to help bring them to this same commitment. In the name of our Lord Jesus, we pray. Amen, and Amen!"

Last Words and Prayer

Dear brothers and sisters, I trust that now that you have read the preceding five chapters, considered carefully the root sins, spirits, and attitudes of Babylon (false religion) such as fear, pride, rebellion, selfishness in all its forms (such as ambition, self-exaltation, and desire for preeminence), unbelief and misbelief (that includes all kinds of error and false doctrine), idolatry, other sins, works of the flesh, and energizing spirits that follow (such as lusts of all kinds — sexual, material, mental, and aspirational), it is important that we realize that even though we may have renounced all of this, that we will still be tempted by these destructive sins and spirits even though we come out of Babylon, as far as our understanding and the Holy Spirit enables us to go. We will always be subject to these things as long as we are in the flesh, and so we must now pray and ever be vigilant to renounce all the works of the flesh, resist every evil spirit, and every sin that so easily might beset us, and to cast out every evil spirit that might have a hold upon us whether in our spirits, our souls, or our bodies!

Also, understanding that iniquities can be passed down upon us from our forefathers (Rom. 5:12-21; Ex. 20:5-6; 34:6-7; Lev. 26:39-43; Jer. 32:17-18; Lam. 5:7; Dan. 9:1-24; Zec. 3:9), but can be forgiven and released from us through confession, repentance, and the blood of the New Covenant (Jer. 31:29-34; Heb. 8:6-13; 10:9-23), it behooves us to pray diligently with understanding concerning our own iniquities, transgressions, and sins, and those of our forefathers. The iniquities, the iniquitous traits, and the curses that have been brought upon us from our ancestors are very real, and we need to be set free!

The psalmist prayed, "**Search me, O God, and know my heart: try me, and know my thoughts: And see if there be any wicked way in me, and lead me in the way everlasting**" (Psa. 139: 23-24 KJV). Concerning the heart, the Lord said, "**The heart is deceitful above all things, and desperately wicked: who can know it? I the LORD search the heart, I try the reins, even to give every man according to his ways, and according to the fruit of his doings**" (Jer 17:9-10 KJV); but praise God He preceded this by saying, "**Blessed is the man that trusteth in the LORD, and whose hope the LORD is. For he shall be as a tree planted by the waters, and that spreadeth out her roots by the river, and shall not see when heat cometh, but her leaf shall be green; and shall not be careful in the year of drought, neither shall cease from yielding fruit**" (Jer. 17:7-8 KJV).

Therefore let us pray and ask the Lord to search our hearts and reveal any sin which we must confess and forsake, and any iniquity that has been brought down to us from our forefathers, and any spirit that may be troubling us which must be cast out and away from us. (And then later we can ask the Lord to help us in prayer for others concerning these same things, but first let us pray for ourselves and the beam that might be in our own eye.)

"Dear God, please search my heart, and reveal any and every sin within me, and forgive me and cleanse me by the precious blood of Your son Jesus! And Heavenly Father, I confess that neither I nor my ancestors have walked in your ways as we should, we have transgressed thy holy law, and therefore thy righteous judgment has come upon us. Forgive me I pray, and also my living relatives; my God, reveal our iniquities, have mercy upon us, and break the bonds of sin and iniquity. As I wait upon You, please reveal by Your Holy Spirit any and every foul, unclean spirit that is within me, that I might cast it out in Your holy name, so that I might walk holy and obediently, without fear or failure all the rest of my days, in Your sight and for Your praise and glory and honor. Amen!

"Thank You, Father, and fill me with Your Holy Spirit, and anoint my eyes to see these realities, and empower me to live as Jesus lived, and be holy as You are holy, and to speak Your words with all boldness while You stretch forth Your hands to heal me and then others, that mighty signs and wonders might be wrought through the name of Thy holy servant Jesus, so that Thy will is done in earth as it is in heaven! Amen, and Amen!" AMEN!!!

APOSTOLIC FOUNDATION SERIES

The following 11 Tapes and 4 Books by John Rothacker comprise our Apostolic Foundation Series. The tapes are just $4.50 each including tax, shipping and handling, and the books are priced as marked.

Tape List	Num. Tapes
Tithes & Offerings	1 Tape
The Church	3 Tapes
How to be Saved - The Bible Way!	1 Tape
The Five-Fold Ministry	3 Tapes
Do You Know the Lord?	1 Tape
Foreign Missions	1 Tape
AFS Books, Tapes, & Literature	1 Tape
	11 Tapes + Album = $40.

Book List	
The Public Ministry of Women	$7.95
A Woman's Headcovering	$3.95
A Woman's Dress	$3.95
"The church"	$11.95
	All 4 books = $20.

11 Tapes + Album & 4 Books = $60.

Additional Tapes & Books Recommended

The Headship of Christ & Unity #13-118
       by: Everett L. "Terry" Fullam, D.D. $5.00 Tape
Unanimity: The Divine Method of Church Government
       by: G. H. Lang $2.95 Booklet
The Churches of God
       by: G. H. Lang $14.95 Book
The Two Babylons
       by: Alexander Hislop $18.99 Book

HOLY NUTRITION

Holy Nutrition #1   "The clean & the unclean"   1 Tape
Teaching and ministry in an assembly on scriptural eating and the difference between the clean and unclean flesh foods.

Holy Nutrition #2*   "Building the House of the Lord!" 1 Tape*
This is a primary study of scriptural teaching and facts and revelations from the Lord on how we are to eat according to the Holy Scriptures and the Holy Spirit!

Whole Leaf Aloe Vera #2*
by: Max Matthewson, M.D. &
John Rothacker, D.D.S.   1 Tape*
This is a teaching and testimony tape on the healing power of our own Manna From Heaven brand of Whole Leaf Aloe Vera.

Wheat & Barley Grass*   1 Tape*
This is a 60 minute teaching tape which I did over our Truth For Today radio program on the importance and healing significance of principally the green grasses.

Water   1 Tape
This is another 60 minute Truth For Today teaching tape on the importance and kinds of water that we should and should not drink.

* Indicates our recommended Health For Today packet tapes with literature.